IMAGES
of America

WHITEMAN AIR FORCE BASE

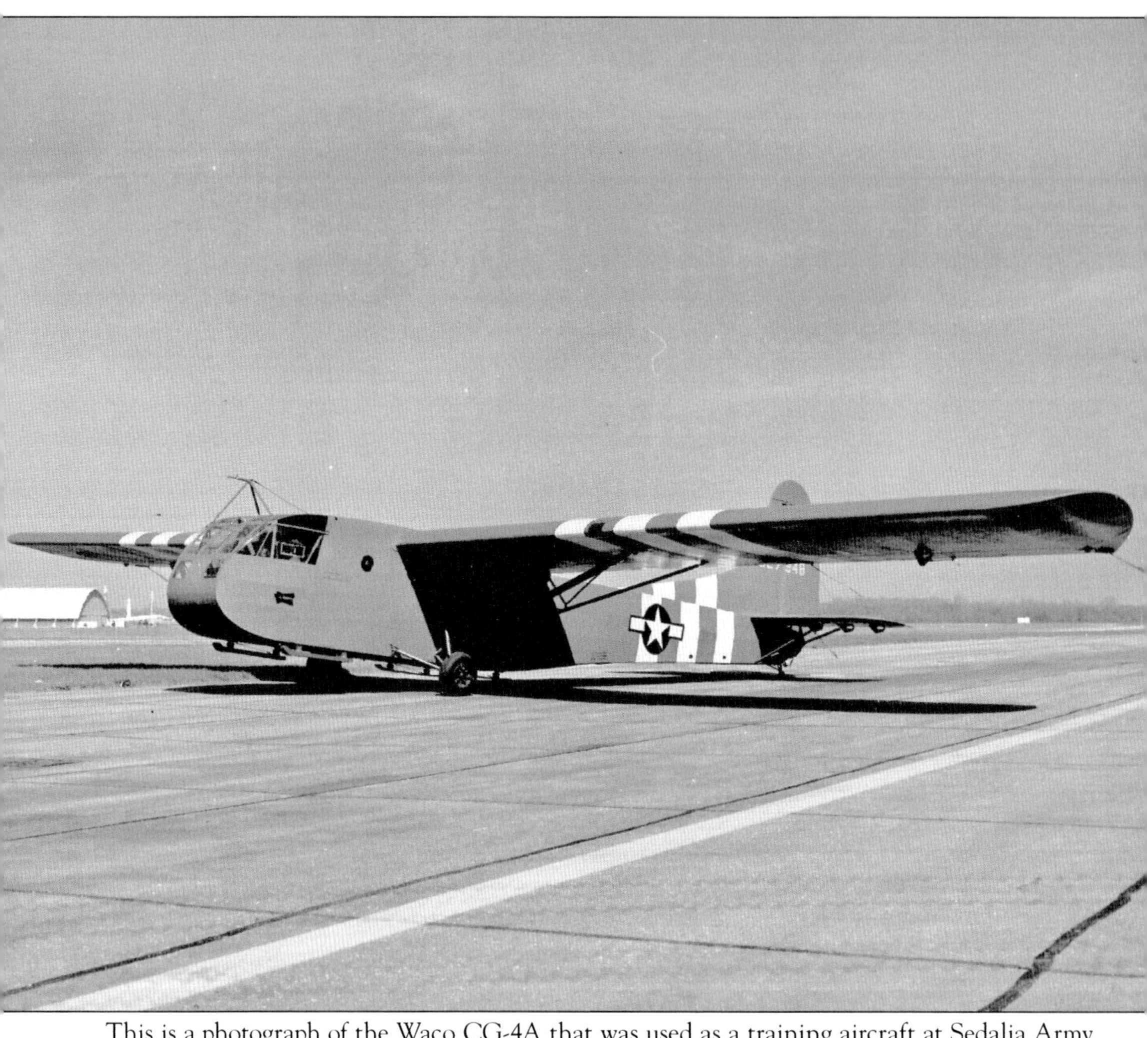

This is a photograph of the Waco CG-4A that was used as a training aircraft at Sedalia Army Air Field during World War II. (Courtesy National Museum of the United States Air Force.)

On the Cover: Pictured is a B-2 on the flight line at Whiteman Air Force Base as maintenance personnel prepare the aircraft for a training mission, with one of the two pilots climbing up the ladder into the aircraft's cockpit. (Courtesy Whiteman Air Force Base, 509th Bomb Wing Public Affairs.)

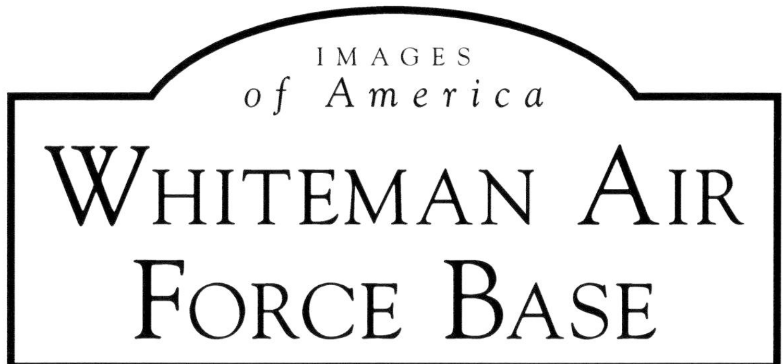

Lt. Col. George A. Larson, USAF (Ret.)
Foreword by Gen. Paul Tibbets IV

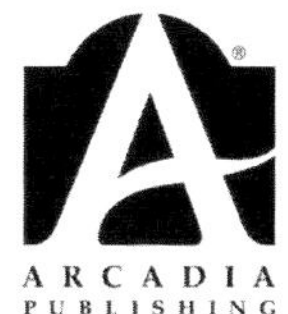

ISBN 978-1-4671-2812-4

Published by Arcadia Publishing
Charleston, South Carolina

Printed in the United States of America

Library of Congress Control Number: 2017950619

For all general information, please contact Arcadia Publishing:
Telephone 843-853-2070
Fax 843-853-0044
E-mail sales@arcadiapublishing.com
For customer service and orders:
Toll-Free 1-888-313-2665

Visit us on the Internet at www.arcadiapublishing.com

This book honors the thousands of men and women who answered the nation's call to arms from World War II to the war on terrorism.

Contents

Foreword

When I first heard George was compiling a book detailing the rich history of Whiteman Air Force Base, I thought it was a fantastic idea. It is no secret that the base holds a place of honor in our nation's history, from supporting our victory in World War II to continuously providing an elite combat capability that can reach any area of the world. However, many are unaware of the full extent of the base's past and its current contributions to US national security.

Originally known as Sedalia Army Air Field, Whiteman later took its namesake to honor 2nd Lt. George A. Whiteman, a former farm boy from the Sedalia area. When the attack on Pearl Harbor began, Lieutenant Whiteman's P-40 aircraft was tragically shot down shortly after liftoff. As one of the first airmen killed during the attack, Lieutenant Whiteman left a lasting legacy of courage not only for his family but also for the airmen at Whiteman Air Force Base.

The following pages help tell the story of the rich history of Whiteman, from its early days of training Waco glider pilots through its evolution into a central point in US strategic deterrence and global strike.

George has done a great job detailing the base's connection to multiple conflicts, beginning with World War II, to the Cold War, and eventually missions in Afghanistan, Iraq, and Syria. Additionally, he illustrates how it has been home to some of the Air Force's most powerful and influential weapon systems, including Minuteman I and II intercontinental ballistic missiles, the B-47 Stratojet, the A-10 Thunderbolt, remotely piloted aircraft, and the world's only stealth bomber, the B-2 Spirit.

Also encompassed in this book is the prestigious history of the 509th Bomb Wing and the story of my grandfather, my hero, who was the commander of the 509th Composite Group and pilot of the *Enola Gay*. Through their heroic actions, the crew of the *Enola Gay* dropped the first atomic weapon used in warfare, accelerating the end of World War II and saving millions of lives and generations of people.

It has been my privilege to spend a combined 12 years in Missouri at Whiteman. I have witnessed firsthand the strategic importance of this base and the supportive communities that surround it.

It is my sincere hope that others will learn of the enduring legacy of Whiteman Air Force Base through the pages contained in this book.

—Brig. Gen. Paul W. Tibbets IV

The views and opinions expressed above are the author's own, were prepared in his personal capacity, and do not reflect the views of the US Air Force, the Department of Defense, or the US government.

Acknowledgments

I want to thank Brig. Gen. Paul Tibbets IV, former commander of the 509th Bomb Wing, for assistance in research on Whiteman Air Force Base. I want to thank the 509th Public Affairs, Historian, Oscar 1 Minuteman Museum on base for photographs, historical documents, and tours of the base. The Air Force Historical Research Agency at Maxell Air Force Base, Alabama, dug through its collection for historical files. The Department of the Army and Air Force historical archives in the Pentagon provided rare photographs. The former Strategic Air Command historian at Offutt Air Force Base allowed me access to files on Whiteman. Trying to pull documents and photographs from 1942 was no easy task, and I appreciate the efforts of Team Whiteman.

INTRODUCTION

As I researched the history of Whiteman Air Force Base, I traced the history of the 509th Composite Group (CG), which included part of my family's military history. During World War II, my father, George W. Larson, volunteered for the US Navy, leaving his wartime industry job at a .50-caliber ammunition production plant in Ankeny, Iowa, where he had a high-priority draft deferment. He could not remain safe at home while so many from Altoona, Iowa, were killed and wounded in combat. He gave up his military deferment, joining the Navy and training as a gunner. After training, while at Pearl Harbor, Hawaii, he was assigned as a replacement to the 135th US Naval Construction Battalion, referred to as the Seabees, to fill out the battalion's construction manpower. The battalion landed on Tinian Island on October 24, 1944. George worked on runway number four, where on August 6, 1945, a 509th CG B-29 took off to drop an atomic bomb on Hiroshima, Japan. Three days later, a second 509th CG B-29 dropped a second atomic bomb on Nagasaki. In 1980, while I was a captain assigned to the 43rd Strategic Wing, Strategic Air Command, Andersen Air Force Base, Guam, as the wing intelligence officer, I brought my father to Guam, and we traveled to Tinian Island. I retraced the World War II footsteps of my father, 36 years after he served on the island, retracing the footprint of the 509th CG on Tinian, especially the two atomic bomb loading pits. All of a sudden, he started talking about his war experiences on the island and the work he did on the 509th Composite Group's composite hut camp, actually meeting Col. Paul Tibbets. It was as if I had been transported back in time to 1944 when my father worked with the 509th, and I flashed forward to my book telling the 509th's history.

As an Air Force lieutenant colonel assigned to the 544th Aerial Reconnaissance Technical Wing, Offutt Air Force Base, Nebraska, I was deputy commander for resource management. My office was in Building D, the former World War II Martin Aircraft B-29 production plant. My office was on the ground floor, adjacent to the former main production line for the Boeing Superfortress. It was from this production line that Col. Paul Tibbets, 509th CG commander, selected his unit's B-29s. I was able to walk over the remaining wood-block flooring on a section of the World War II Martin bomber plant where the 509th's atomic-delivery-capable B-29s were built and think about what my father did to build the runways and facilities they used to drop the two atomic bombs on Japan to end World Wat II. Interestingly, part of my classified Air Force training was that of a conventional and nuclear weapons weaponeer officer, along with many classified nuclear operations. While assigned to the Joint Chiefs of Staff at the Pentagon, I supported the 509th Bomb Wing's operations. I have a connection with the 509th that extends from 1944 to 2017, pushing me onward to research and write the history of Whiteman Air Force Base.

During World War II, I Troop Carrier Command pilots and personnel trained with the Waco Aircraft Company (WACO) CG-4A glider, Curtiss C-46, and Douglas C-47 cargo/troop transports. The CG-4A was the Army's first stealth aircraft flown in combat. The glider was built of wood covered with fabric, was unarmed, and was vulnerable to enemy small arms, with disastrous results from hard crash combat landings. Whiteman Air Force Base is preserving its military heritage as a group of volunteers restores a WACO CG-4A glider from parts recovered in Kansas City, Missouri. Plans are to create a museum around the glider, maintaining the early history of the base.

The Cold War with the Soviet Union brought rapid changes, including a new name, Whiteman Air Force Base. The Strategic Air Command (SAC), 340th Bomb Wing (BW), was equipped with the turbojet Boeing B-47 Stratojet medium bomber and the piston KC-97 Stratofreighter (aerial tanker) to stand nuclear alert, supported by the storage of nuclear weapons inside a highly secure and specialized weapons storage area (WSA). Whiteman also supported SAC satellite nuclear alert operations by the supersonic B-58 Hustler delta-wing bomber and KC-135A Stratotanker.

Whiteman was home to the 150 Minuteman I and later Minuteman II intercontinental ballistic missiles (ICBMs) of SAC's Wing IV, part of the nation's nuclear triad, manned by a professional cadre of missileers. It was hard duty that continues today with three active Minuteman III missile wings deterring a nuclear attack on the United States. With the Strategic Arms Reduction Treaty (START), Minuteman II ICBMs were removed and launch facilities and underground launch control centers destroyed except for Whitman's Oscar-01, preserved as a museum to those who served as missileers and supported the missiles of Whiteman. It was SAC's only on-base missile alert facility with the associated underground launch control center, which monitored the Oscar squadron's 10 Minuteman III ICBMs.

The 509th was reborn as an Air Force Global Strike Command (AFGSC) bomb wing flying the Northrop B-2 stealth bomber. With 20 B-2s in the Air Force's only B-2 bomb wing, Whiteman closes the historic loop from the silent glider wings of the WACO CG-4A to modern stealth technology. The B-2 can strike any target in the world, arriving over the target undetected and destroying multiple targets with highly accurate precision-guided munitions. Whiteman airmen share the B-2 with the Missouri National Guard's 131st BW. The 131st BW is the only nuclear certified National Guard unit.

Whiteman is a multi-mission base, vital to keeping the United States free from potential enemies, at the same time reducing operational costs to the Department of Defense. The 442nd Fighter Wing flies the A-10, a powerful ground attack aircraft. The 20th Reconnaissance Squadron flies the unmanned, remotely controlled MQ-1B Predator to provide ground support in overseas locations, supporting America's war on terrorism. To maintain B-2 pilot proficiency, the 394th Combat Training Squadron operates the T-38 Talon, providing a high-performance, low-cost-per-flying-hour aircraft for the 509th BW. Pilots can train in all flight environments, also using the full-motion B-2 simulators to fly combat missions and practice emergency flight procedures. The B-2s are a high-cost national asset flown by extremely qualified pilots with outstanding maintenance and support personnel. North Korea has tested atomic weapons, short- and medium-range ballistic missiles, and in July 2017, demonstrated an ICBM with the range to attack Alaska, Hawaii, and most of the nations in the Pacific; nuclear deterrence has become even more important as nuclear threats are reappearing from a new group of nations, led by North Korea and Iran.

Whiteman Air Force Base supports the 1st Battalion, Army Reserve, which flies AH-64D Apache Longbow helicopters. In 2014, the battalion, which has served in Afghanistan, won the Outstanding Reserve Unit award. After more than 60 years, Whiteman Air Force Base continues the heritage of the 509th Composite Group. From the WACO CG-4A glider and the Boeing B-29 Superfortress to the Northrop B-2 stealth bomber, Whiteman Air Force Base blends a World War II–era base with modern technology to attack targets with stealth. Whiteman Air Force Base embraces the concept that "Freedom is not free," requiring professionals to secure the United States 24 hours a day. While finishing my research on the base, eating breakfast in the modern dining facility, I recognized a former Cold War adversary, a Russian general who was visiting the base as part of the Russian START investigation team that visits nuclear installations around the United States. He was part of my Air Force career as an intelligence officer.

The heritage of the 509th Bomb Wing sets the standard of maintaining America's freedom, assaulted by increasing external threats once thought extinguished. The 509th's mission is to provide strategic deterrence, global power, and combatant commanders anytime, anywhere. The dedicated professionals of the 509th BW play a major role in America's global power and long-range strike mission by developing a B-2 combat force capable of delivering rapid, decisive, and survivable air power. The Northrop B-2 Spirit stealth bomber represents a dramatic advancement in technology and achievement of major milestones in the Air Force bomber modernization program. The top secret bomber brings massive firepower to bear in a short time, anywhere on the globe, through previously determined and designed impenetrable defenses. Whiteman Air Force base is a key linchpin in America's global war on terrorism and gives potential adversaries knowledge that no target is immune.

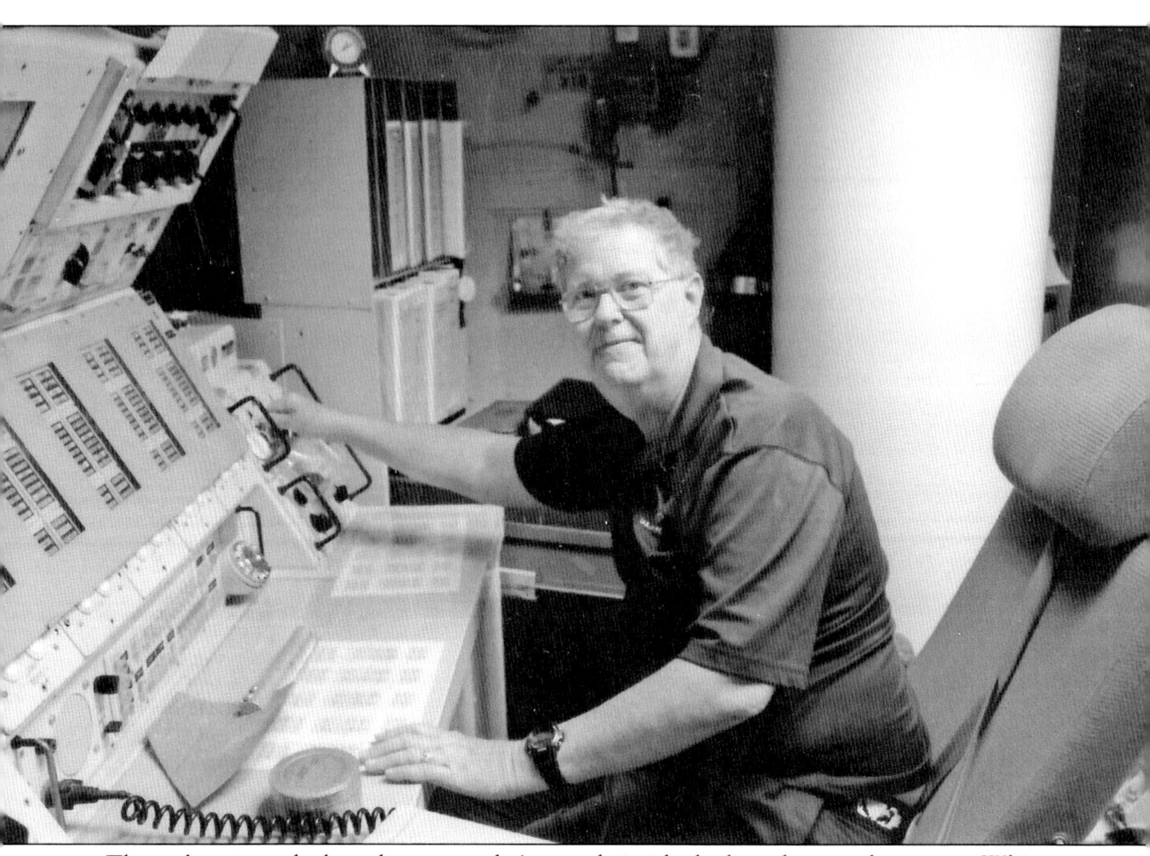

The author sits at the launch commander's console inside the launch control center on Whiteman Air Force Base. (Author's collection.)

One

Sedalia Army Air Field, Early History 1942–1946

In the spring of 1942, a US Army site section board, consisting of Army officers, examined possible sites around Sedalia, Missouri, for a proposed glider training station. At that time, the Army Air Forces (AAF) were attempting to locate sites for air bases to accommodate their expanding tactical air strength to fight a world war. One of the organizations that needed bases was I Troop Carrier Command (I TCC), organized on April 30, 1942, to train combat troop carrier units and crews. In order to carry out its training program, I TCC needed 12 airfields. The board considered several sites, including the Missouri State Fairgrounds in Sedalia and a spot near Dresden, but it considered these not capable for expansion.

On August 8, 1942, the training base was activated. The new airfield was placed under jurisdiction of I TCC at Stout Field, Indianapolis, Indiana. The primary mission of the airfield was the activation of troop carrier groups and advanced training of glider pilots. By September 1942, the airfield was ready for use. The first tactical organizations to be trained at the airfield were 50th Troop Carrier Wing (TCW), which established its headquarters on the airfield, and 89th Troop Carrier Group (TCG), together with its components. The base was one of eight dedicated to training WACO CG-4A glider pilots. Eventually, the base was named Sedalia Army Air Field, Warrensburg, Missouri. Training from January through March 1943 was centered on the transition from C-47s to C-46s and different phases in combat crew training.

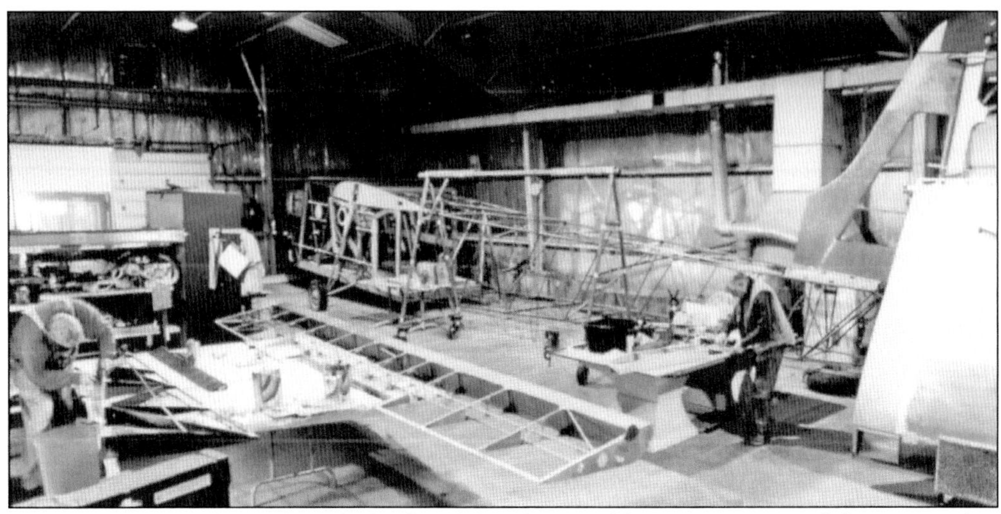

A WACO glider is being brought back to life. This World War II training glider was used at Sedalia Army Air Field during World War II. Today, the facility is called Whiteman Air Force Base, and the 509th Bomb Wing is attempting to maintain its historic past. (Courtesy Whiteman Air Force Base, 509th Bomb Wing Public Affairs.)

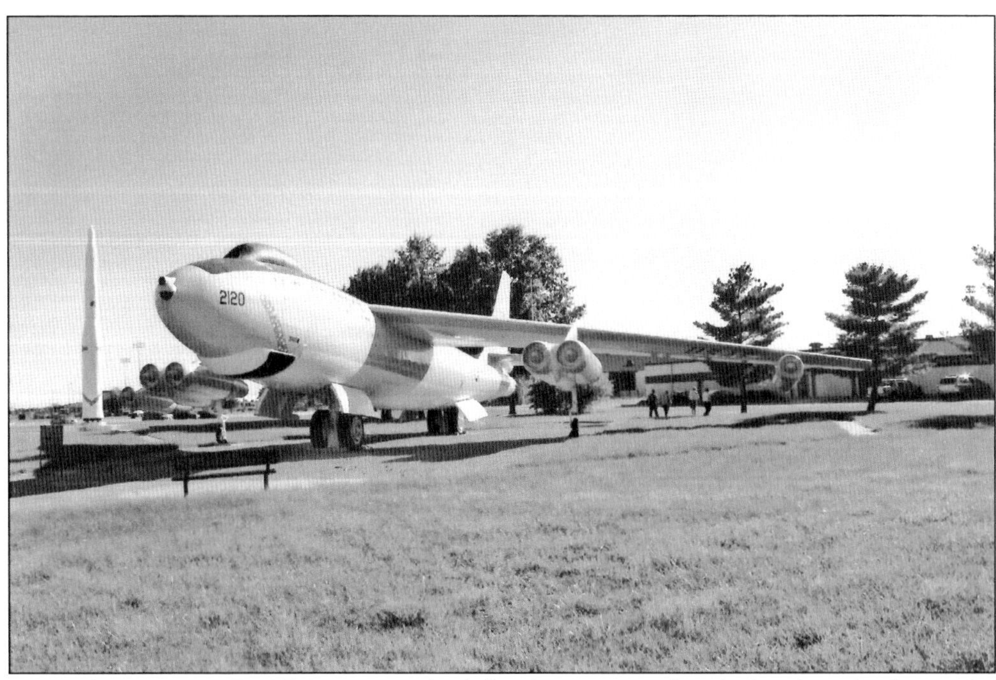

Pictured is a Boeing B-47E Stratojet, which has been restored and placed on display in the Whiteman Air Force Base Air Park to represent the time when these medium bombers were assigned to the base. (Author's collection.)

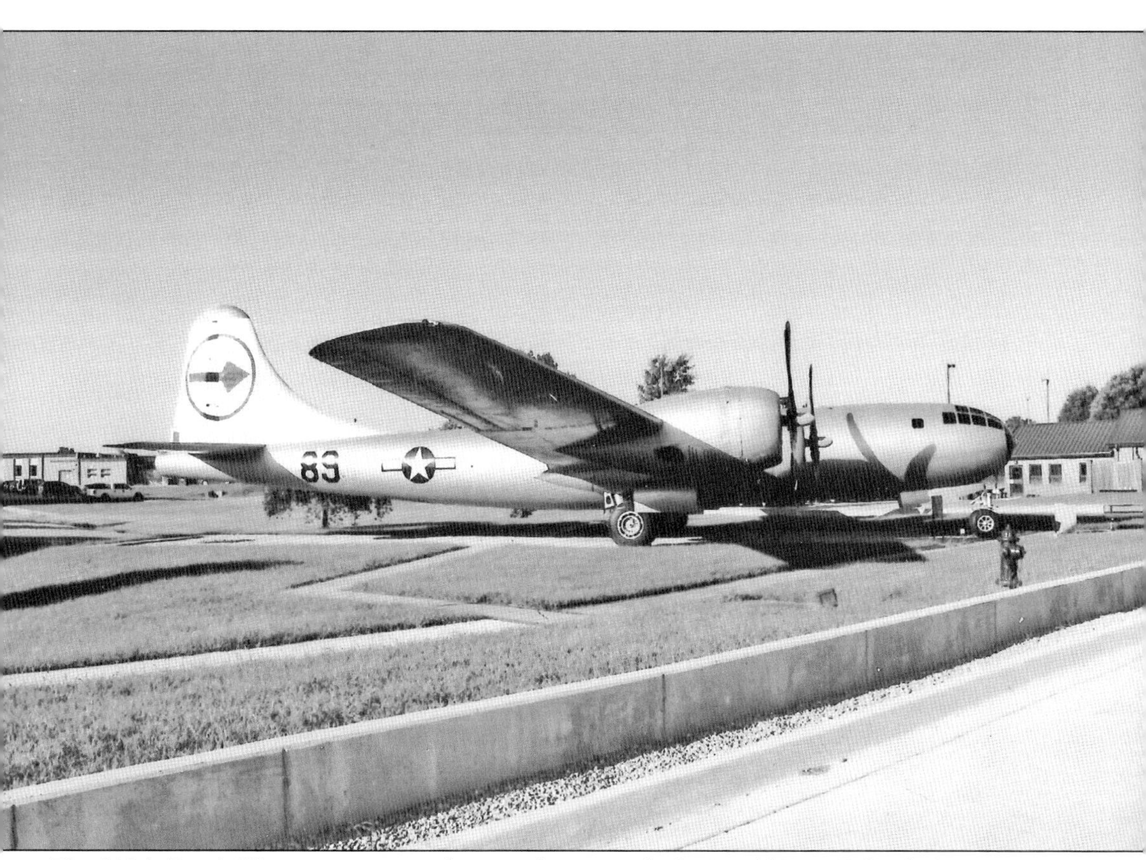

The 509th Bomb Wing maintains its historical roots with the World War II 509th Composite Group on Tinian island with this restored Boeing B-29 Superfortress, on display at Whiteman Air Force Base alongside the main security access gate. (Author's collection.)

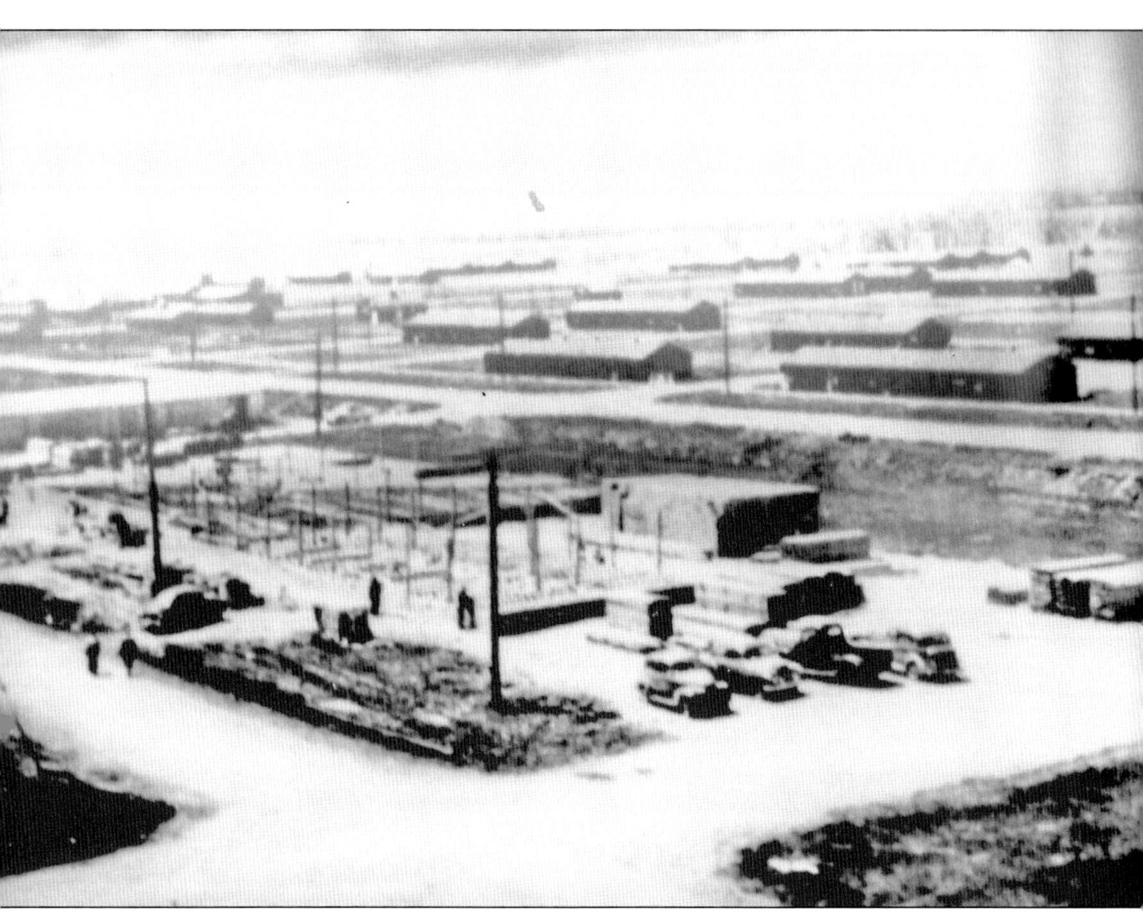

These rows of wood barracks provided housing for thousands of Army trainees who were temporarily assigned to the base. The secure storage area is visible in the foreground. (Courtesy Whiteman Air Force Base, 509th Bomb Wing Public Affairs.)

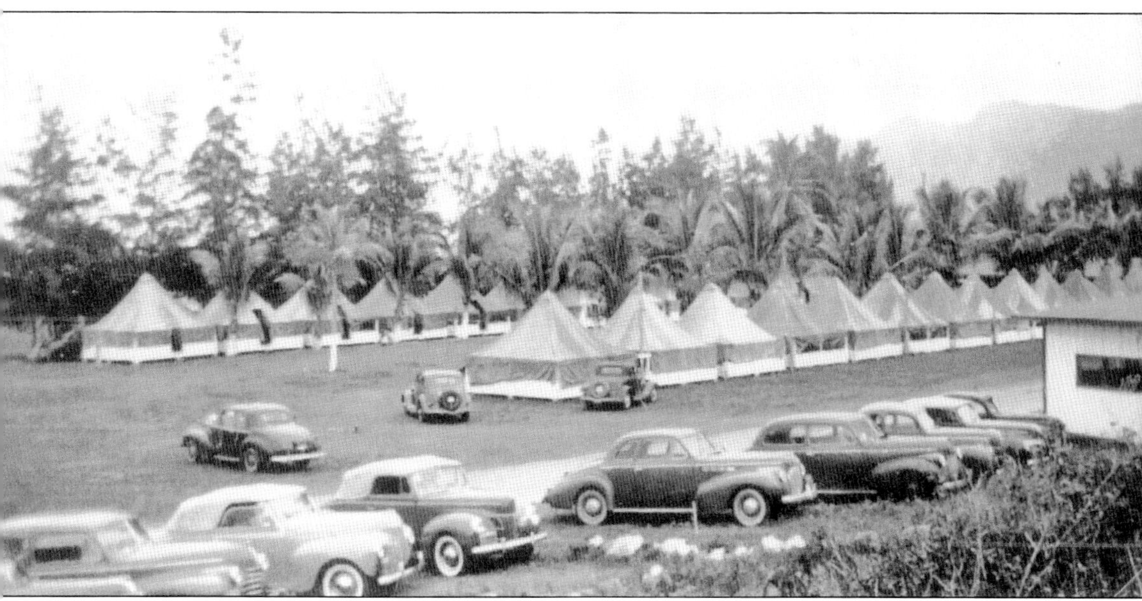

Early in 1942, four-man pyramid tents were erected to house glider pilots and paratroopers training with gliders and C-47s at Sedalia Army Air Field until wood barracks were built. (Courtesy US Army.)

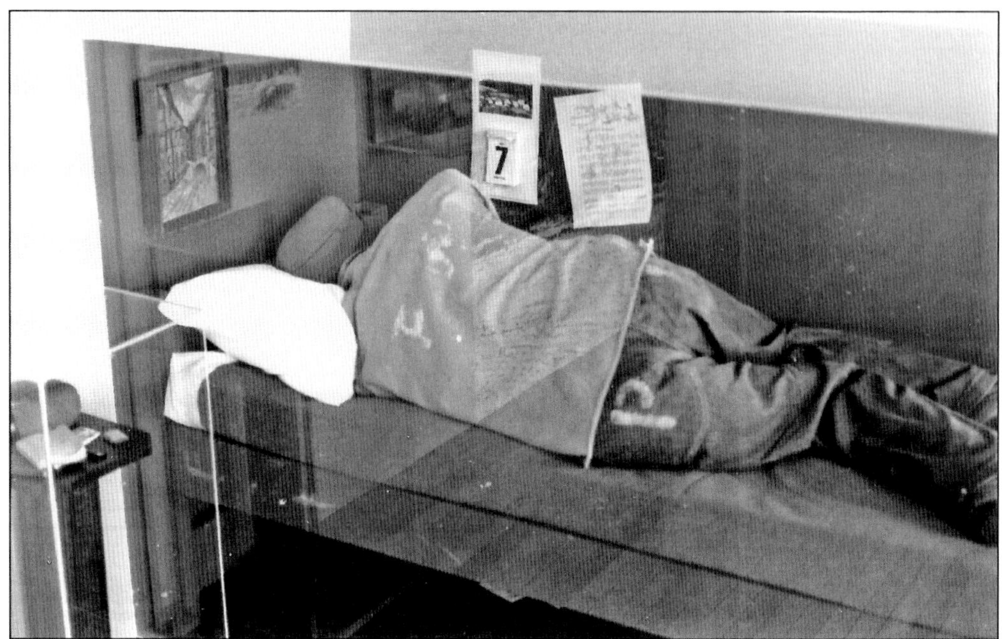

A mannequin of a World War II German POW wears Army-issued clothes. "PW" was painted on the back and front of the POW's shirt and pants. Each POW was issued basic Army clothes but was allowed to retain his uniform. (Author's collection.)

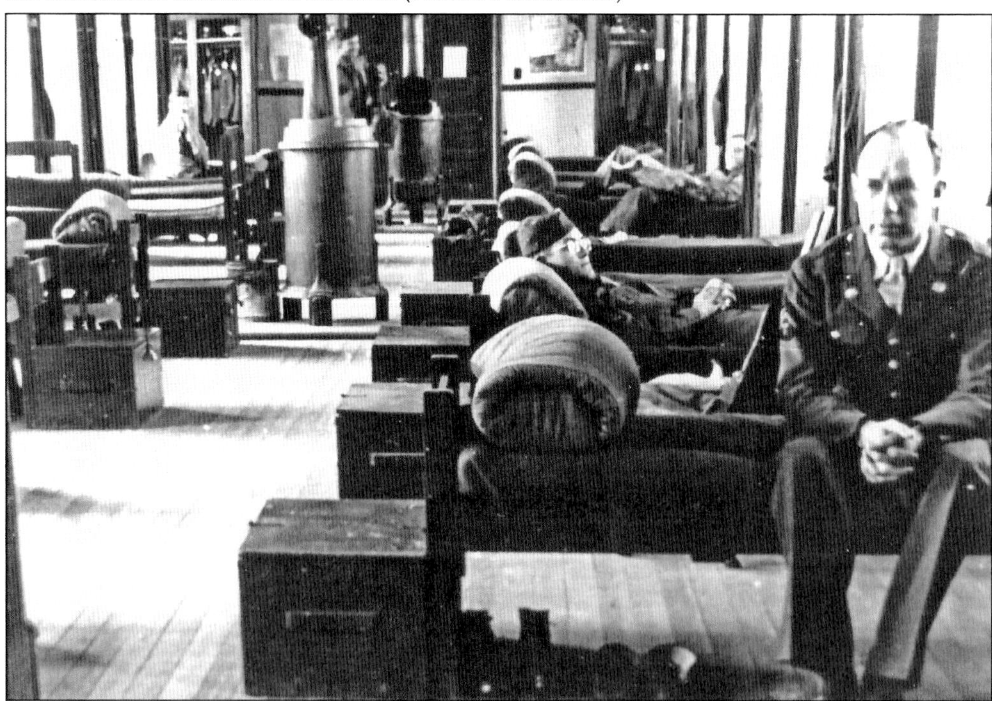

Shown here is a typical POW barracks built by the US Army, with a double row of bunks, footlockers, and clothes hanging on the walls. The barracks were equipped with coal- or woodstoves for heat and had a wood floor set on concrete blocks or posts to prevent tunneling for escapes attempts. (Courtesy US Army.)

Two

Sedalia Army Air Field, I Troop Carrier Command Training 1942–1947

Although the US Army in 1923 and Navy in 1930 looked at the feasibility of using gliders, their interest died. The War Department in 1940–1941 again looked into gliders as the threat of war with Germany, Italy, and the Empire of Japan grew. In the Army's original operational concept, glider pilots would be pulled from existing rated pilots. The shortage of qualified pilots killed this option, especially with the War Department requested 6,000 glider pilots. The CG-4A glider was the mainstay of the AAF glider forces during World War II. Nearly 18,800 were produced from 1942 to 1945, built by 16 prime contractors with many subcontractors. These contractors had to limit aluminum in the construction of the gliders, built out of more than 70,000 parts, with wood and fabric as the primary materials.

The CG-4A became one of the AAF's boldest aerial weapons of World War II to deliver troops, equipment, and cargo behind enemy lines in a stealth mode. Interesting, I TCC training at Sedalia Army Air Field operated decades before the assignment of the Northrop B-2 stealth bomber to the same location, now Whiteman Air Force Base (AFB); both are considered stealth aircraft. The CG-4A was pulled to altitude by the AAF's twin-engine Curtiss C-46 Commando or Douglas C-47 Dakota/Skytrain, towed to the designated drop or release zone, and released for the two pilots to glide to a silent landing behind enemy lines. Once the pilots were on the ground, the landing zone was secured to allow follow-up landings delivering troops, equipment, ammunition, and supplies. Operational gliders could be snatched airborne from the secured landing area to fly out wounded personnel. When glider pilots arrived at Sedalia Army Air Field, they went through a specialized glider training program that included combat training to prepare them to fight on the ground once they landed their glider, prior to their transport back to their base.

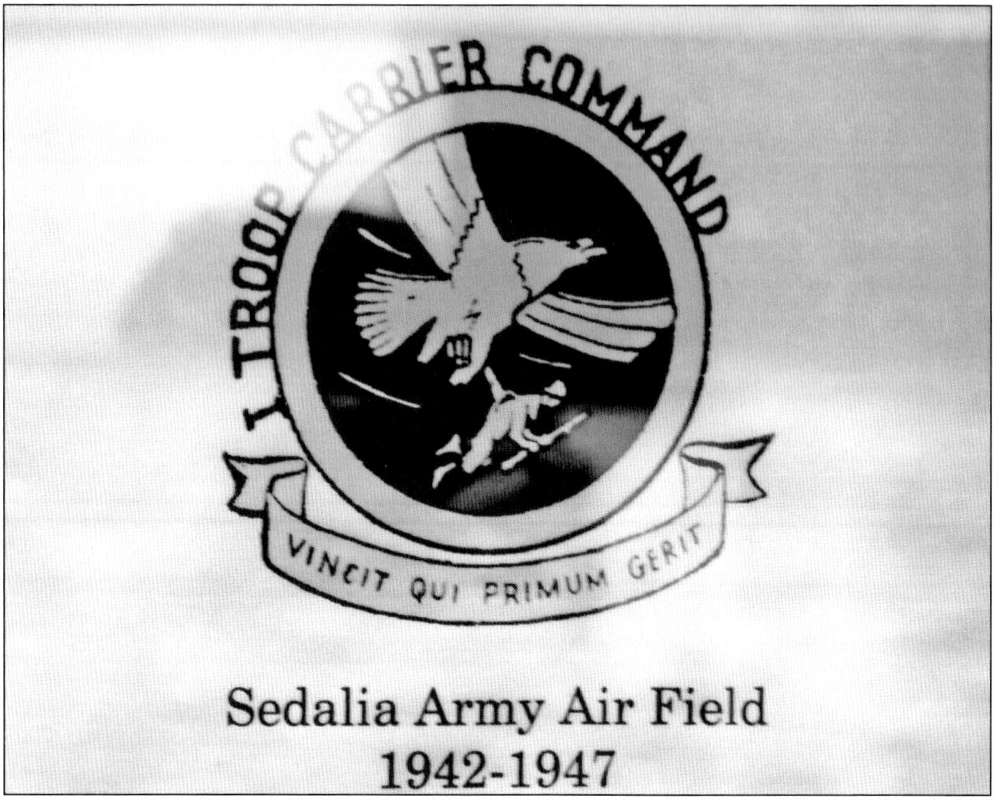

I TROOP CARRIER COMMAND

VINCIT QUI PRIMUM GERIT

Sedalia Army Air Field
1942-1947

Pictured is the World War I Troop Carrier Command shield. (Courtesy 509th Wing Public Affairs.)

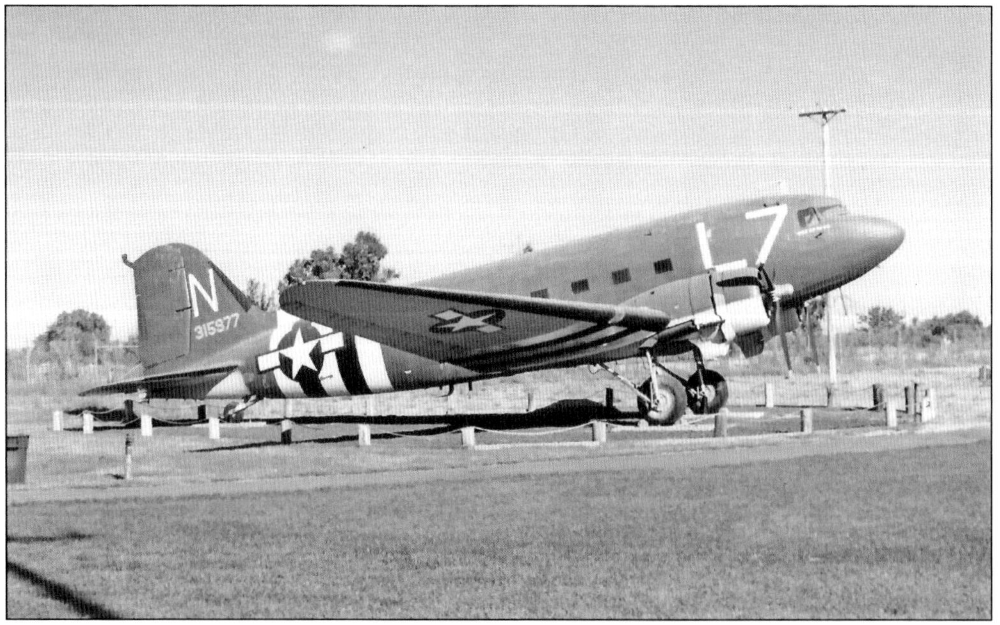

This Douglas C-47 transport/tow aircraft is on display at the Castle Air Museum in Atwater, California. (Author's collection.)

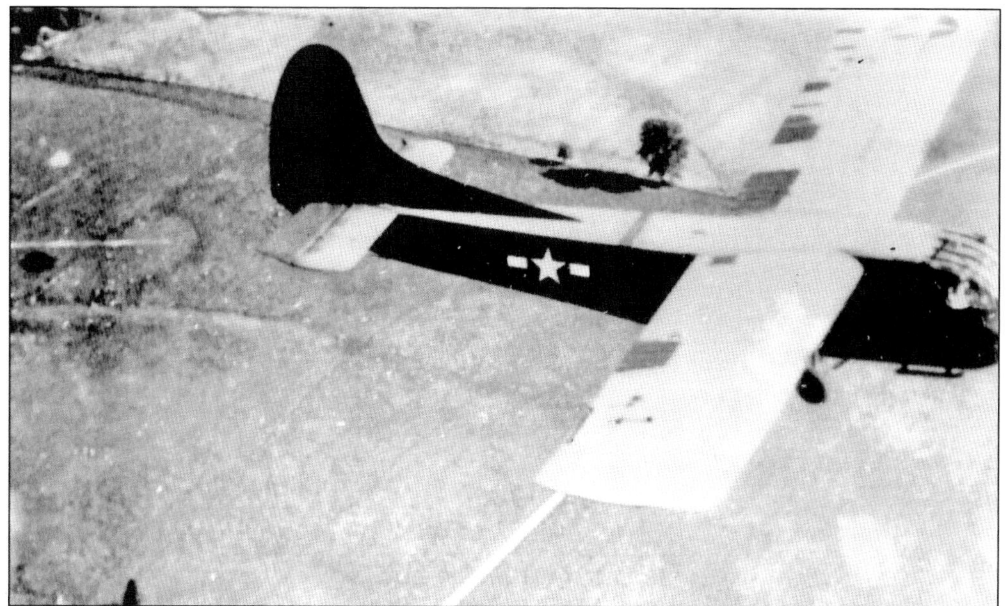

This WACO CG-4A glider was released from its C-47 tow ship near Sedalia Army Air Field, then glided to a designated spot landing on the runway. (Courtesy Whiteman Air Force Base, 509th Bomb Wing Public Affairs.)

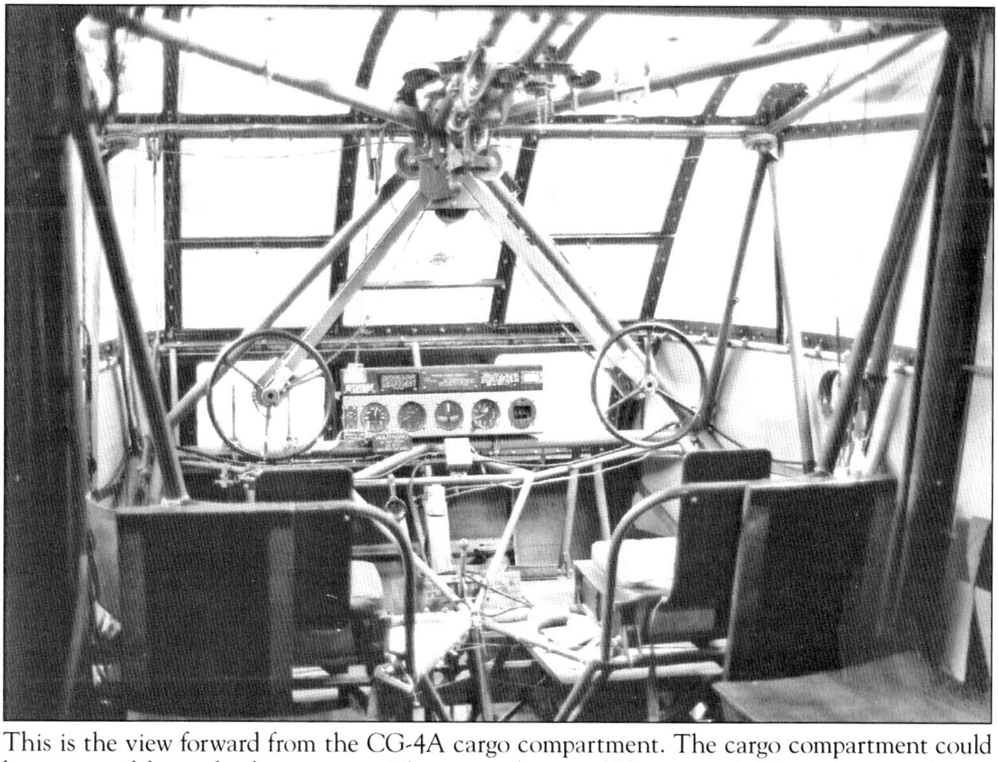

This is the view forward from the CG-4A cargo compartment. The cargo compartment could be converted for medical evacuation. Three stretchers could be suspended from the aircraft's top fuselage ribs on each side of the cargo area. The glider is on display at the Silent Wings Museum in Texas. (Author's collection.)

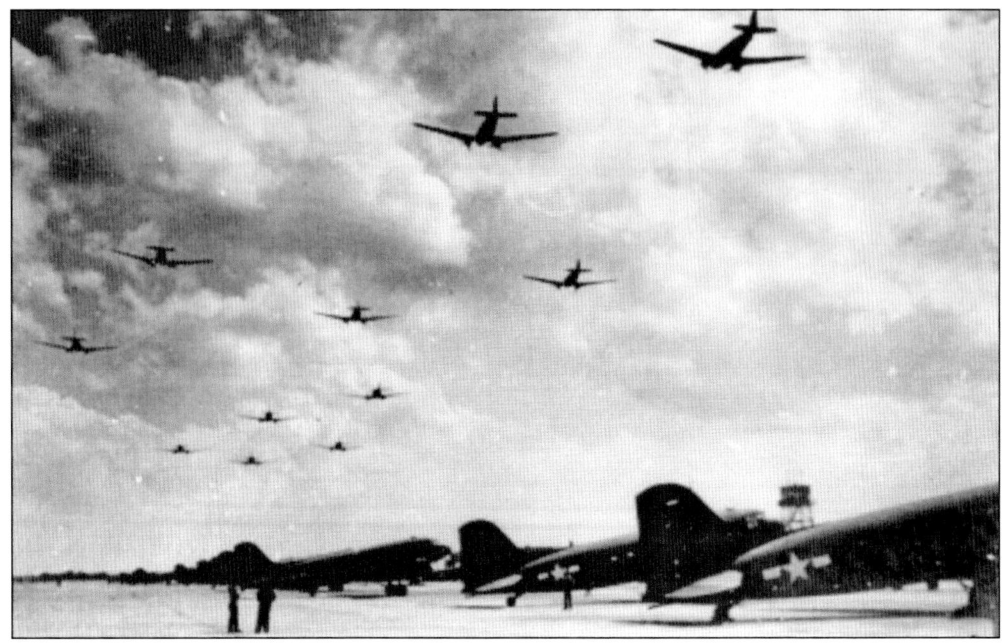

These C-47s are over the Sedalia Army Air Field flight line in formation, part of an air show during the base's open house. Other C-47s are parked on the flight line. The flight line operations tower is visible above the parked C-47s. (Courtesy Whiteman Air Force Base, 509th Bomb Wing Public Affairs.)

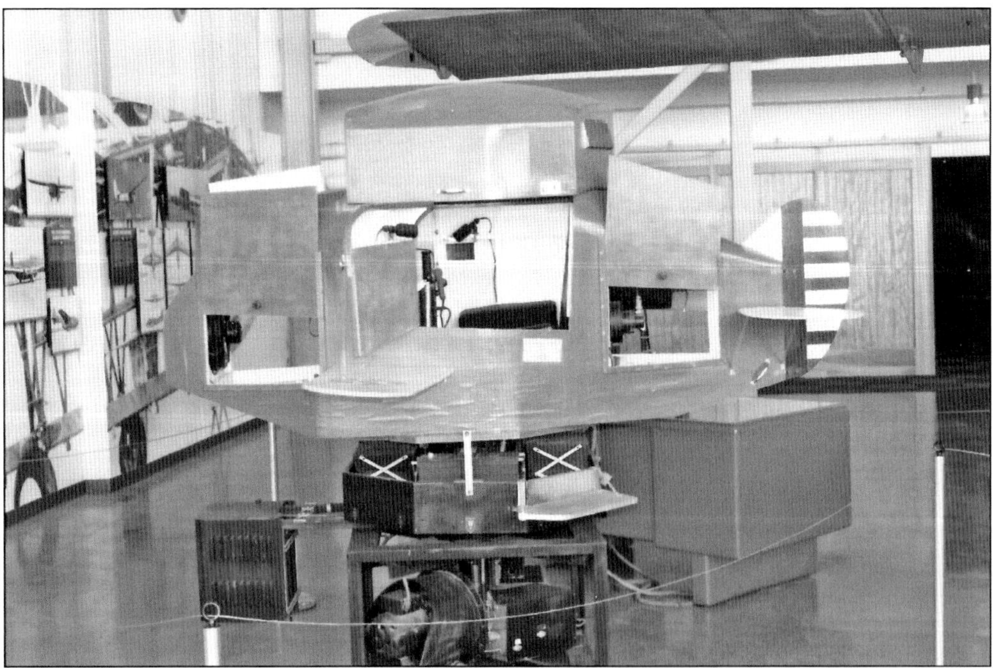

During World War II, the Link trainer was mass-produced to train pilots on instrument flying, often referred to as blind flying. The Link trainer provided pilots, sitting inside an enclosed cockpit, with a full-motion trainer with the feel of an actual aircraft. This restored Link trainer is on display at the Silent Wings Museum. (Author's collection.)

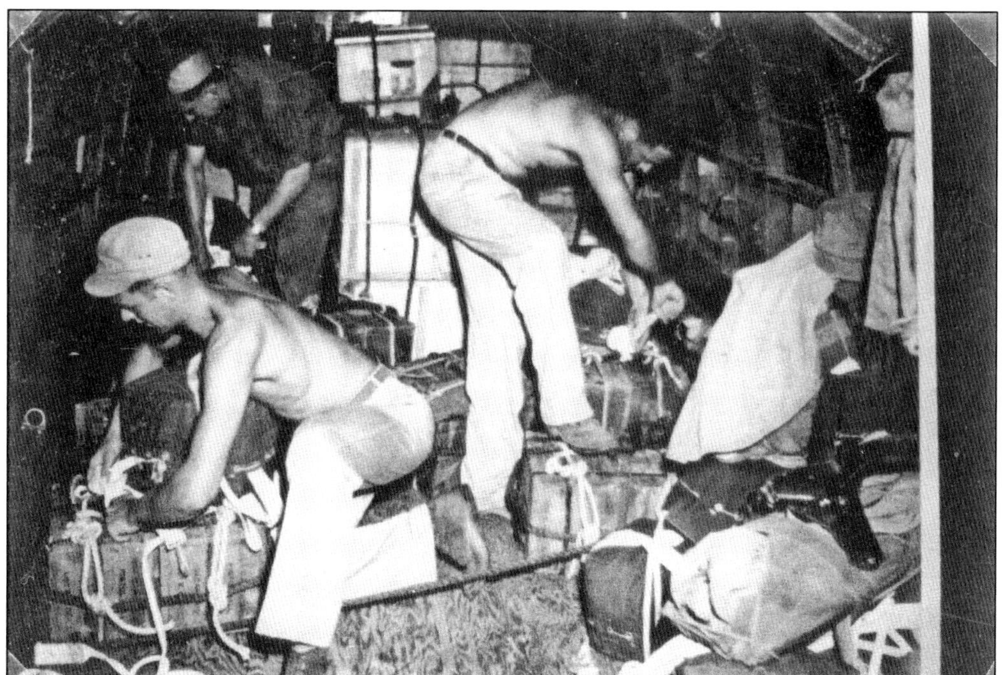

These aircrew enlisted personnel are pushing bundled equipment with parachutes that will be opened by static lines attached to the aircraft's fuselage door frame. During summer training months, it was hot inside the C-47, as noted by the lack of shirts on the crew in the C-47's cargo compartment. (Author's collection.)

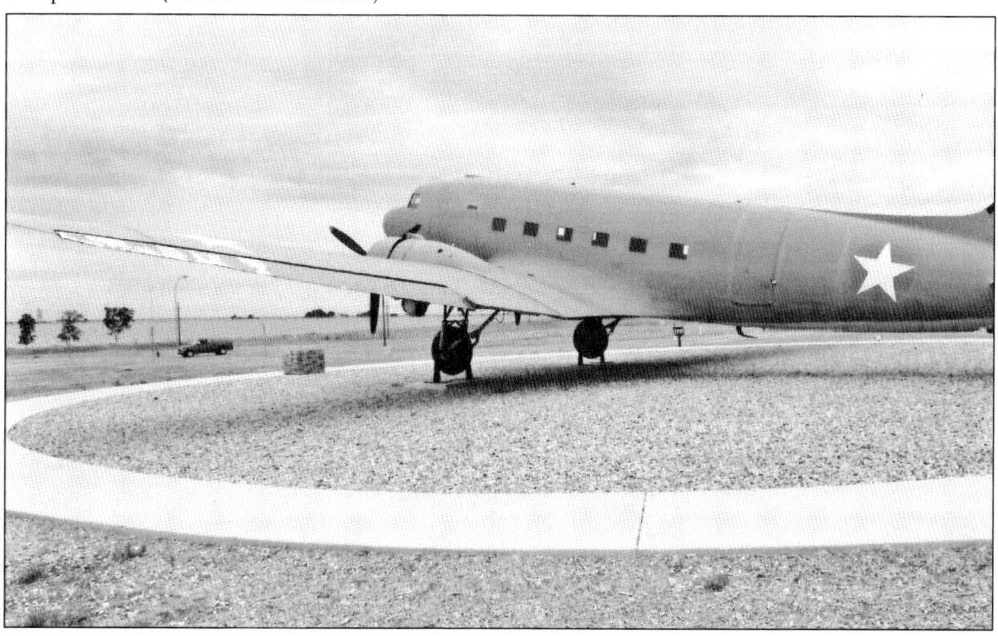

This Douglas C-47 is on static display at the Dakota Territory Air Museum in Minot, North Dakota. The C-47, the backbone of the US Army's airborne forces support, was ideal for towing the WACO CG-4A glider behind enemy lines. There were never enough C-47s to meet the demand of the United States and its allies during World War II. (Author's collection.)

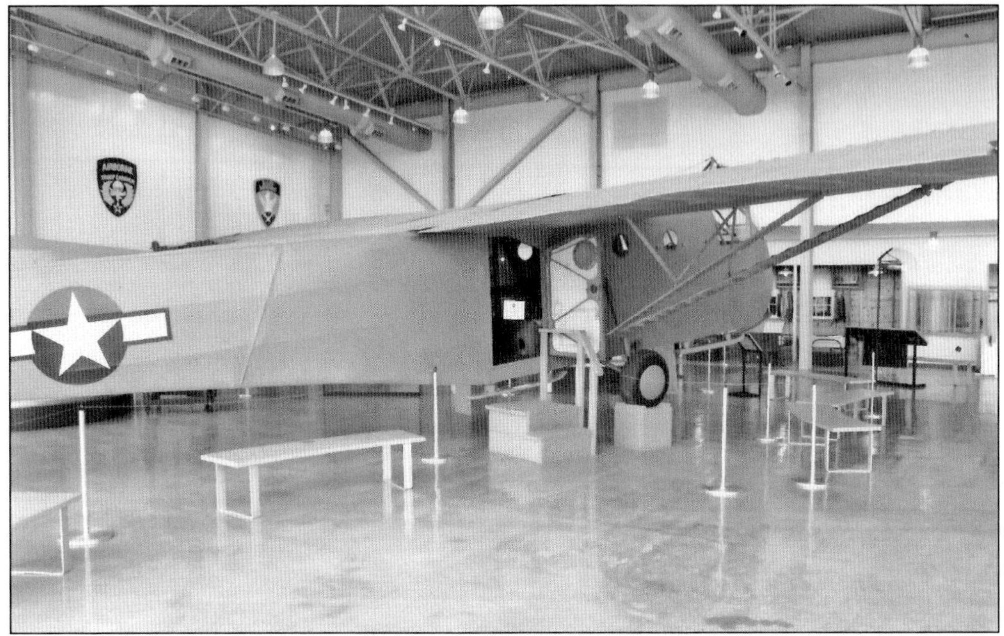

Pictured is a restored WACO CG-4A glider on display at the Silent Wings Museum. The wood-and-fabric aircraft transported troops and equipment behind enemy lines, bypassing heavy defenses. The glider became part of the fluidity of World War II combat. The aircraft used limited steel tubing in its construction, with wood ribs for the wings covered with fabric. (Author's collection.)

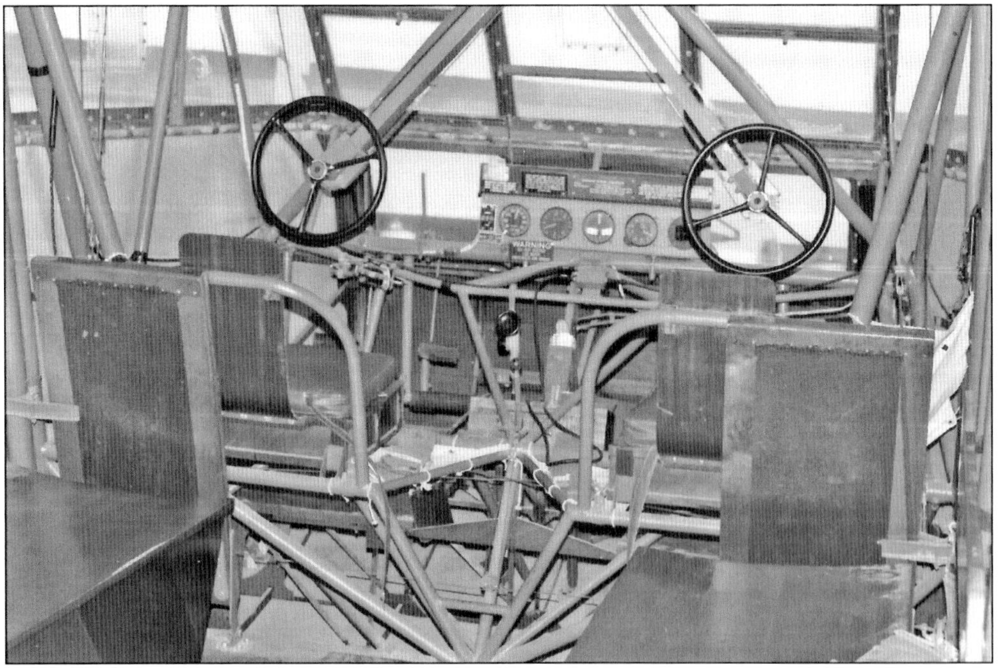

This close-up view looks from the WACO glider's cargo/troop compartment into the pilots' compartment. Controls were simple, allowing the pilots to maintain tow position behind the C-47 and, when cut loose, to complete a landing into a designated area. The cockpit was not designed for pilot comfort. (Author's collection.)

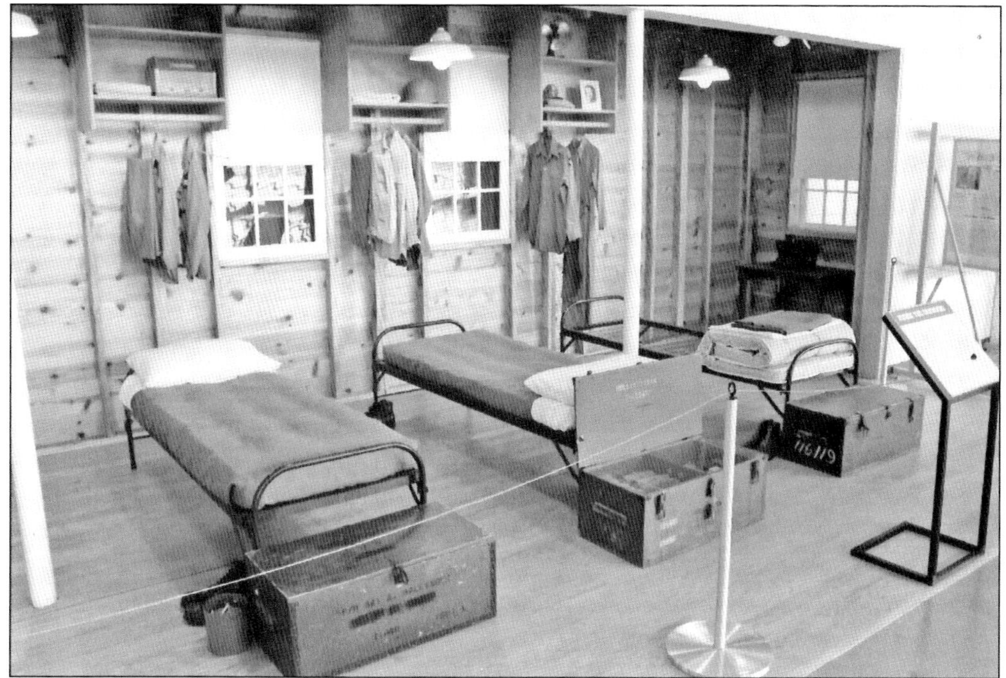

Army barracks were sparse, filled with limited furnishing for those assigned to Sedalia and other Army training bases. This display includes World War II clothes hanging on the wall, with shelves above. Army cots, shown here, were single beds covered with rough blankets, one pillow, and sheets. Wood footlockers were at the foot of the cots. (Author's collection.)

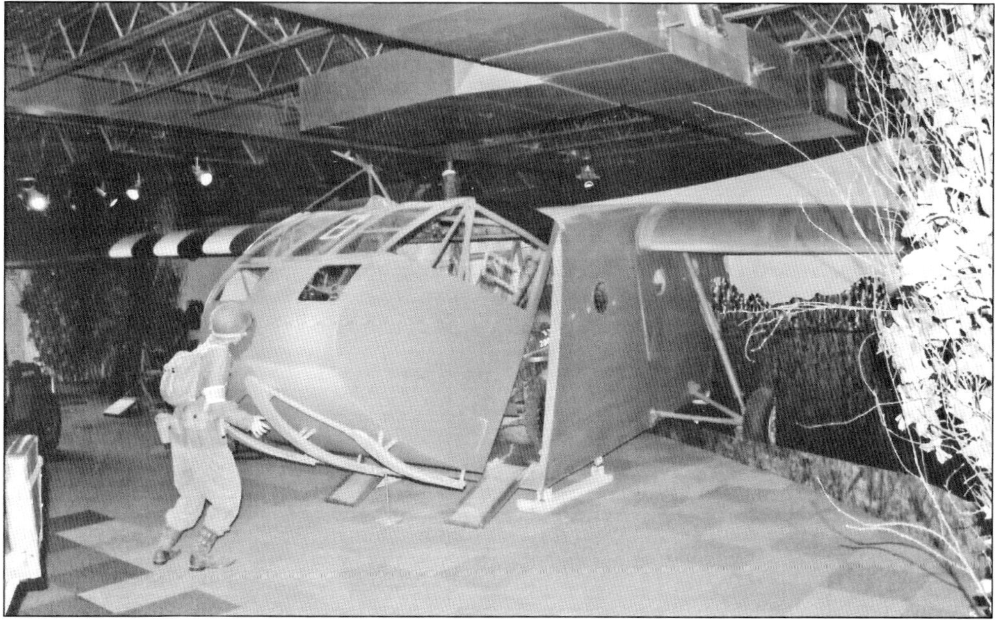

The WACO glider has a unique feature. The nose compartment, containing the two pilots' controls, could be released and raised, allowing large pieces of the equipment to be loaded and unloaded through the front. This WACO glider is on display at the Silent Wings Museum. (Author's collection.)

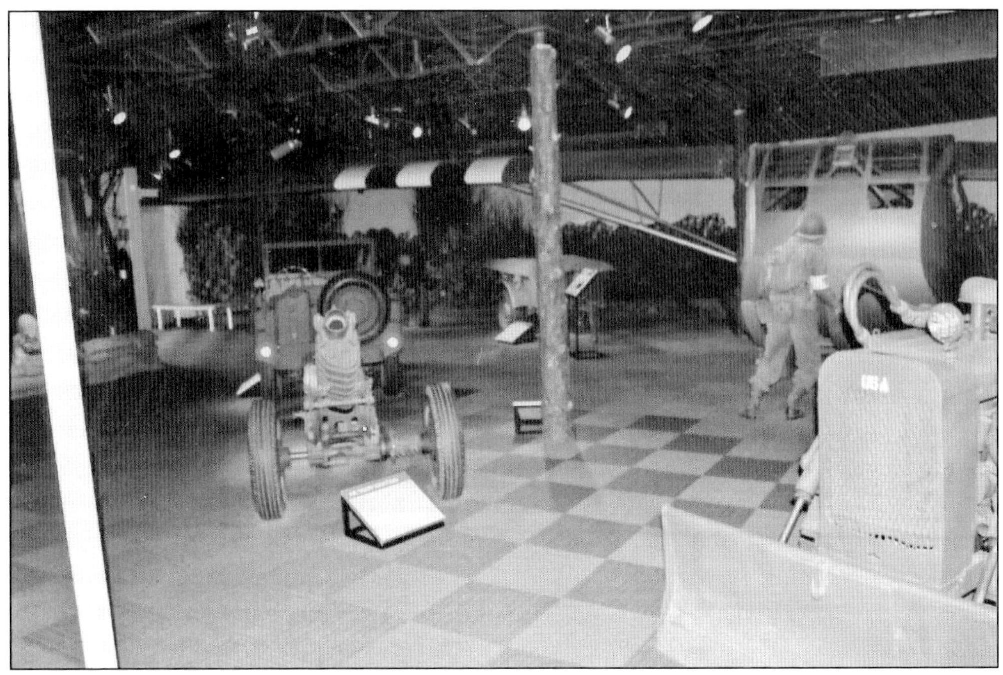

The WACO glider was able to haul equipment, like this 75-millimeter field artillery piece, needed by the airborne and glider troops once on the ground to defend themselves from heavily armed enemy troops. This gun is on display at the Silent Wings Museum. (Author's collection.)

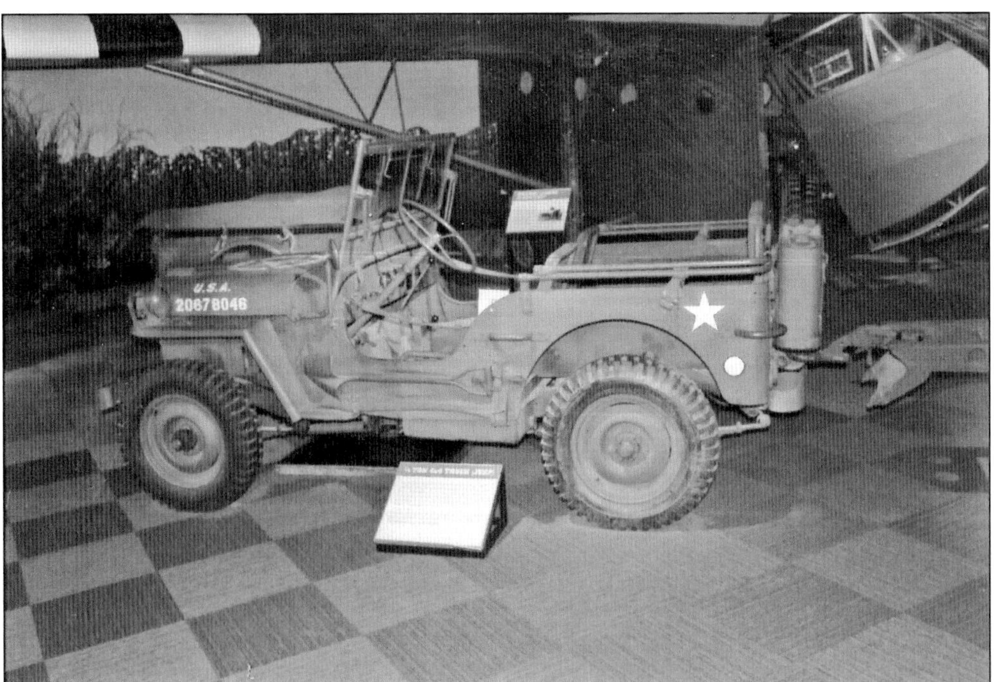

To tow the 75-millimeter artillery piece and light trailers, the WACO glider could also deliver the versatile Army jeep. It could be quickly unloaded from the glider once the front compartment was raised and provided mobility for airborne troops when on the ground. (Author's collection.)

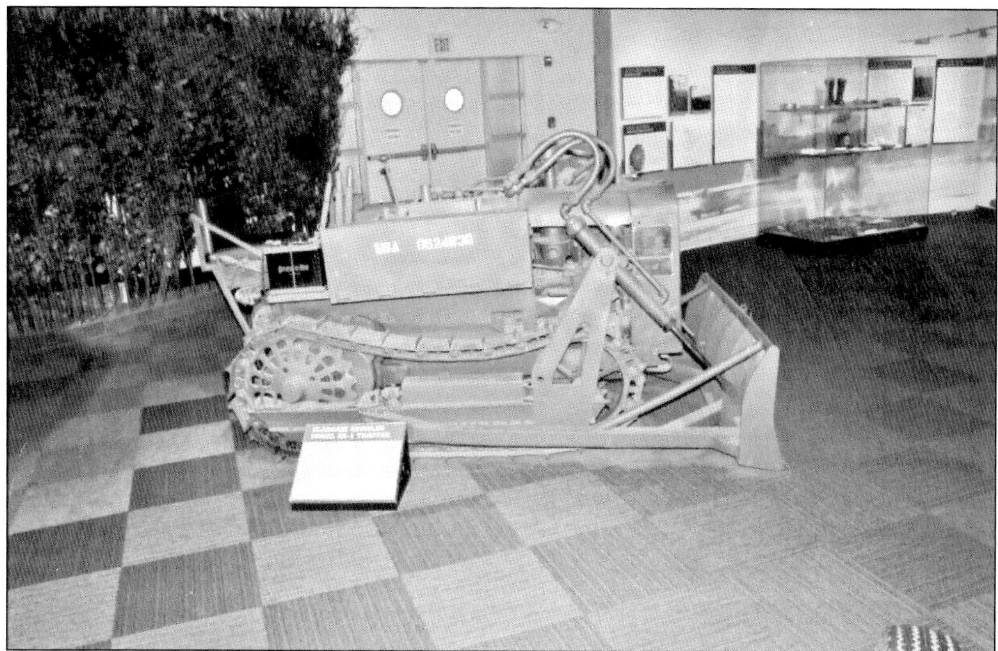

The heaviest equipment, nearly maxing out the glider's cargo capacity, was this mini-bulldozer. It was often used to clear the landing area of badly damaged and smashed gliders to allow follow-on operations. The bulldozer is on display at the Silent Wings Museum. (Author's collection.)

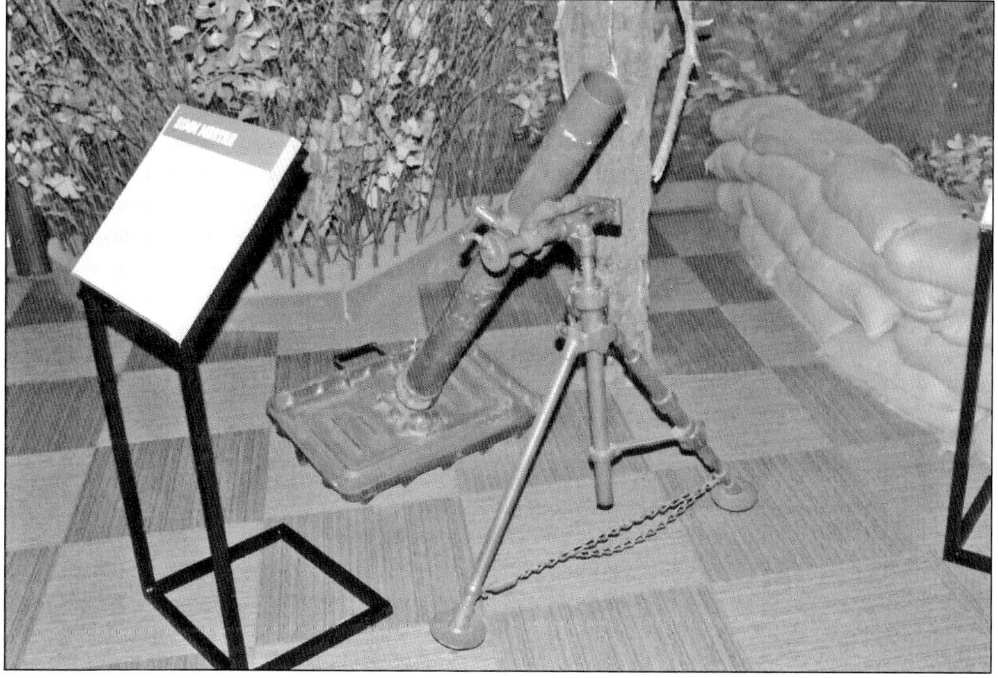

The WACO glider could deliver the Army's heavy mortar, needed to provide fire support to hold off enemy troops. Troops had to be trained to properly secure the mortar so that on rough landings it would not become a deadly projectile inside the glider. This one is on display at the Silent Wings Museum. (Author's collection.)

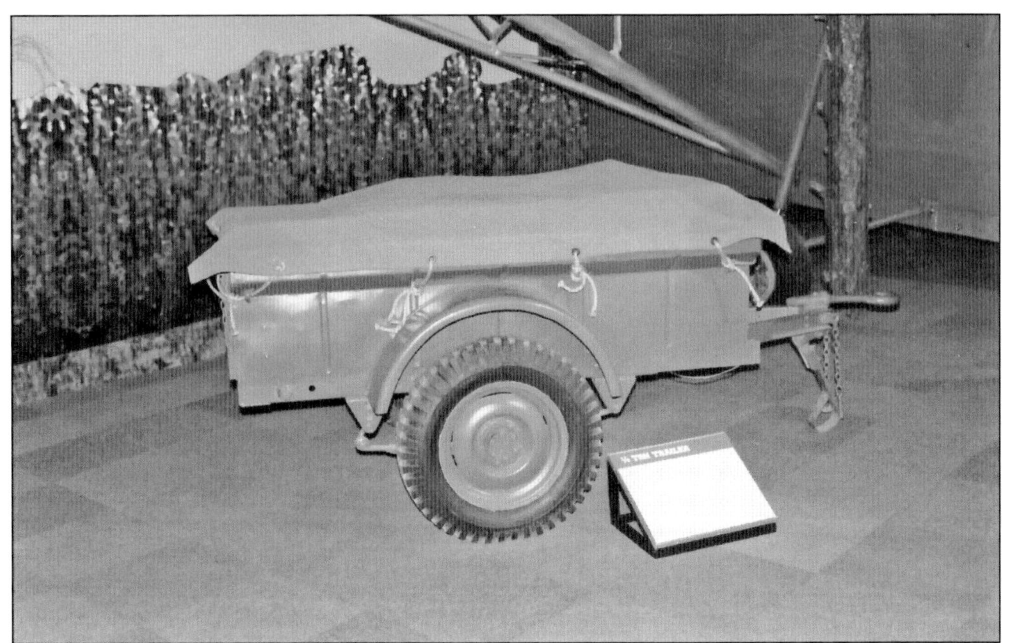

The Army's light utility trailer could be carried by the WACO glider, loaded with ammunition, food, medical supplies, communications equipment, and whatever the airborne troops needed. The trailer could be quickly unloaded and hooked to a jeep. This trailer is on display at the Silent Wings Museum. (Author's collection.)

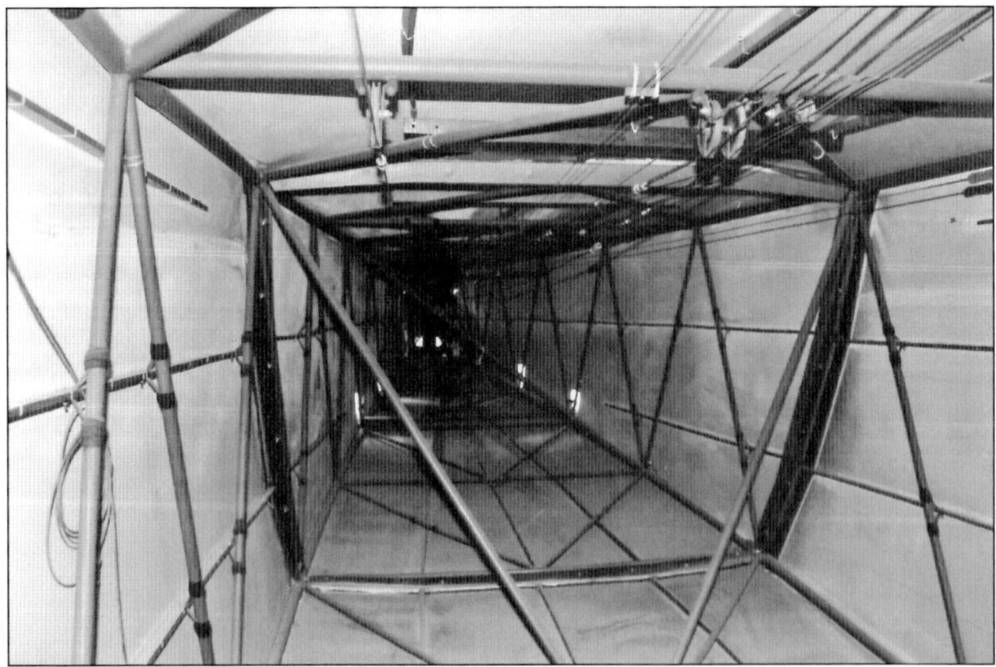

This view from the rear cargo compartment of the WACO glider toward the rear fuselage shows the steel tubing and fabric covering. The glider proved to be a remarkably tough aircraft, surviving all but the most drastic landings. This glider is on display at the Silent Wings Museum. (Author's collection.)

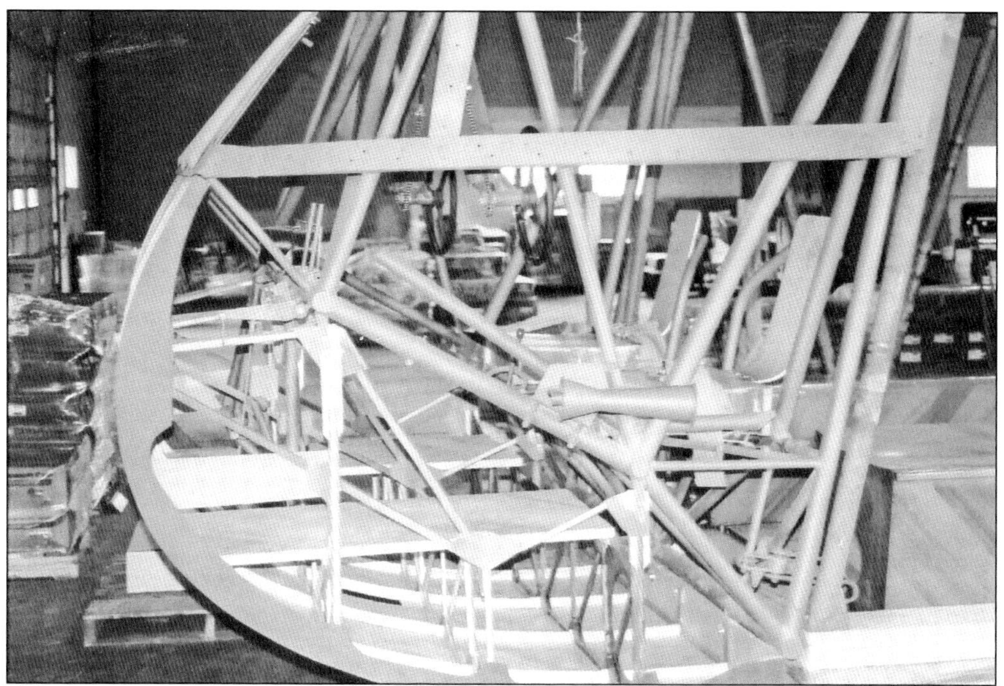

Shown is the interior steel and wood framework of the glider's fuselage. The wood floor is installed. One end of the Villaume Industries Warehouse in Minneapolis has been turned into a restoration workshop. The company built gliders during World War II. (Author's collection.)

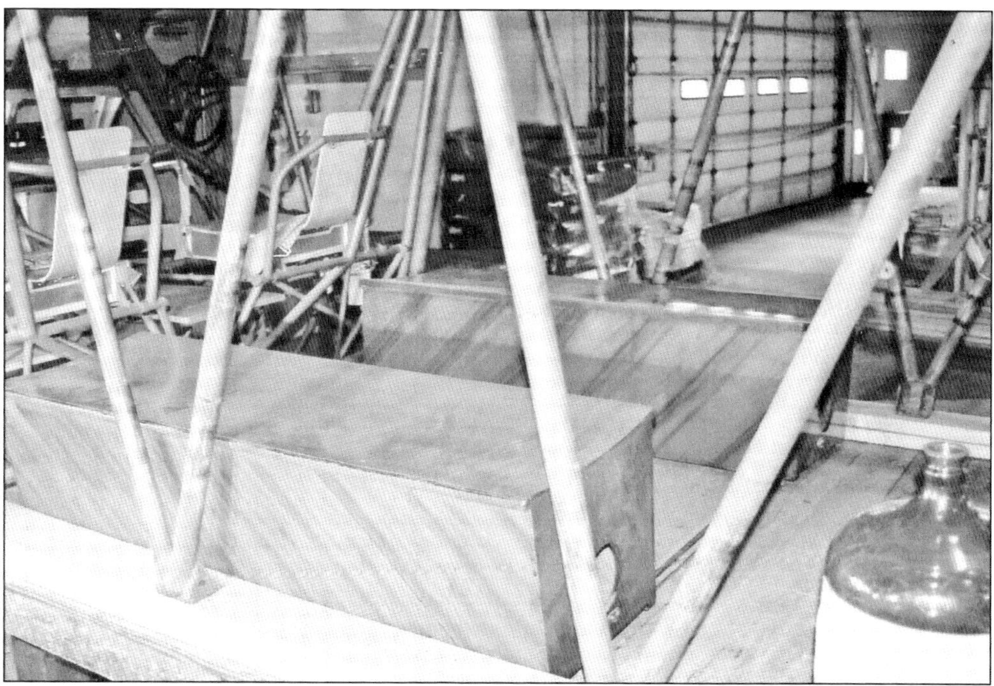

Once completed, the fuselage bottom and wood flooring would be attached to this section. (Author's collection.)

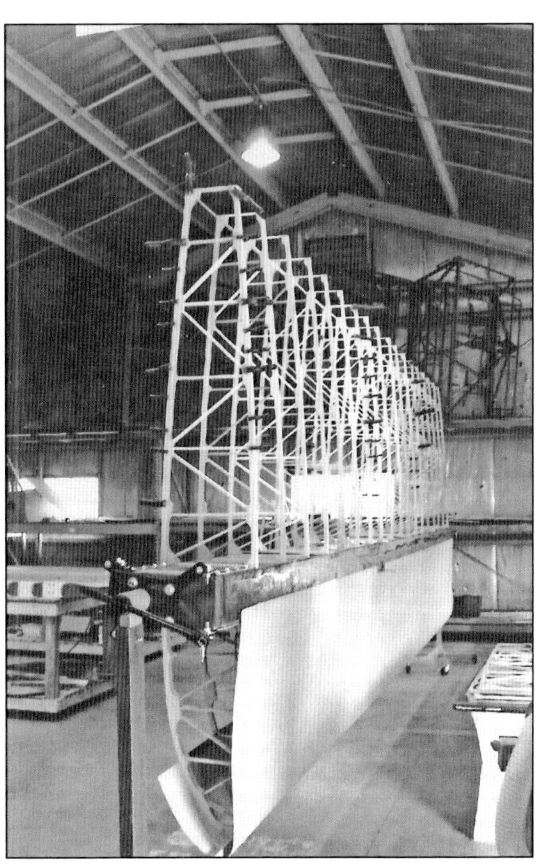

These glider wing ribs are near the final restoration process. Light plywood is steamed and bent to begin covering the wing's wood ribs. (Courtesy restoration volunteer Clifford Taylor, USAF, Ret.)

This is a finished outboard section of a WACO glider's wing, complete with fabric covering. Since 2006, the WACO glider has been under restoration by volunteers, which continues in 2017. (Courtesy restoration volunteer Clifford Taylor, USAF, Ret.)

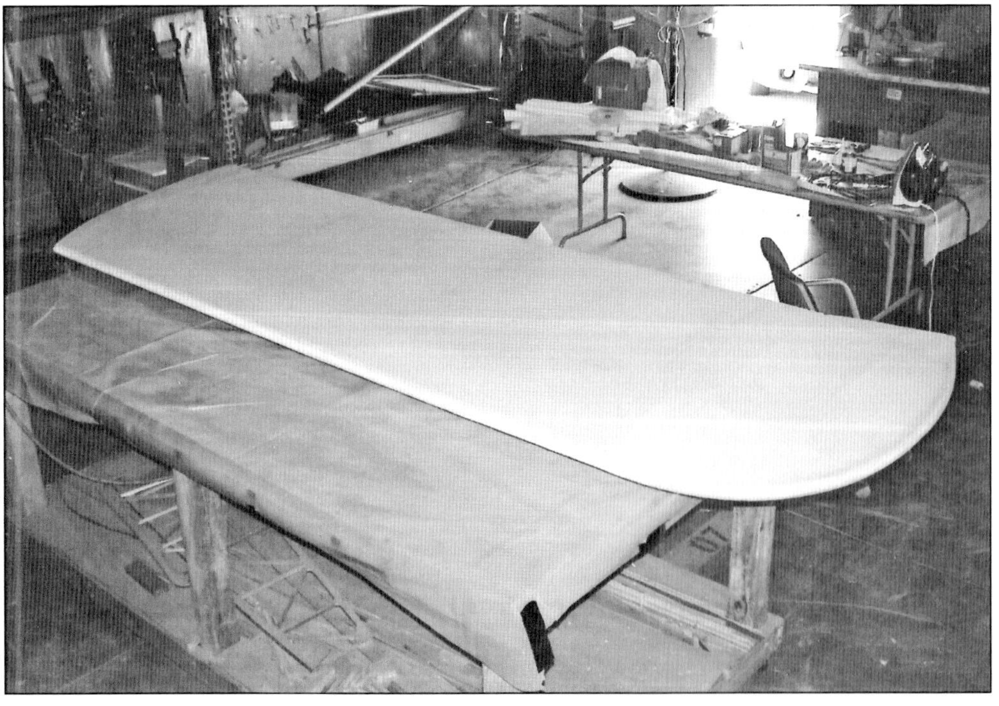

Three

The Cold War Comes to Missouri, Strategic Air Command 1947–1969

After representatives of the Japanese Empire signed the Allied terms of unconditional surrender on the US Navy battleship *Missouri* in Tokyo Bay, Japan, on September 2, 1945, World War II officially ended, and operations at Sedalia Army Air Field declined, with many buildings abandoned. In December 1947, the base was placed on inactive status and its name changed to Sedalia Air Force Auxiliary Field. As the Cold War between the United States and Soviet Union intensified, air bases inside the United States were needed to protect SAC's nuclear bomber deterrent force. SAC activated the 4224th Air Base Squadron (ABS) to supervise the rehabilitation and construction of a new base, now called Sedalia Air Force Base. The 4224th ABS continued its activities until October 20, 1952, when it was inactivated while turning over the base to the 340th BW. SAC scheduled the 340th BW to receive the command's newest aircraft, the Boeing B-47 Stratojet and KC-97 Stratofreighter. Construction workers completed repairs to the 1942 runway and other base support and improvement facilities in November 1953.

The first B-47 landed on the new runway in March 1954, flown from Lockbourne AFB, Ohio. The 340th BW trained bombardment crews, refueling crews, and units for the performance of global bombardment operations, and equipped units for the accomplishment of their assigned missions. The wing consisted of the 486th Bombardment Squadron (BS), 487th BS, 488th BS and 489th BS. On December 3, 1955, Sedalia AFB became Whiteman AFB, named to honor 2nd Lt. George A. Whiteman. The 340th BW transitioned to the B-47E in late 1955, retaining this variant until 1963.

With the phase-out of the B-47 and KC-97 at Whiteman, SAC used the base for the 43rd BW's B-58s to stand satellite nuclear alert. The B-58s were home based and on nuclear strip alert at Carswell AFB, Texas, and Little Rock AFB, and were occasionally dispersed to Grissom AFB, Indiana, and Whiteman AFB. It was becoming obvious in 1969 that SAC needed to protect its nuclear bomber forces, and periodic dispersal added to targeting problems for Soviet ICBMs. Whiteman was an ideal choice; in the center of the United States, it provided maximum time to launch the B-58s under an impending Soviet ICBM attack.

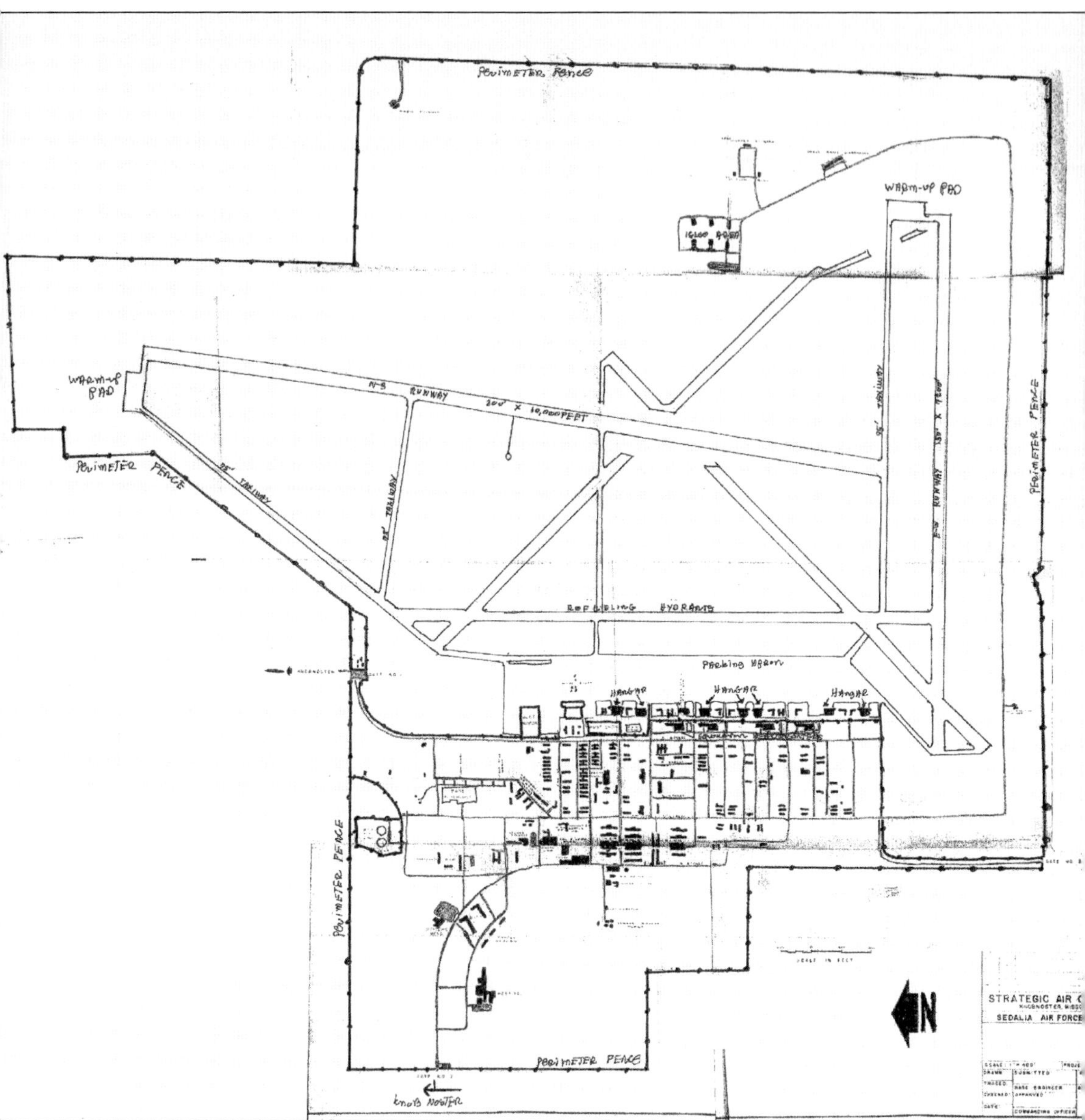

The US Army Corps of Engineers provided this construction layout of Sedalia Air Force Base for the Strategic Air Command to develop its installation, using World War II buildings, along with modifications to two existing buildings and new construction to meet SAC's needs. (Courtesy Offutt Air Force Base, Strategic Air Command Historian Archives.)

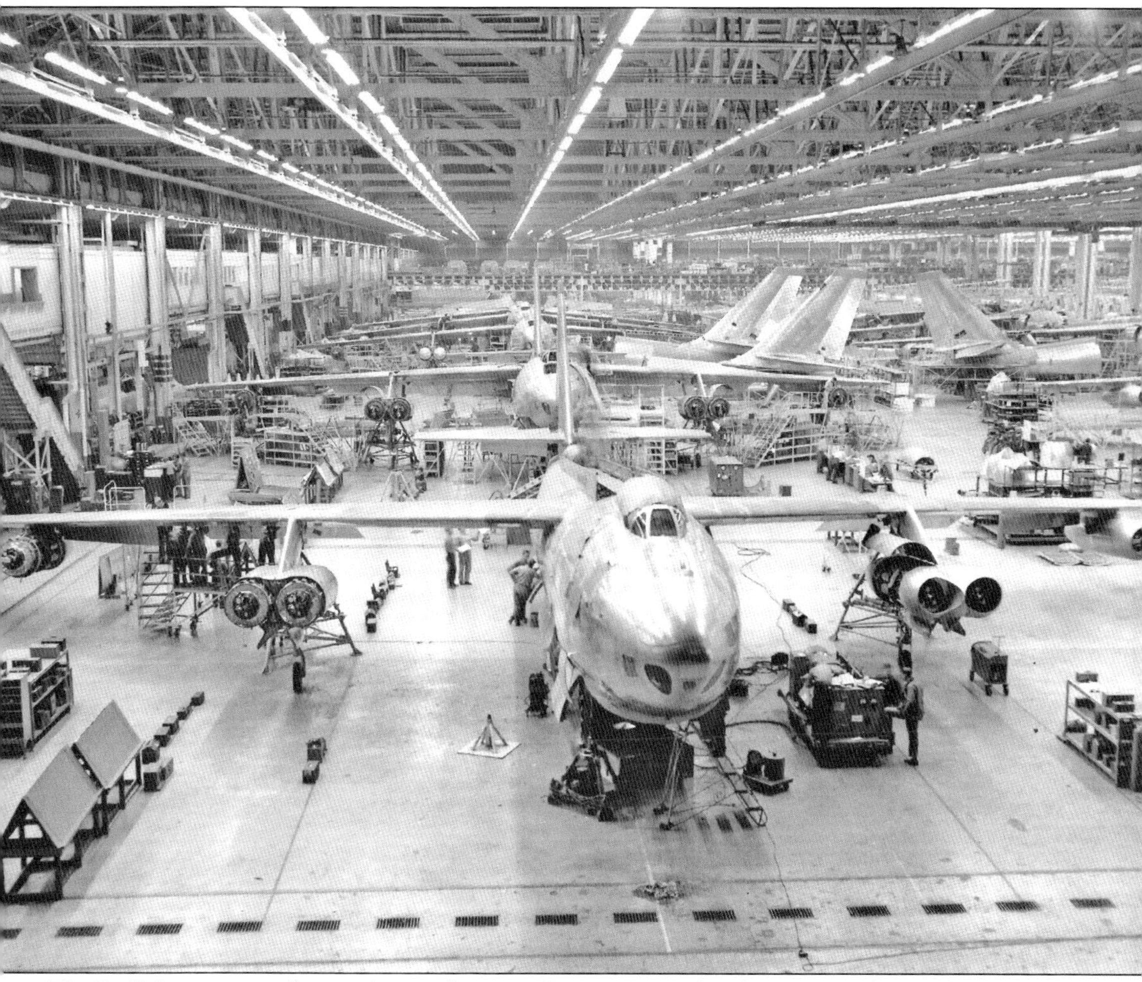

The B-47 Stratojet production line is shown at Boeing Aircraft's plant in Seattle, Washington. This medium bomber's manufacturing run was the largest since World War II to meet SAC's need to replace its piston-powered B-29s, B-36s, and B-50s. (Courtesy Boeing Aircraft Archives.)

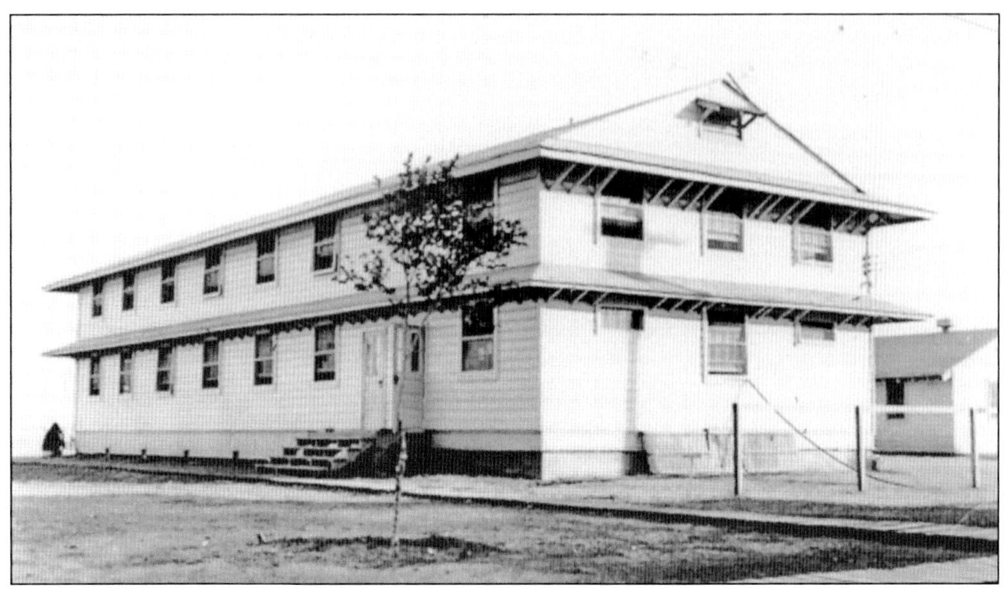

New airmen dormitories were constructed on the base in the Group A base building project. These slowly replaced two-story wooden World War II barracks, as shown in the photograph. (Courtesy Maxwell Air Force Base, Alabama, Air Force Historical Research Agency.)

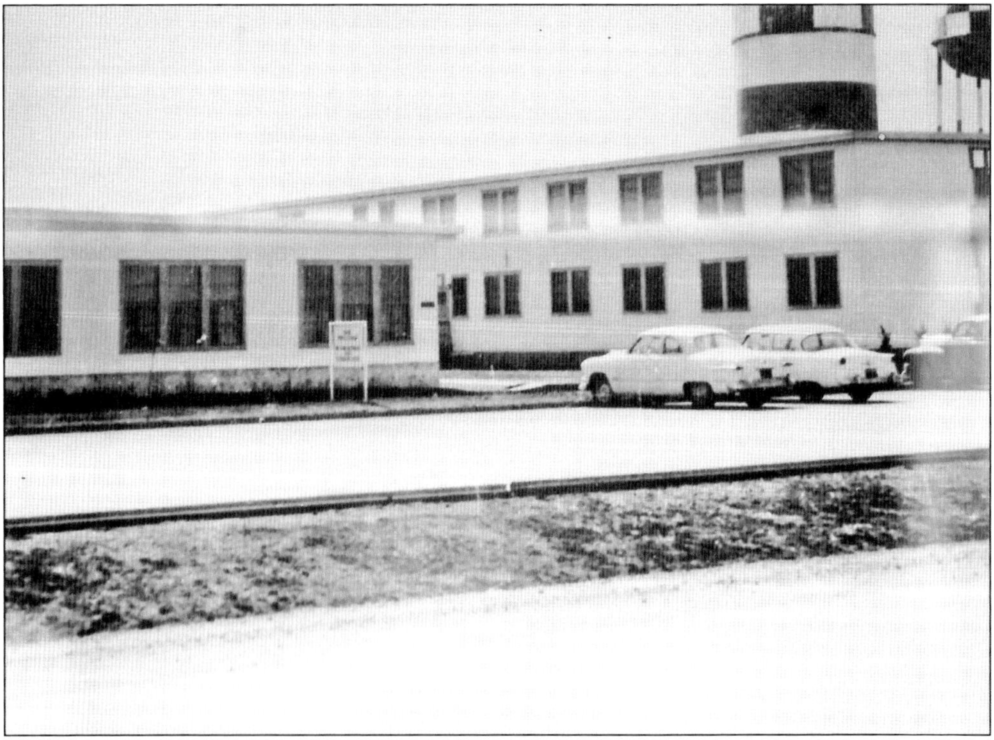

SAC operations required new buildings to coordinate B-47 and KC-97G training and alert operations. The new operations building followed standard 1950s Air Force base construction. These buildings could be rapidly erected. (Courtesy Whiteman Air Force Base, 509th Bomb Wing Public Affairs.)

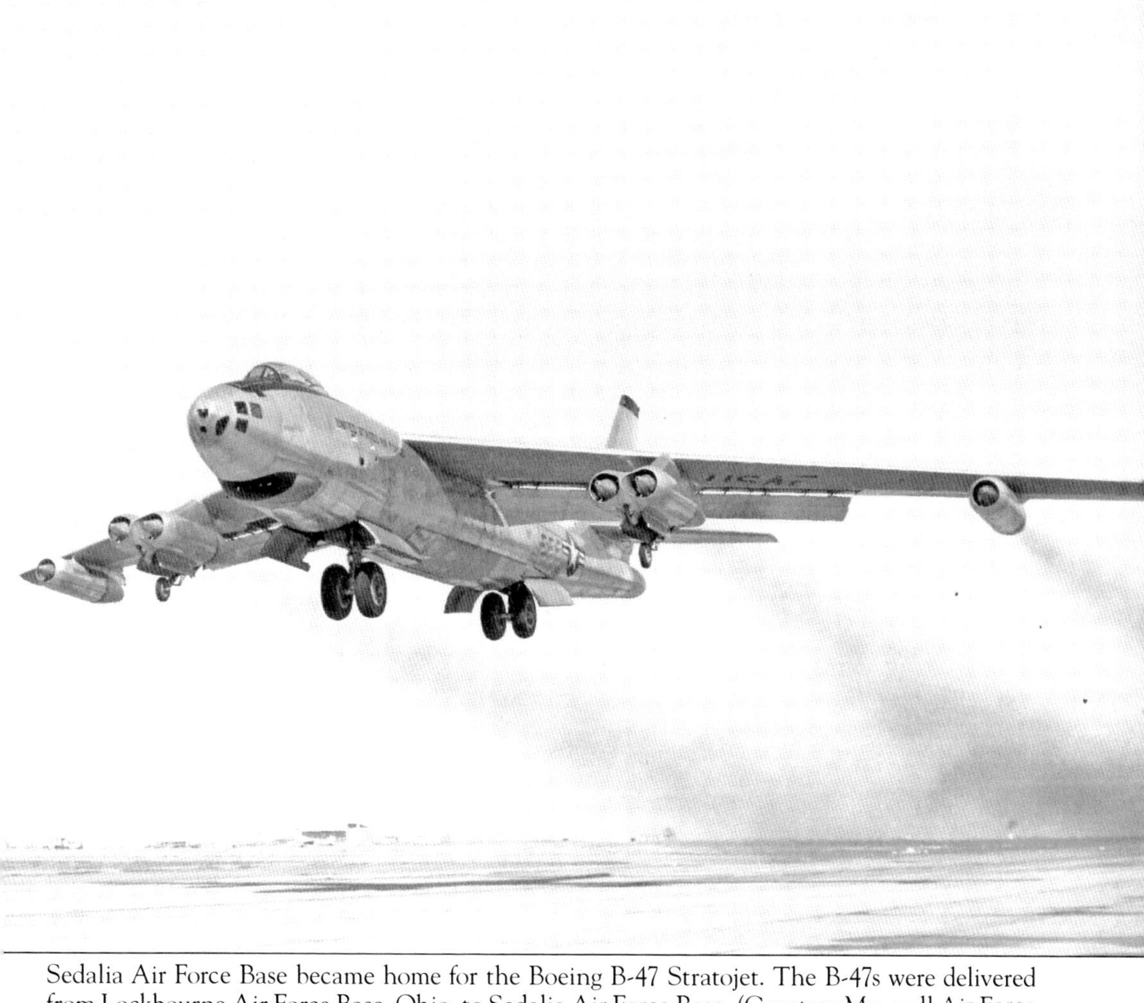

Sedalia Air Force Base became home for the Boeing B-47 Stratojet. The B-47s were delivered from Lockbourne Air Force Base, Ohio, to Sedalia Air Force Base. (Courtesy Maxwell Air Force Base, Alabama, Air Force Historical Research Agency.)

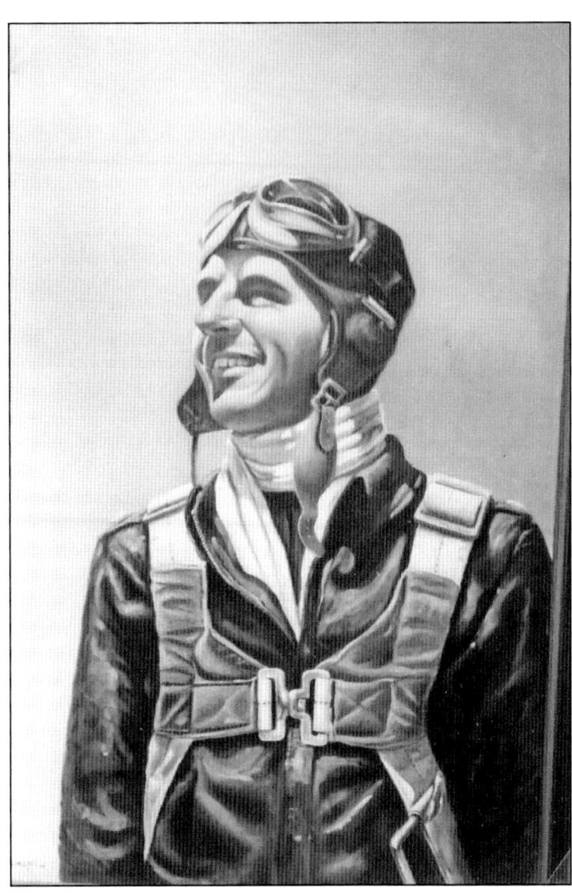

Second Lt. George A. Whiteman was stationed at Bellows Air Field, Oahu, Hawaii, before the Japanese attack on Pearl Harbor on December 7, 1941. (Courtesy Whiteman Air Force Base, 509th Bomb Wing Public Affairs.)

This Curtiss P-40 Warhawk is on display at the National Museum of the United States Air Force. This is the type of pre–World War II fighter flown by 2nd Lt. George A. Whiteman at Bellows Air Field. (Author's collection.)

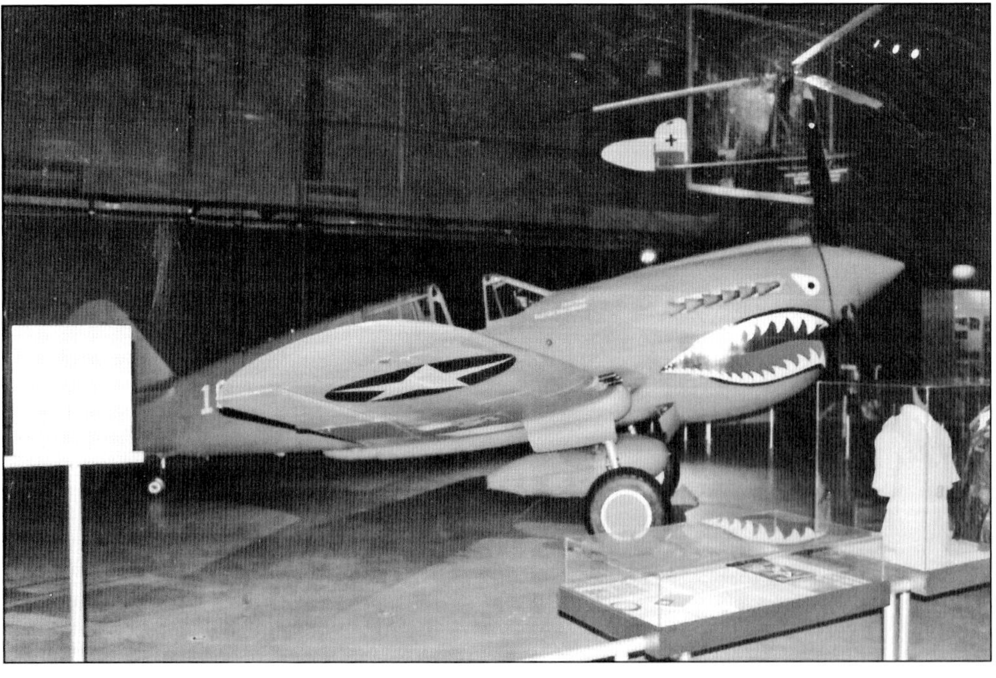

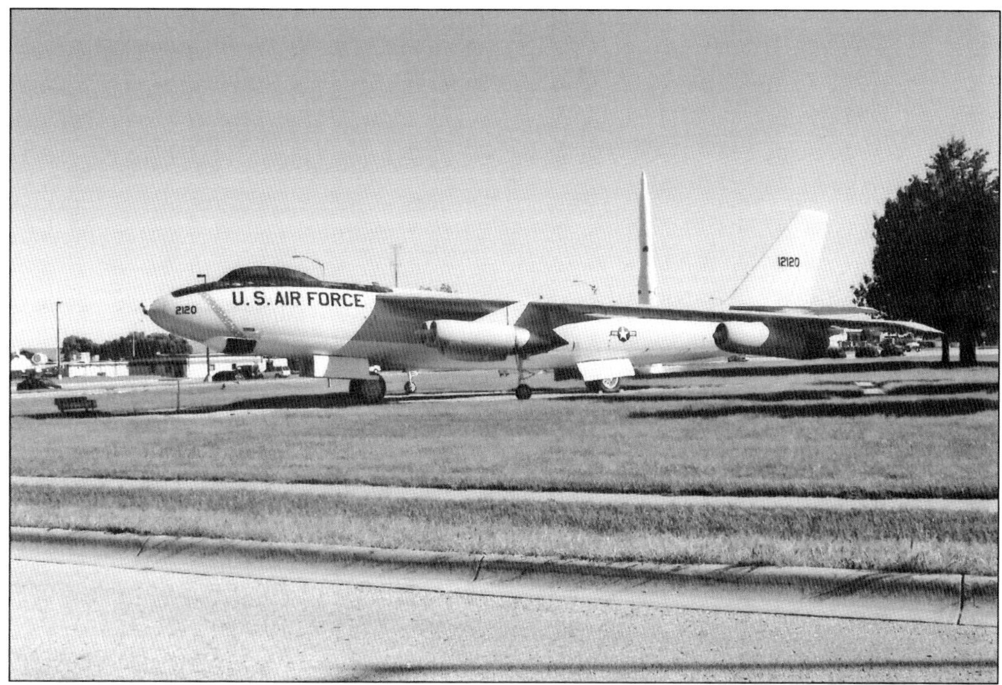

This Boeing B-47E Stratojet is on display at Whiteman Air Force Base Air Park. The B-47E equipped the 340th Bombardment Wing on Whiteman AFB to implement SAC's nuclear alert to maintain the nation's nuclear deterrence. (Author's collection.)

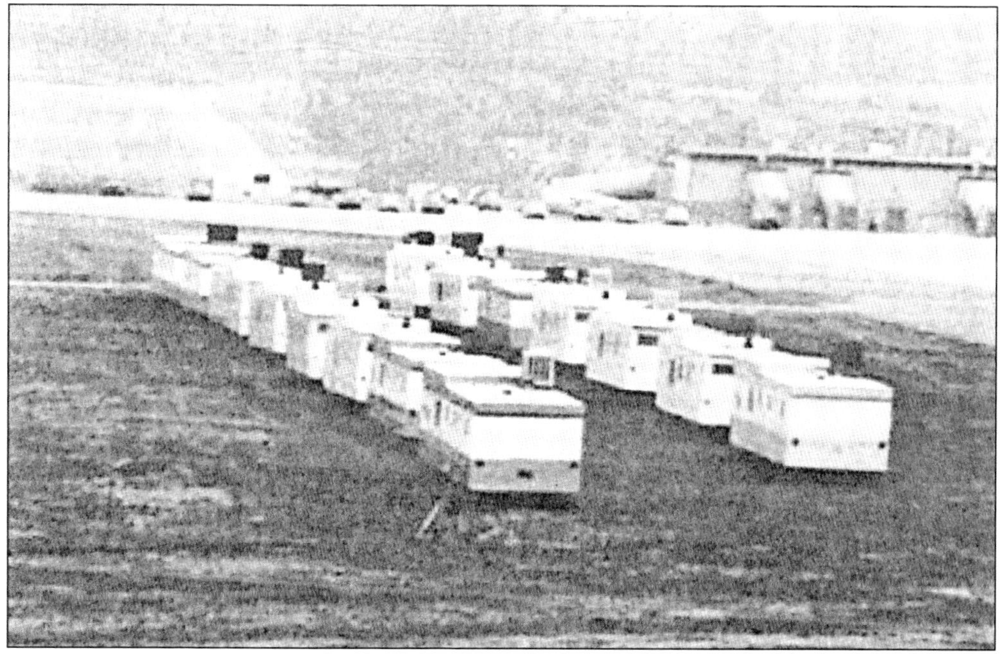

This is a rare photograph of the Cold War grouping of two rows of temporary alert crew trailers at Griffiss Air Force Base, New York, in 1964. At the time of the photograph, they were not in use, because the new, permanent alert facility in the background had recently been completed. (Courtesy Maxwell Air Force Base, Alabama, Air Force Historical Research Agency.)

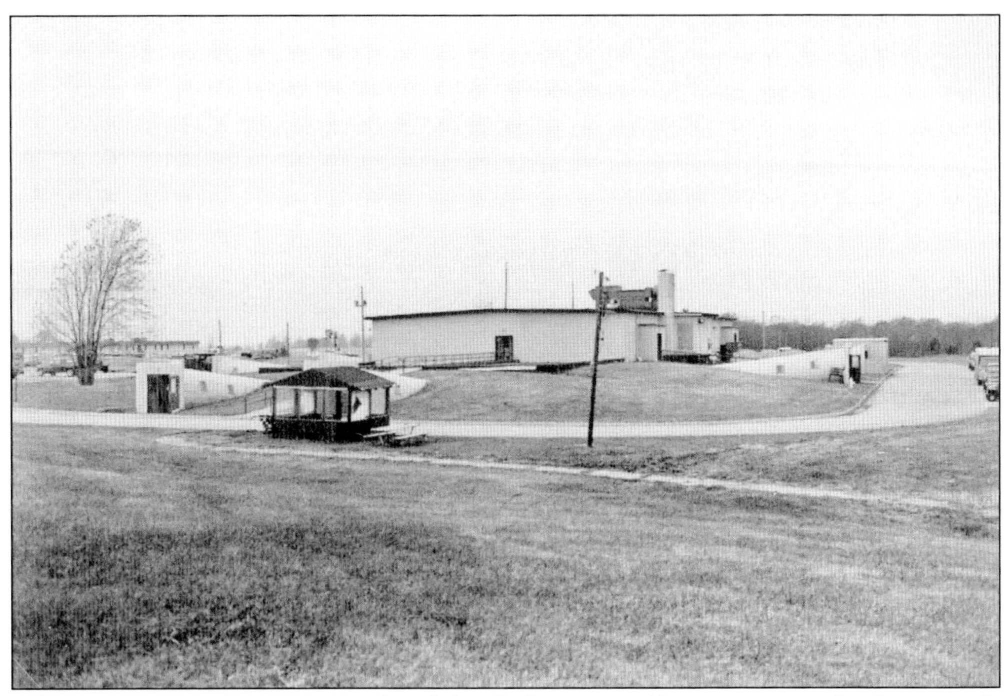

Whiteman Air Force Base's semi-hardened alert facility, pictured here, was retained and is currently used as a storage building. The corrugated steel tubes provided an exit from the facility when the klaxon sounded to get alert crews to their aircraft for takeoff. (Courtesy Whiteman Air Force Base, 509th Bomb Wing Public Affairs.)

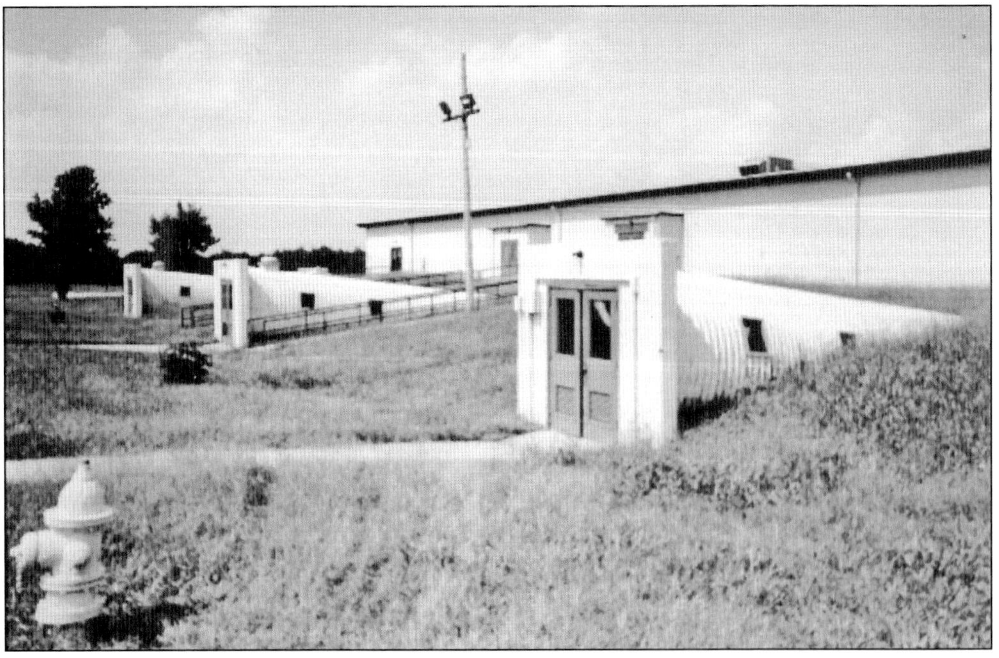

This is a close-up view of the alert crew exit ramps at Griffiss Air Force Base. The construction was standardized throughout SAC bases and used on the Whiteman AFB bomber alert facility, referred to as the "Mole Hole." (Courtesy Whiteman Air Force Base, 509th Bomb Wing Public Affairs.)

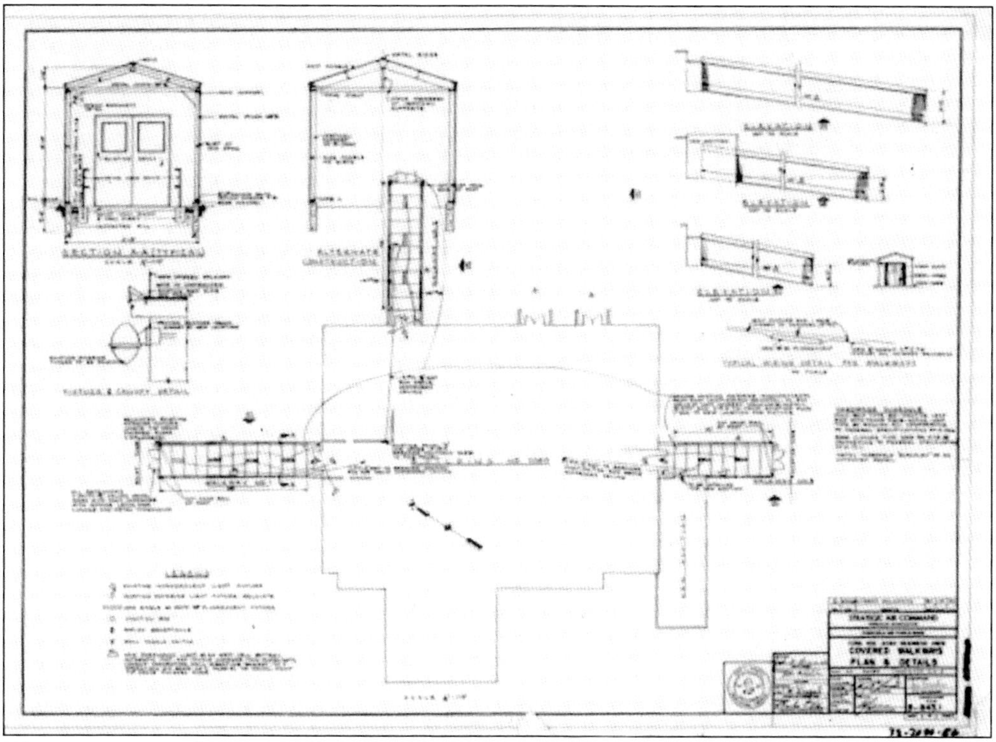

This engineering drawing of the Whiteman Air Force Base alert facility shows exit ramps onto the flight line, where cocked bombers and tankers were parked to respond to a SAC launch on warning order. (Courtesy Offutt Air Force Base, Strategic Air Command Historian Archives.)

This interior room at the former Whiteman AFB Cold War alert facility was used as a sleeping room. The partially underground building also contained areas for recreation, crew study, a kitchen and dining hall, and administrative offices. (Courtesy Whiteman Air Force Base, 509th Bomb Wing Public Affairs.)

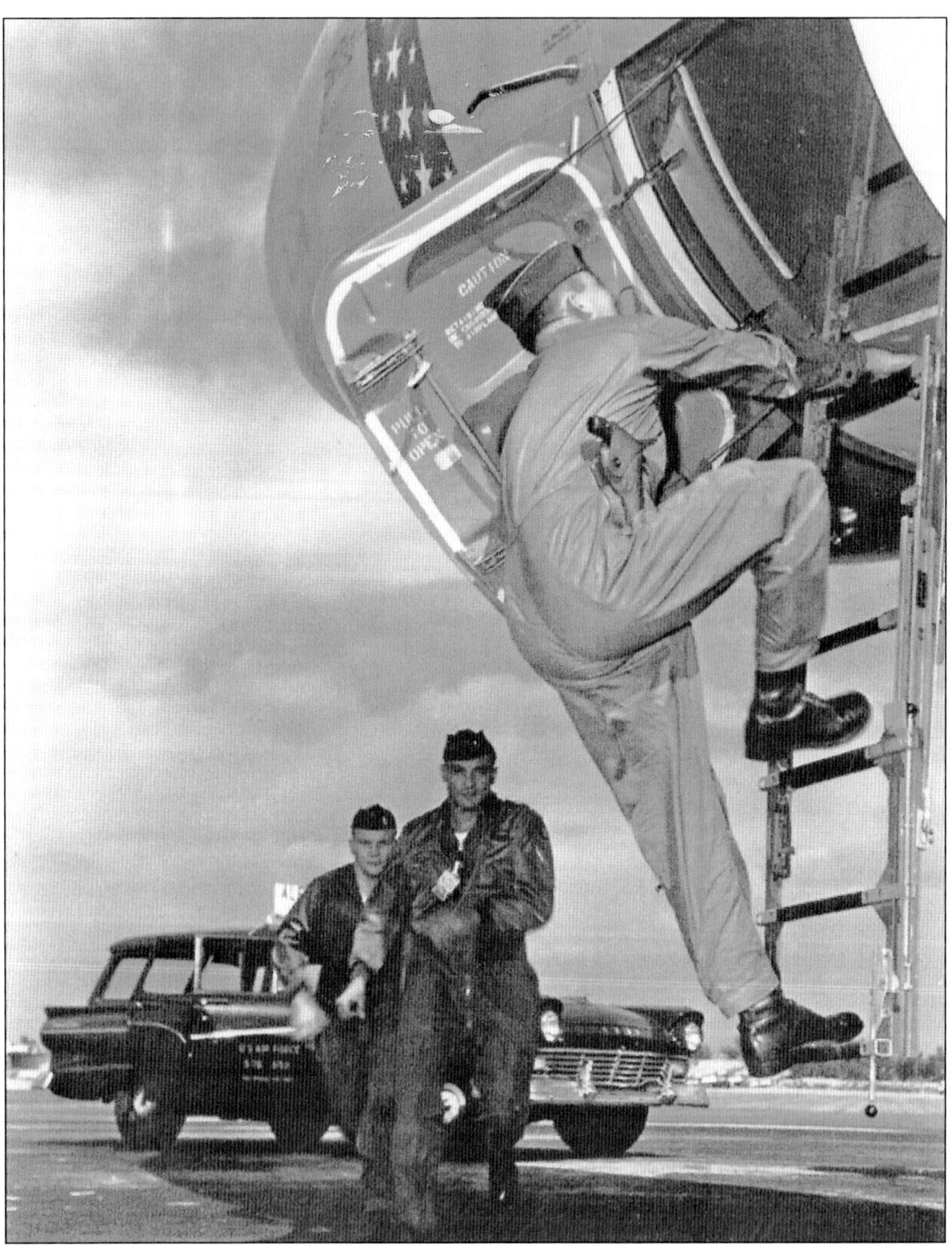

This is a staged Strategic Air Command Public Affairs photograph of a three-man B-47 alert crew arriving at their aircraft. The pilot climbing into the B-47 is wearing a sidearm, which is kept inside the aircraft when on alert. (Courtesy Offutt Air Force Base, Strategic Air Command Historian Archives.)

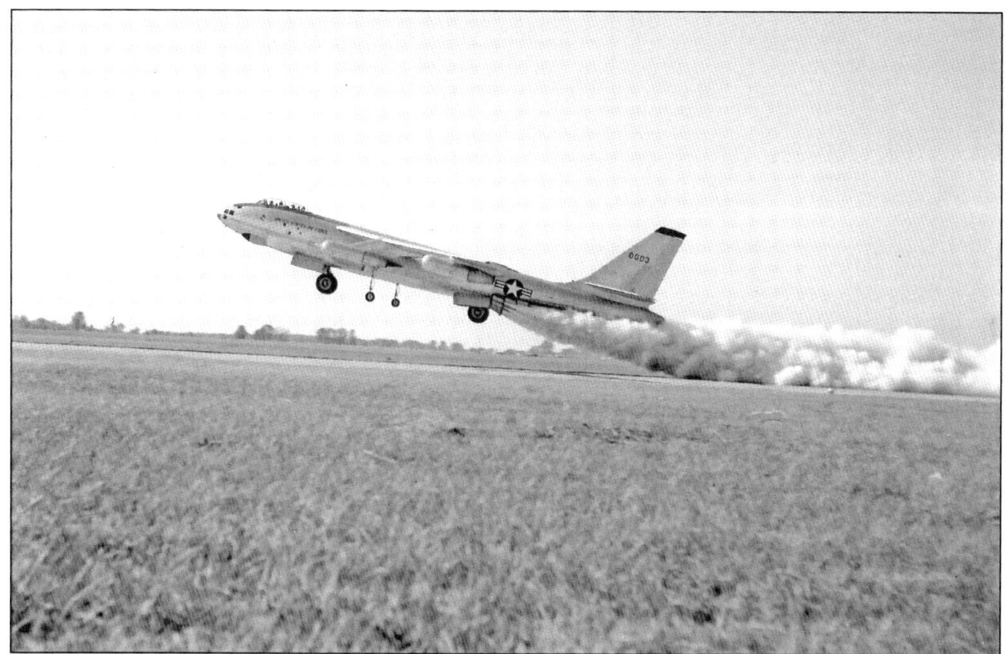

To decrease takeoff distance when loaded with the heavy early nuclear weapons, Boeing engineers provided jet-assisted takeoff (JATO) rockets. For the B-47B, they were installed internally in the aircraft's fuselage, and with the B-47E, they were attached externally and jettisoned after takeoff. (Courtesy Boeing Aircraft Historical Archives.)

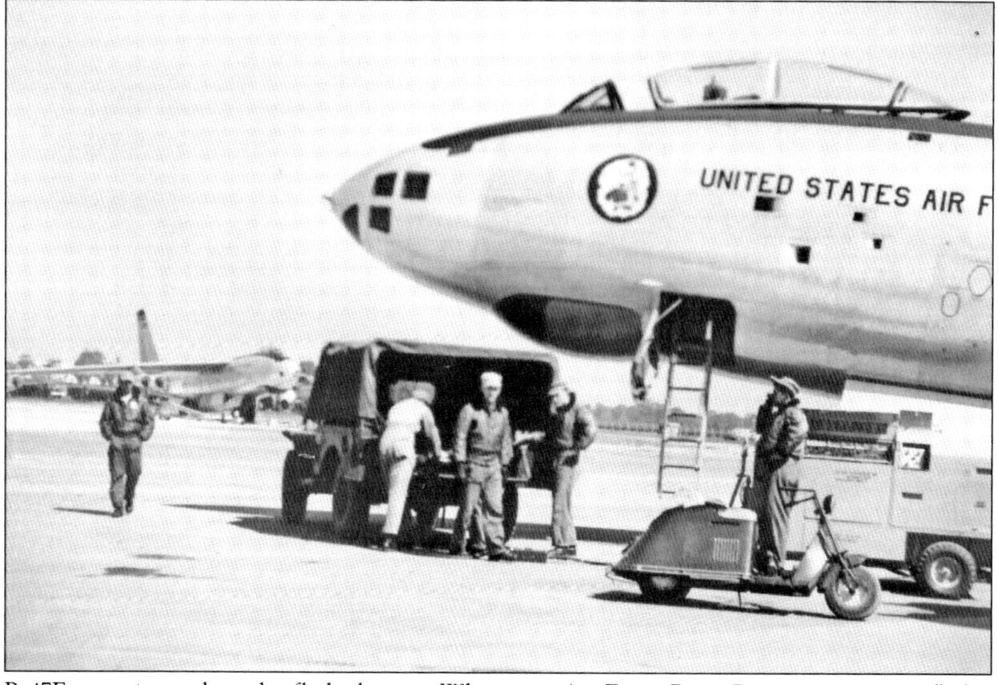

B-47Es are pictured on the flight line on Whiteman Air Force Base. Prior to a training flight, there was always a lot of maintenance personnel and equipment and other aircraft parked nearby. (Author's collection.)

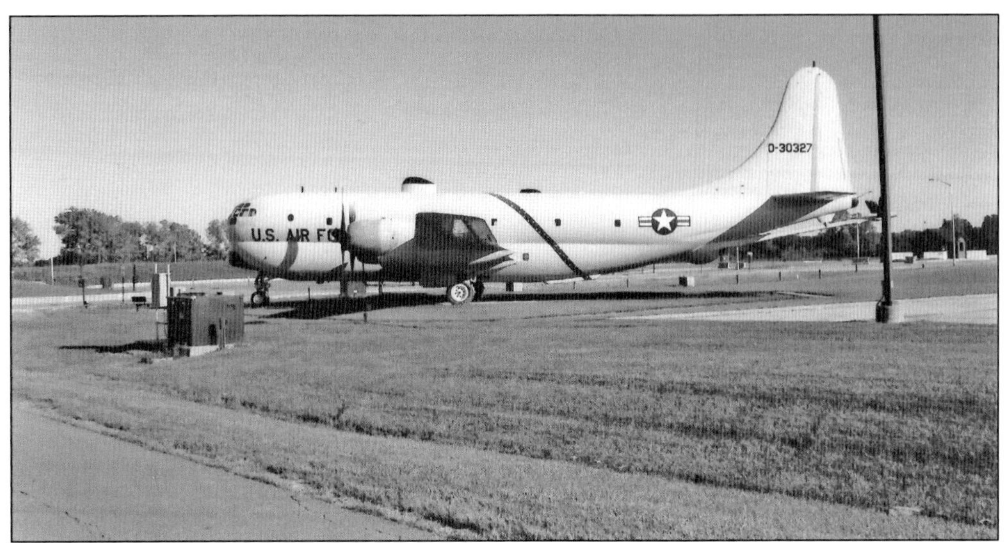

This Boeing KC-97G Stratofreighter tanker is on display at Whiteman Air Force Base Air Park. The tanker had been modified with the installation of two Pratt & Whitney turbojet engines on each wing, outboard of the two piston engines, creating the KC-97L. At Whiteman, the jet engines were removed to create the piston-only KC-97G. (Author's collection.)

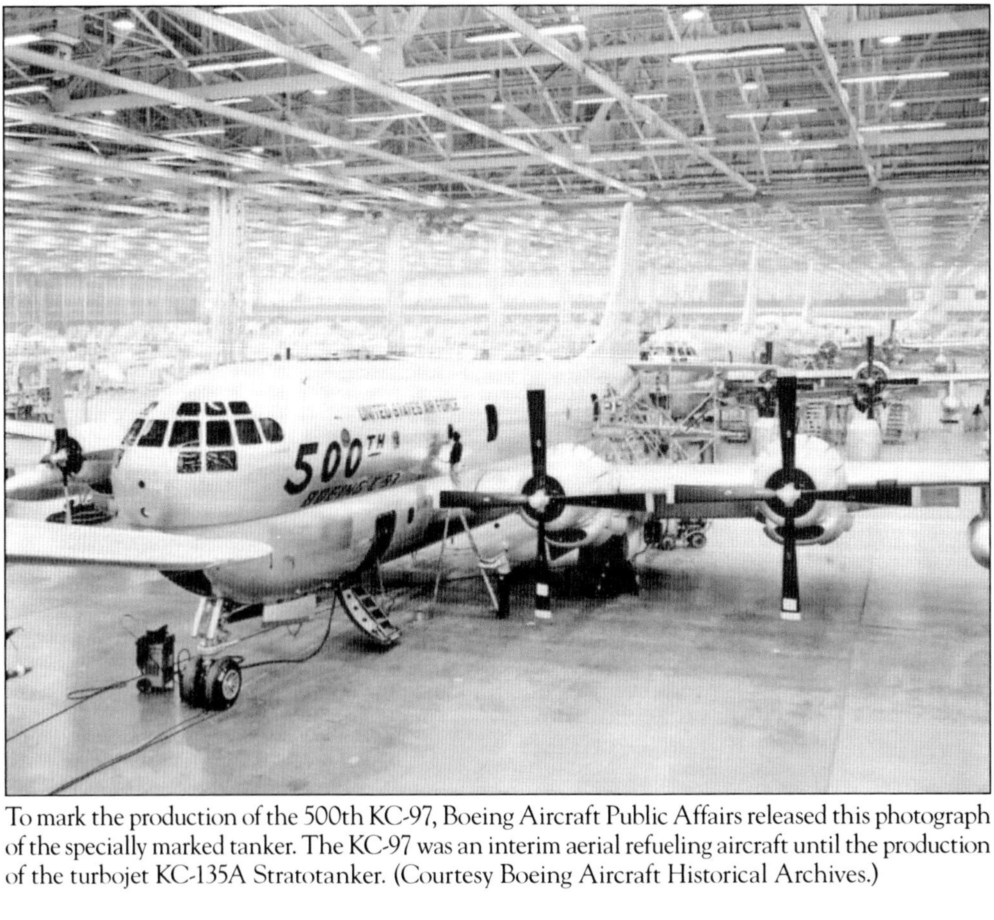

To mark the production of the 500th KC-97, Boeing Aircraft Public Affairs released this photograph of the specially marked tanker. The KC-97 was an interim aerial refueling aircraft until the production of the turbojet KC-135A Stratotanker. (Courtesy Boeing Aircraft Historical Archives.)

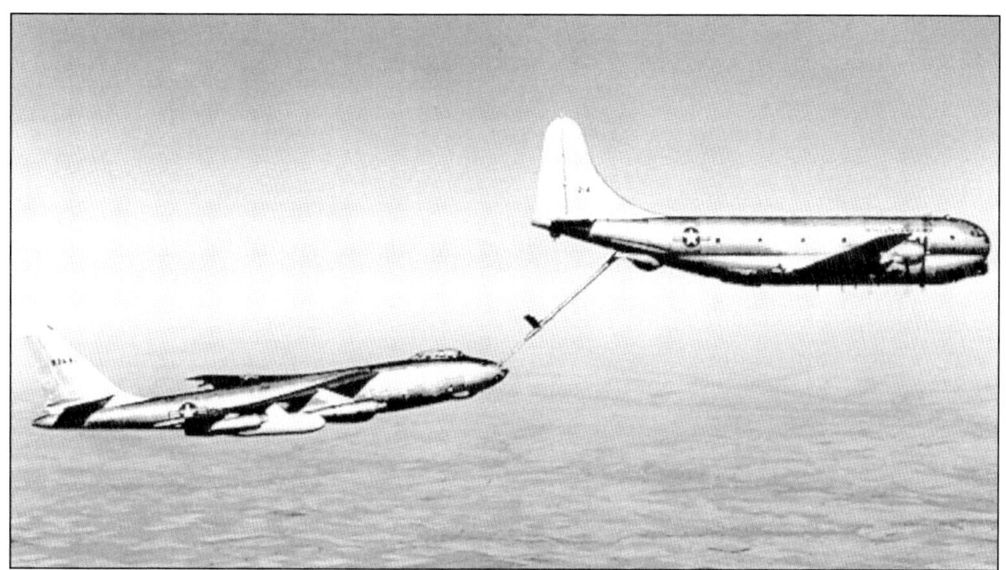

Pictured is a KC-97 refueling a B-47E. The piston-powered tanker was not as fast as the B-47. The refueling connection would be made at high altitude, then the connected bomber and tanker would dive for the tanker to increase speed and complete the aerial refueling. (Courtesy Offutt Air Force Base, Strategic Air Command Historian Archives.)

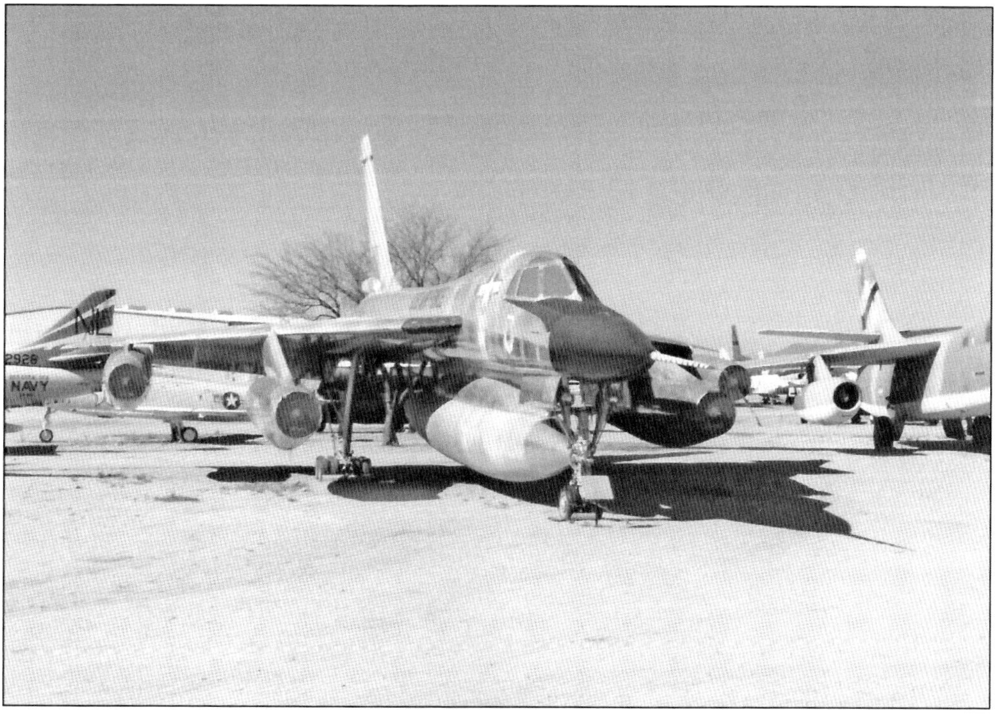

For a brief time, the Strategic Air Command operated the Convair B-58 Hustler, a supersonic delta-wing bomber. This aircraft is on display at the Pima Air Museum at Tucson, Arizona. Nuclear weapons were carried in the pod underneath the fuselage, which required a high-clearance tricycle landing gear, giving it a fragile appearance. (Author's collection.)

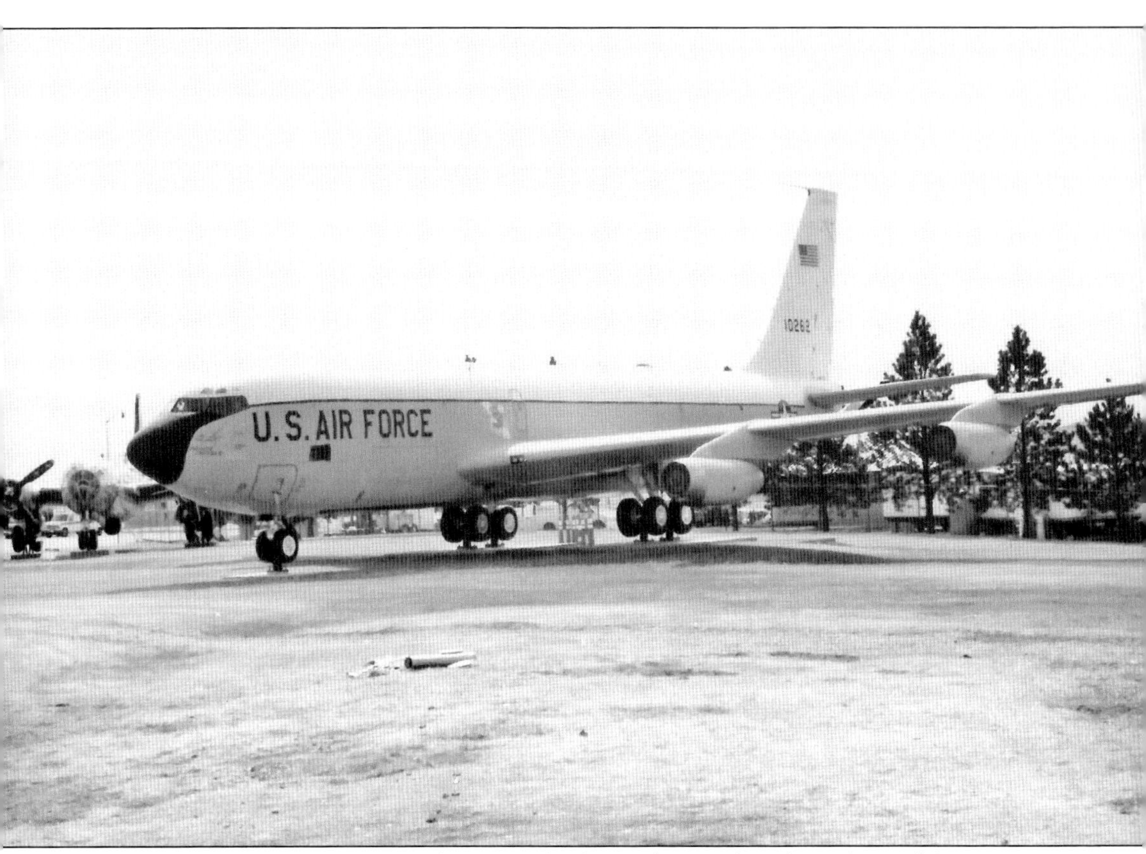

This Boeing KC-135A Stratotanker is on display at the South Dakota Air and Space Museum, outside the main gate to Ellsworth Air Force Base, South Dakota. The KC-135A was the Strategic Air Command's aerial refueling aircraft. (Author's collection.)

Four

MINUTEMAN INTERCONTINENTAL BALLISTIC MISSILE, 351ST STRATEGIC MISSILE WING 1961–1997

In June 1961, the Department of Defense selected Whiteman AFB to host an LGM-30 Minuteman ICBM wing. The 351st Strategic Missile Wing (SMW) operated the LGB-30B Minuteman I ICBM from 1963 to 1967 and the LGM-30F Minuteman II ICBM from 1966 to 1995. The 351st SMW consisted of the 508th Strategic Missile Squadron (SMS), 509th SMS, and 510th SMS.

The first Minuteman IB arrived at Whiteman AFB from the Boeing production plant at Hill AFB, Utah, on January 14, 1964. On June 29, 1964, the final flight of Minuteman IB missiles went on alert, bringing the 351st SMW to full operational SAC alert status. Starting on May 7, 1966, and throughout the rest of the year into 1967, the Air Force replaced Whiteman's Minuteman IBs with Minuteman IIs. The swap out and transition was completed in October 1967, making Whiteman the first Minuteman wing to upgrade to the Minuteman II.

On September 28, 1991, Pres. George H.W. Bush ordered Minuteman II missiles to be taken off alert and the facilities destroyed in compliance with START. This ended Whiteman's status and nuclear deterrence mission as a Minuteman II installation and initiated a complicated and expensive destruction and removal process of the missile facilities. The Air Force scheduled the deactivation of the 351st SMW to begin in 1992. Whiteman AFB Historian files provided the August 1992 plan for the deactivation of the Minuteman II missile wing at Whiteman Air Force Base. The plan sets out specifics on how the missiles would be removed and the facilities destroyed. It goes through a complicated process that was reviewed by Russian inspectors once completed to verify compliance with START. For all launch control facility sites, other than Oscar-01, the Air Force left site security fences and support buildings intact. On December 8, 1993, the wing's first launch control support building and associated underground facilities, India-01, were shut down. On May 7, 1993, the last Minuteman II missile, located at Juliet-03, was removed from its site. On July 31, 1995, the 351st SMW was inactivated. The final launch facility, Hotel-11, was imploded on December 15, 1997.

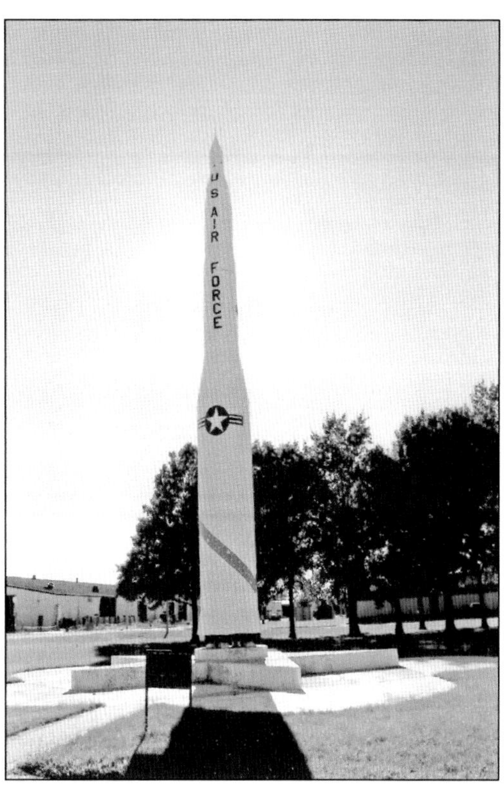

This Minuteman II ICBM is on display at the Whiteman Air Force Base Air Park. (Author's collection.)

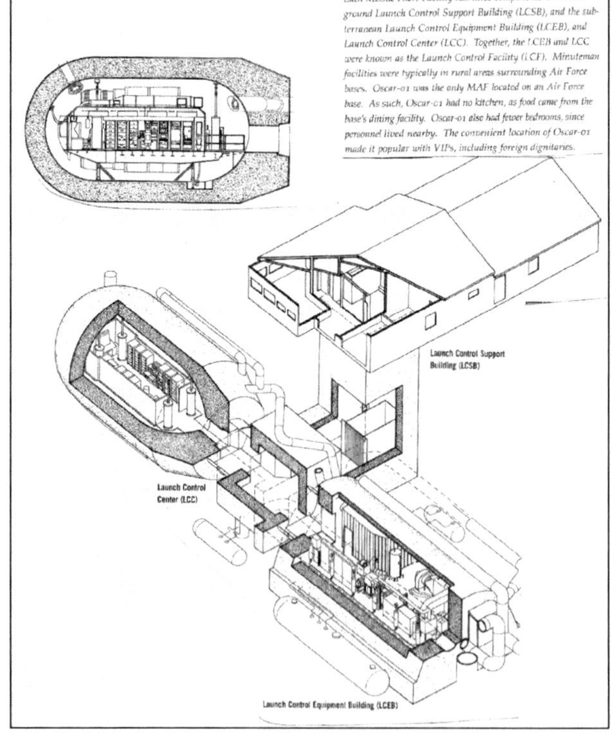

This is an engineering drawing of an aboveground launch control support building (LCSB), underground launch control center (LCC), and launch control equipment building (LCEB). (Courtesy Whiteman Air Force Base, 509th Bomb Wing Historian Archives.)

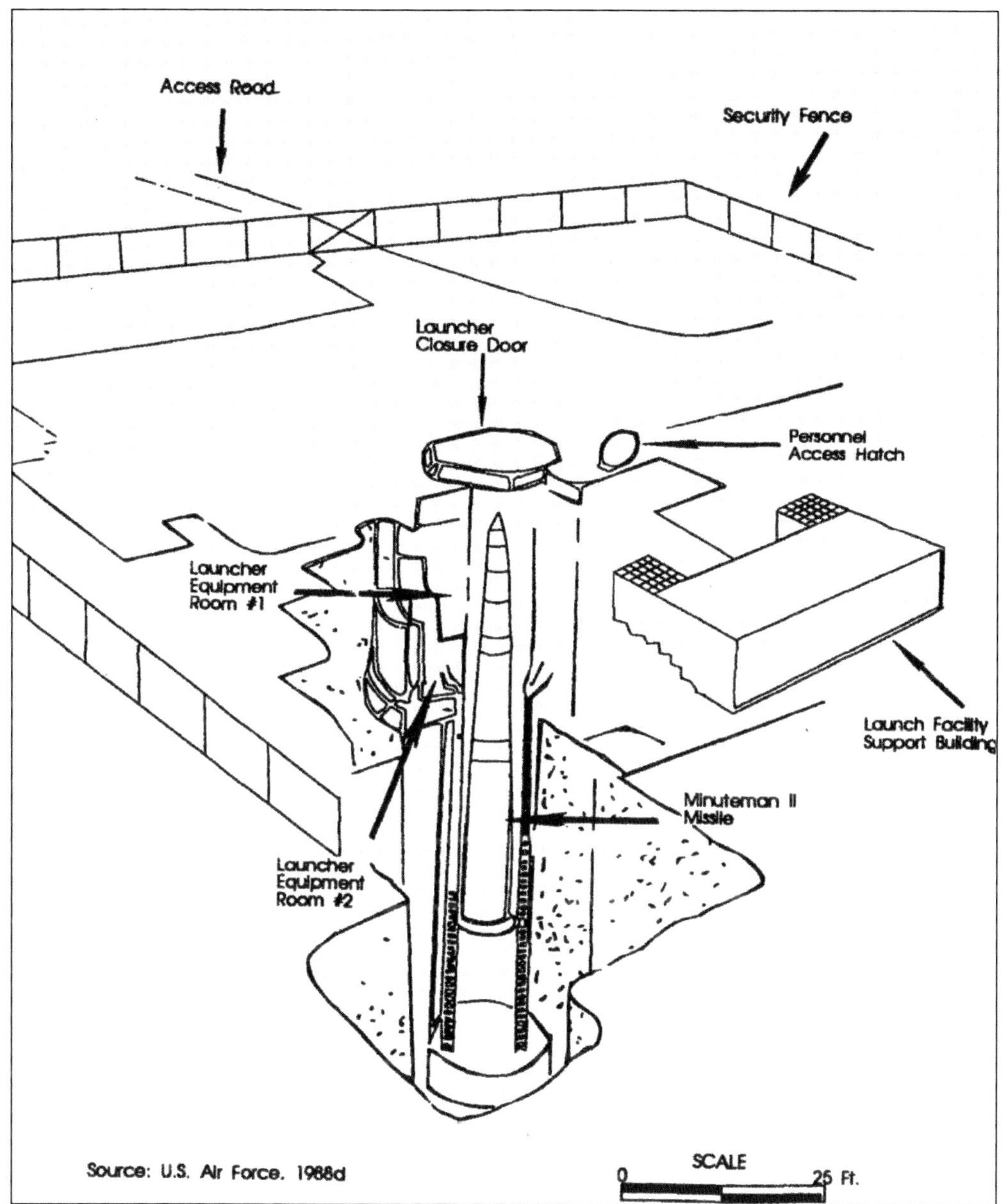

This engineering drawing details a launch facility and associated security area around the underground missile facility. (Courtesy Whiteman Air Force Base, 509th Bomb Wing Historian Archives.)

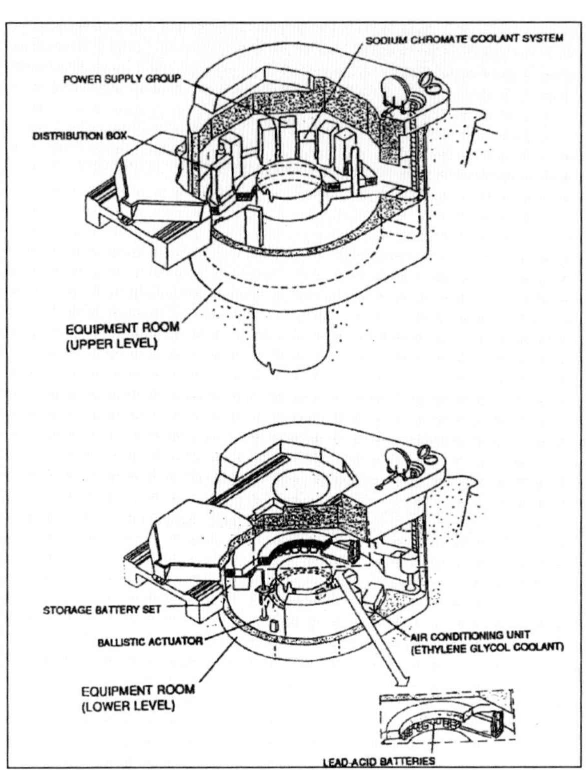

Pictured is an engineering drawing of a Minuteman missile launcher's headworks. (Courtesy Whiteman Air Force Base, 509th Bomb Wing Historian Archives.)

This is a cutaway engineering drawing of a launch facility. (Courtesy US Department of the Interior, National Park Service, Denver, Colorado.)

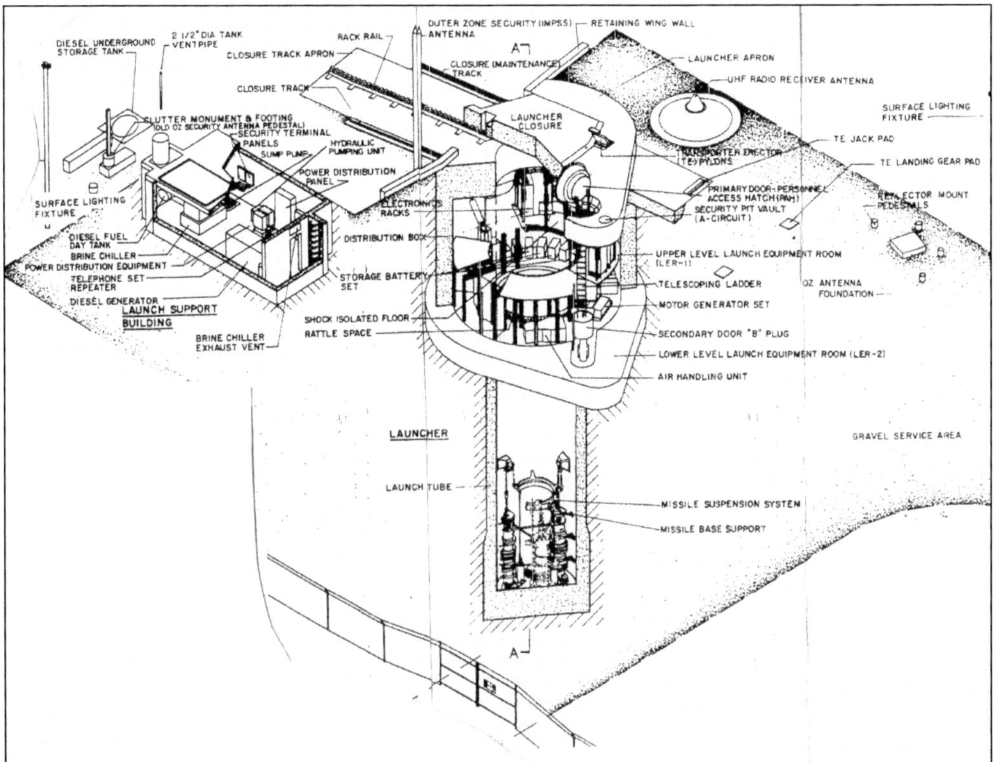

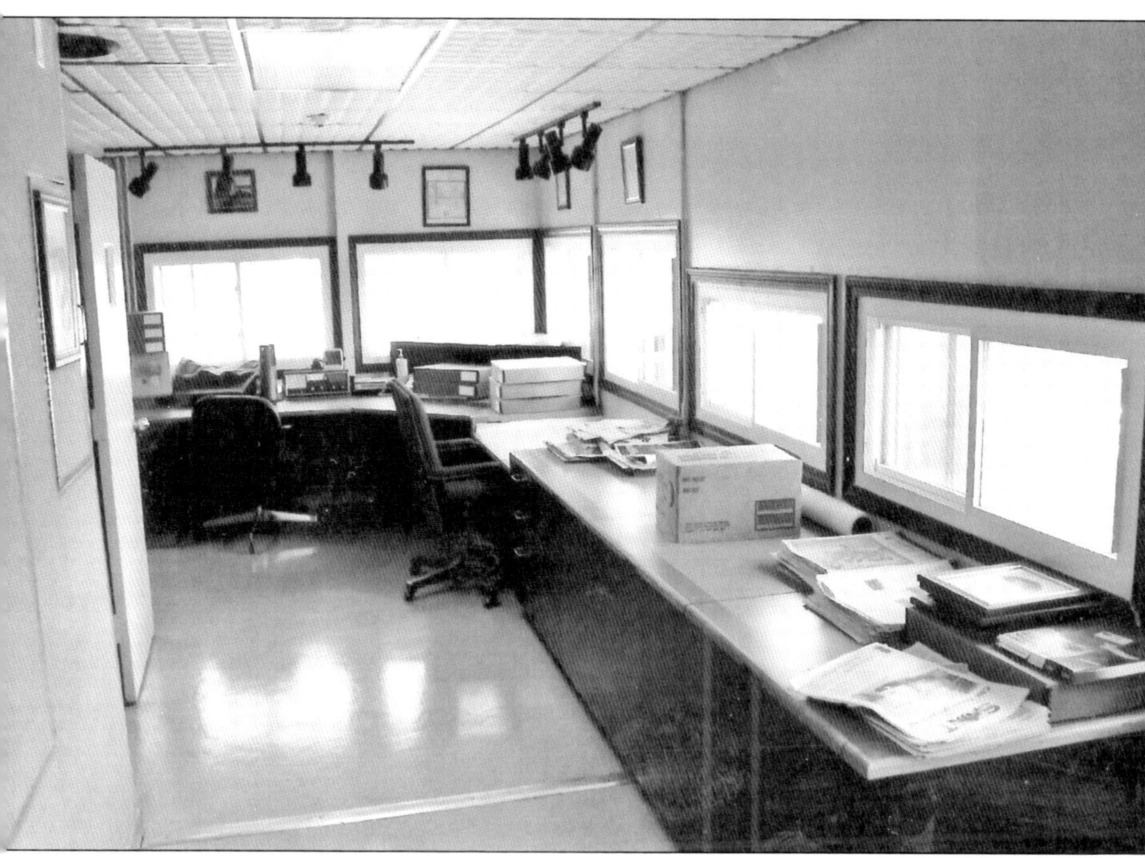

This close-up photograph shows an operational Minuteman III launch facility at Whiteman Air Force Base, which was built to standard engineering plans followed for construction of ICM sites. (Author's collection.)

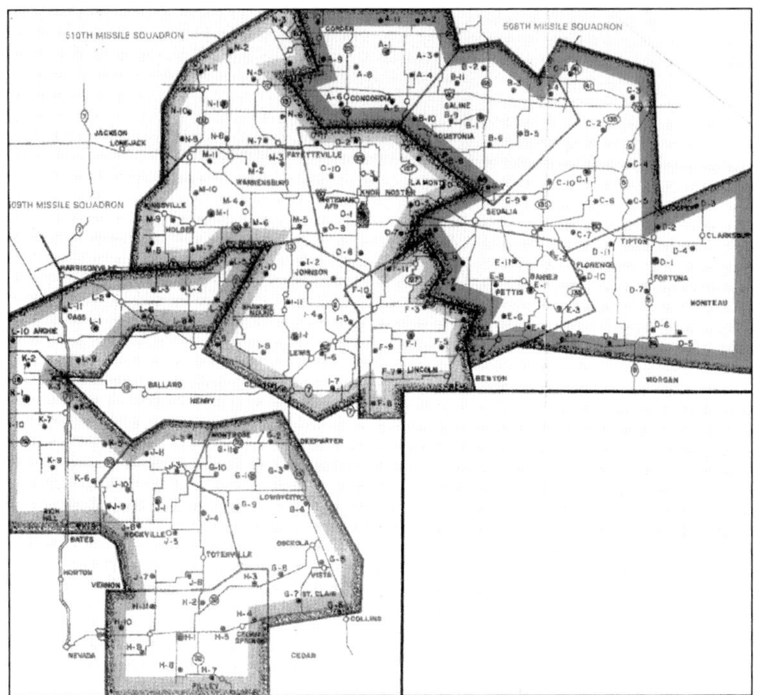

The 351st Strategic Missile Wing at Whiteman Air Force Base consisted of the 508th, 509th, and 510th SMS. Each squadron controlled 50 missiles. (Courtesy Whiteman Air Force Base, 509th Bomb Wing Historian Archives.)

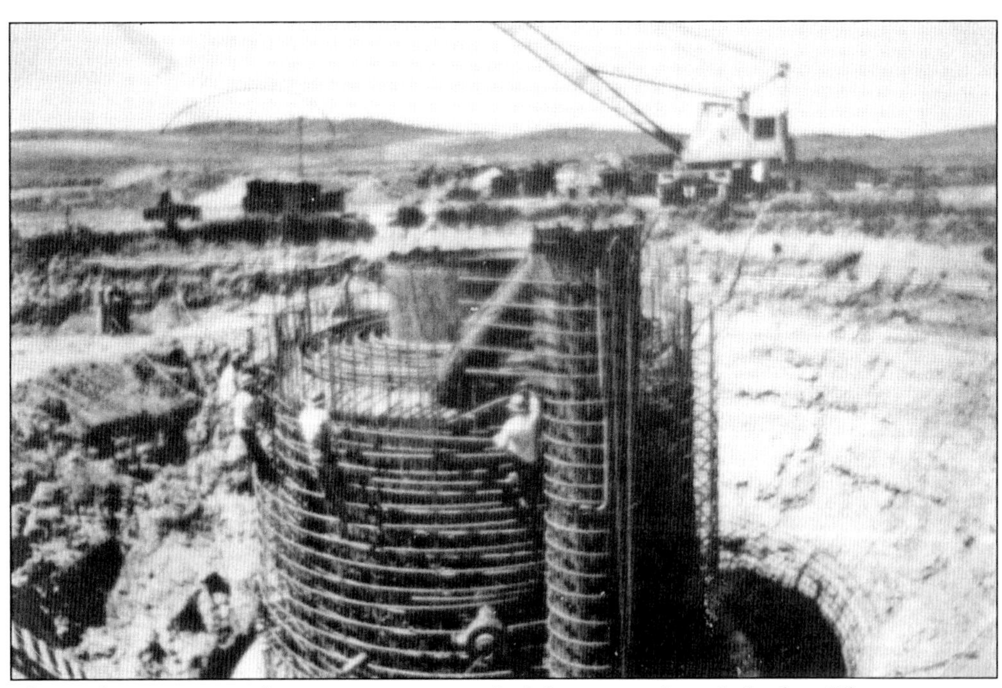

This is the excavation during construction of a Minuteman launch facility. The excavation was wide and deep. Tons of steel wrapped the silo prior to concrete being poured to provide a hardened facility designed to protect the Minuteman ICBM inside from the ground shock and blast overpressures caused by nuclear detonations. (Author's collection.)

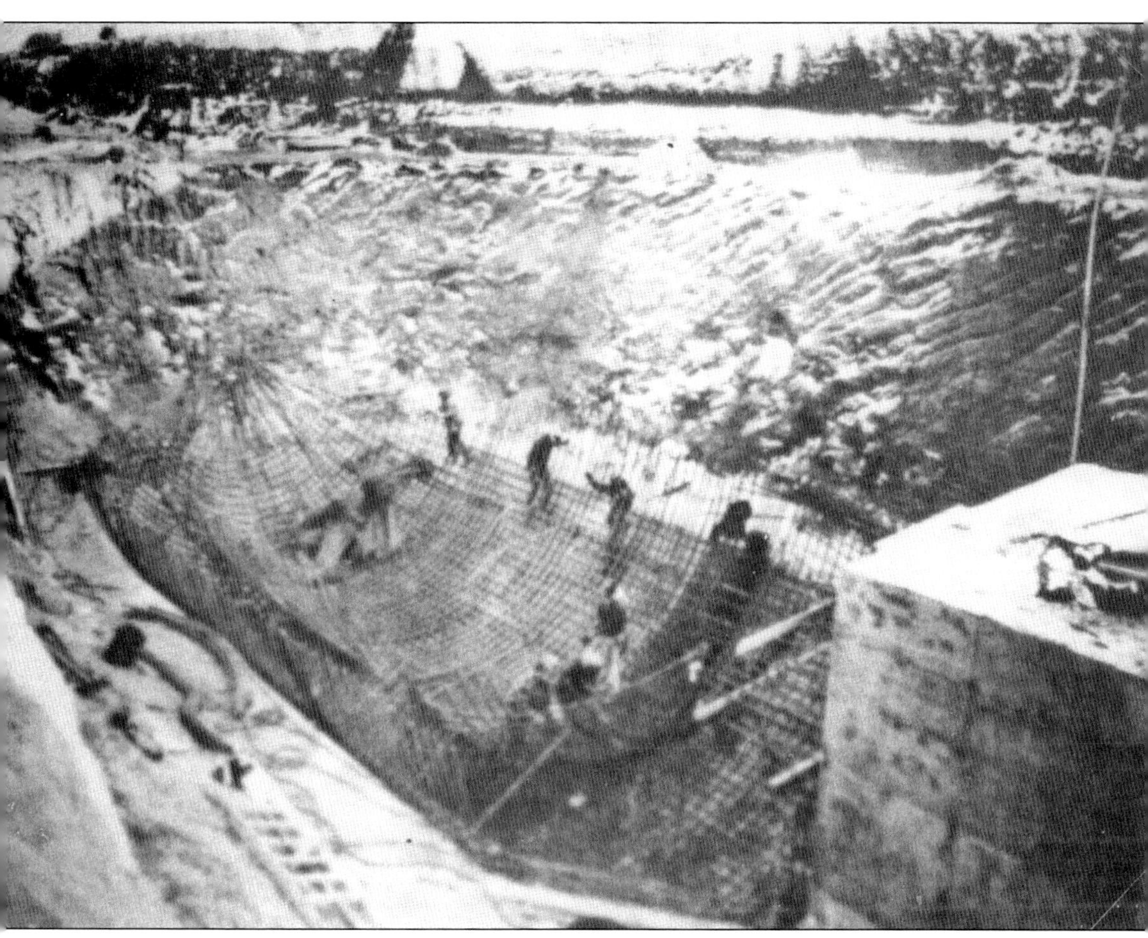

The excavation and construction of the launch control center capsule is pictured here. (Author's collection.)

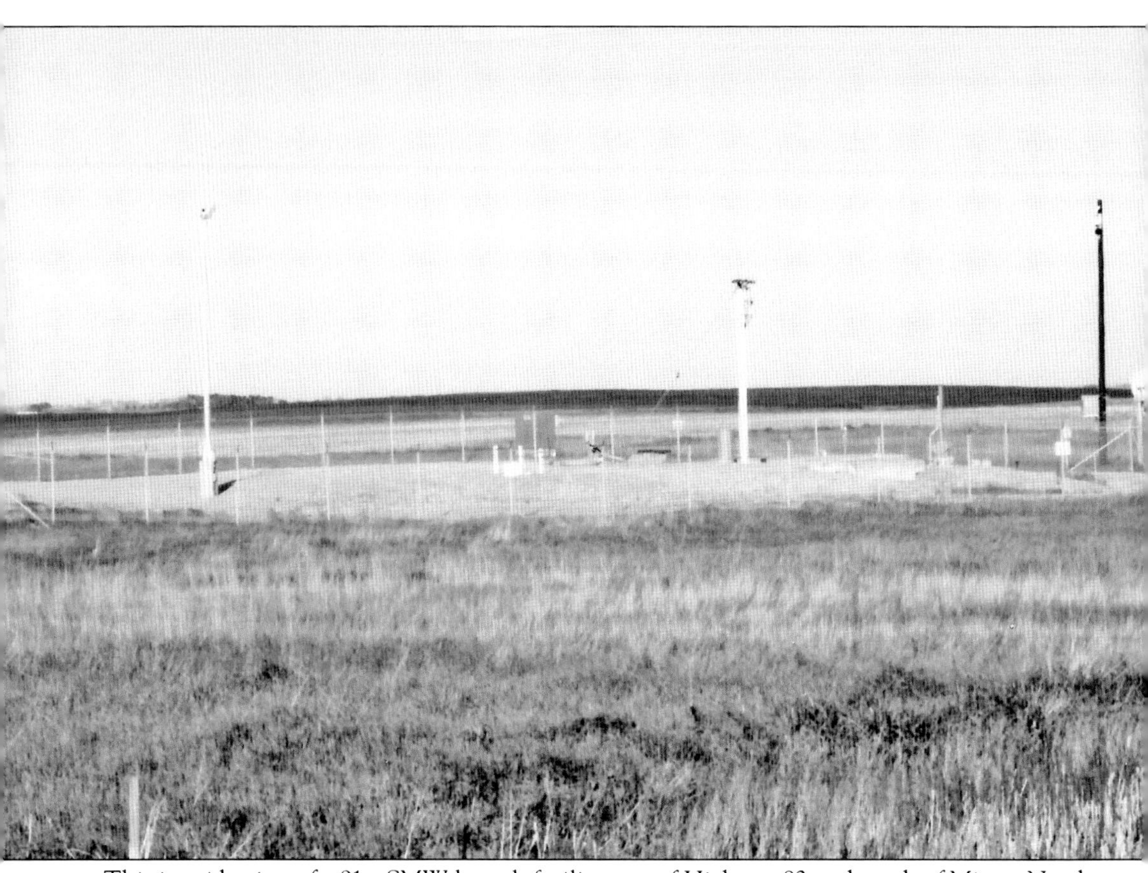

This is a side view of a 91st SMW launch facility east of Highway 83 and south of Minot, North Dakota on Minot Air Force Base. The photograph shows the clean external appearance of the launch facility. The tall tower near the launcher closure is the outer zone security antenna. (Author's collection.)

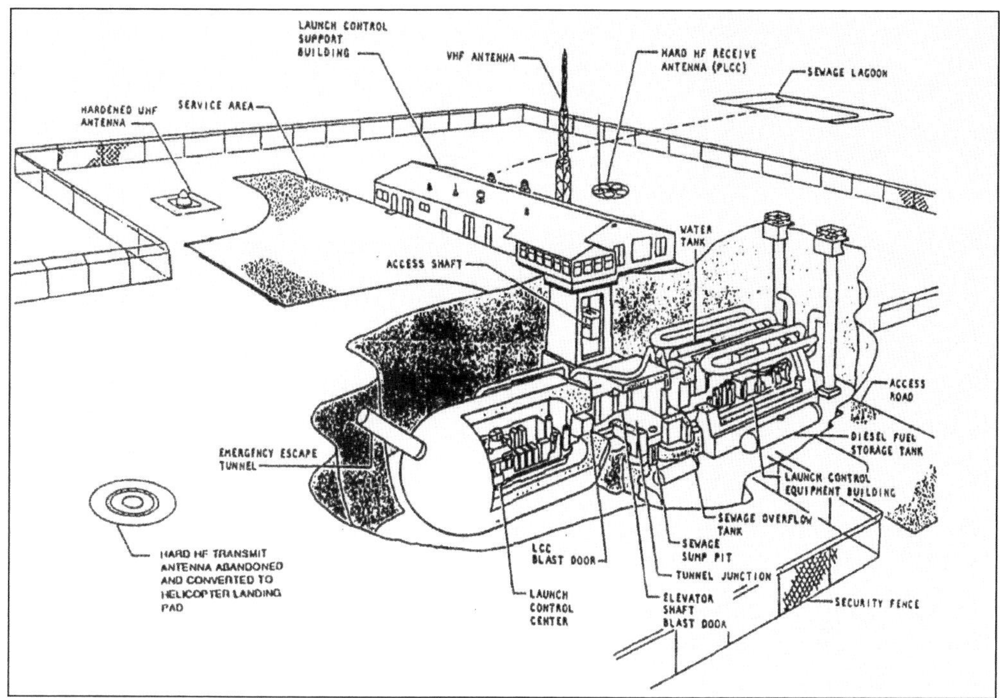

The LCSB, shown at ground level, is a standard one-level, ranch-style wood building. The LCC and LCEB are 40 feet underground. (Courtesy Whiteman Air Force Base, 509th Bomb Wing Historian Archives.)

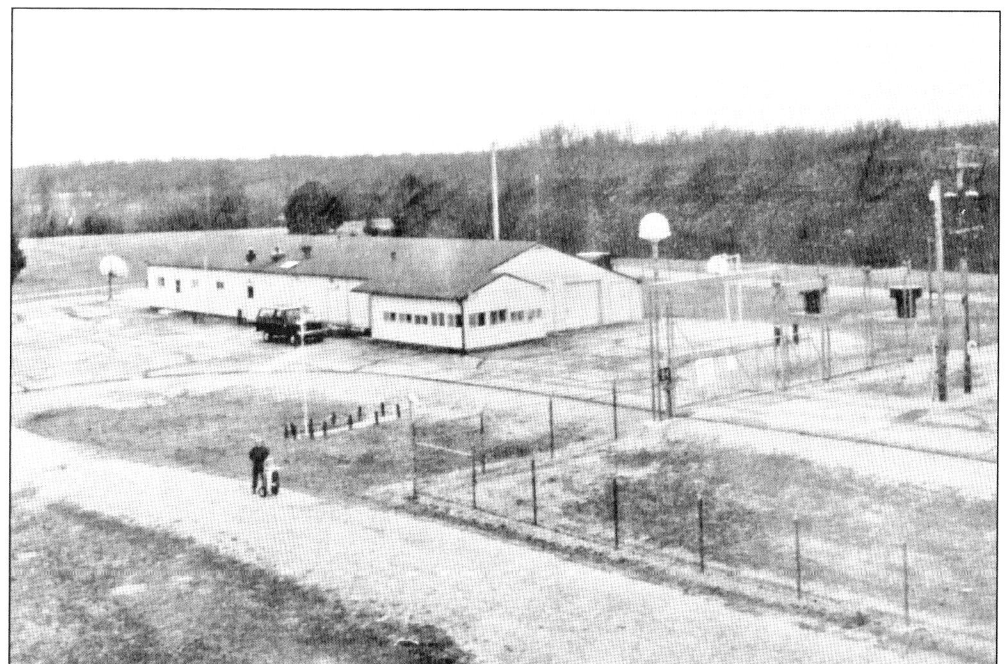

Shown is the Oscar-01 LCSB on Whiteman Air Force Base. Forty feet underneath are the LCC and LCEB. Oscar-01 was the only on-base LCSB, LCC, and LCEB. Security fencing isolated the facility. (Courtesy Whiteman Air Force Base, 509th Bomb Wing Public Affairs.)

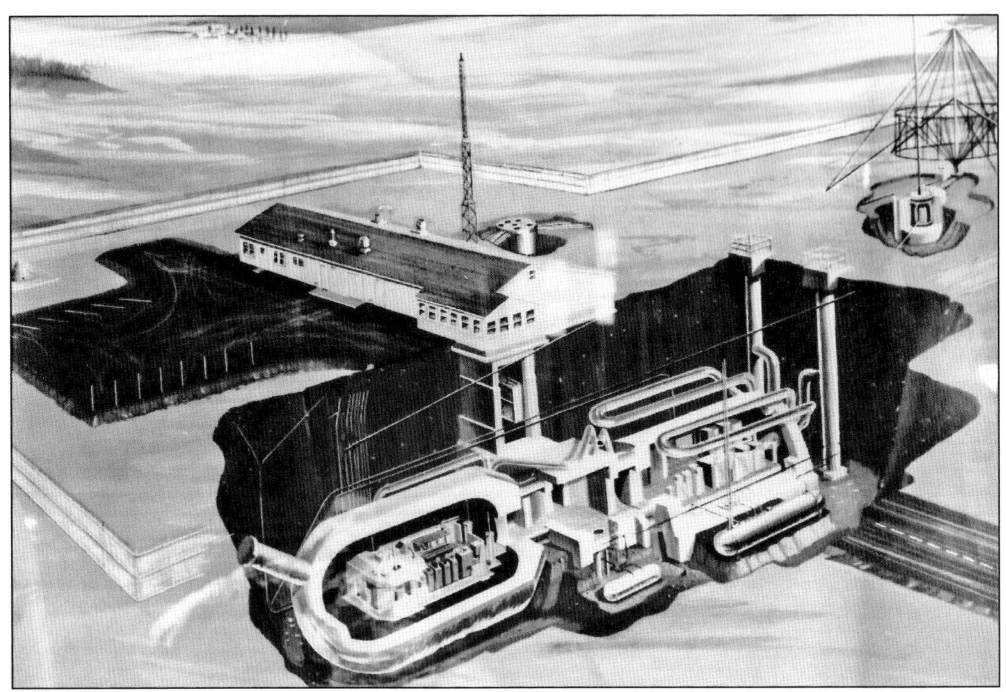

This is a conceptual drawing of Oscar-01 on Whiteman Air Force Base. (Courtesy Whiteman Air Force Base, 509th Bomb Wing Public Affairs.)

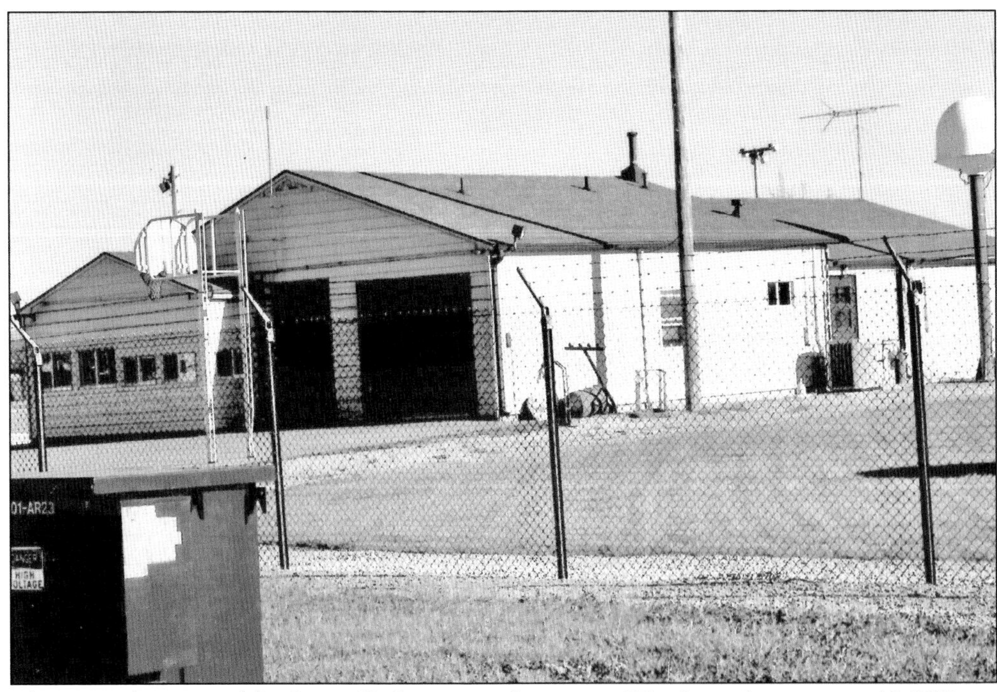

This is another view of the Oscar-01 aboveground structure. The formerly operational LCSB was retained as it was during its missile operations, allowed under START as a nonoperational facility after the deactivation of the 351st Strategic Missile Wing in 1992. (Author's collection.)

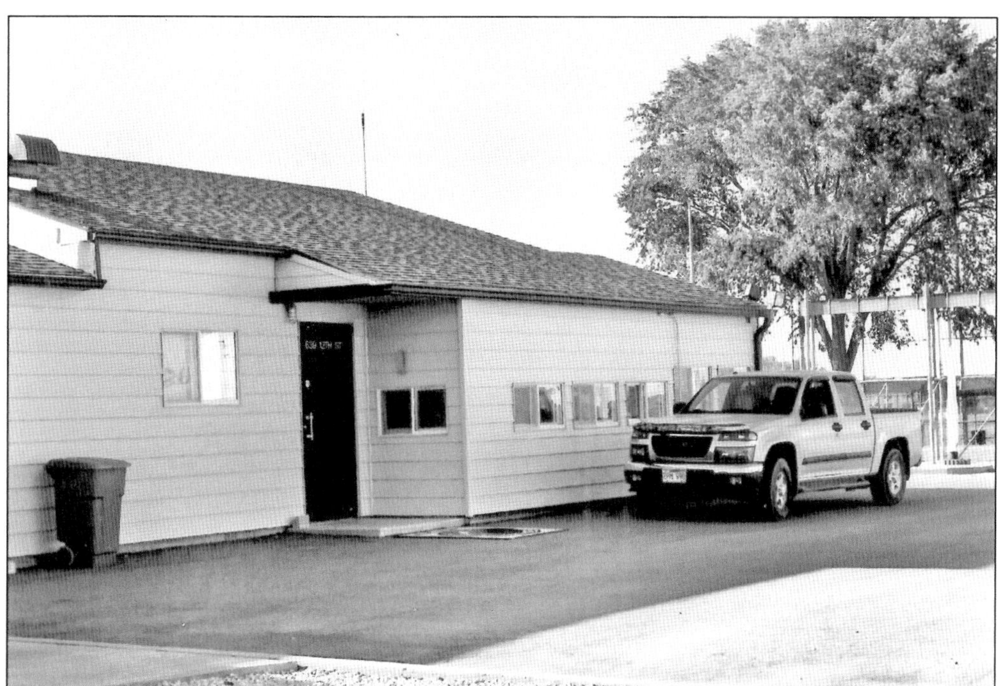

Only a simple entrance into Oscar-01 is provided. The structure hides the former Cold War underground missile control capsule, manned 24 hours a day, seven days a week, to provide immediate contact with the surrounding 10 Minuteman ICBMs in their launch facilities. (Author's collection.)

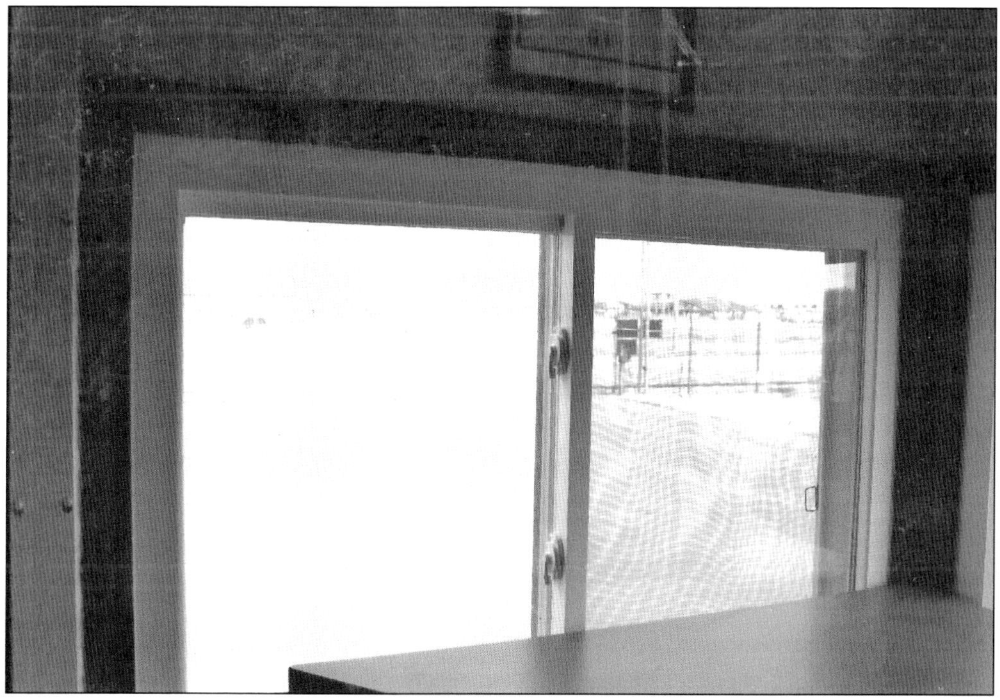

The view from inside the security force control room looks towards the remotely controlled sliding vehicle security access into Oscar-01. (Author's collection.)

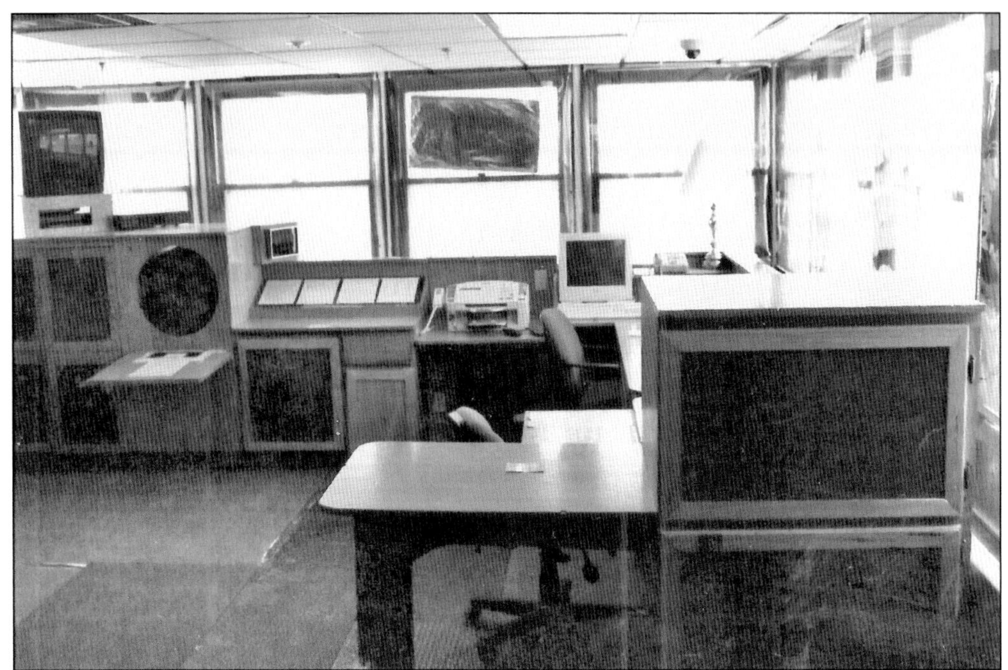

This is the security force control room. When the 351st Strategic Missile Wing was deactivated, equipment inside was removed. The windows remained, showing the view of the exterior along with the work desks. To the left is the entrance to the platform for the freight elevator and ladder to the underground facility, 40 feet below. (Author's collection.)

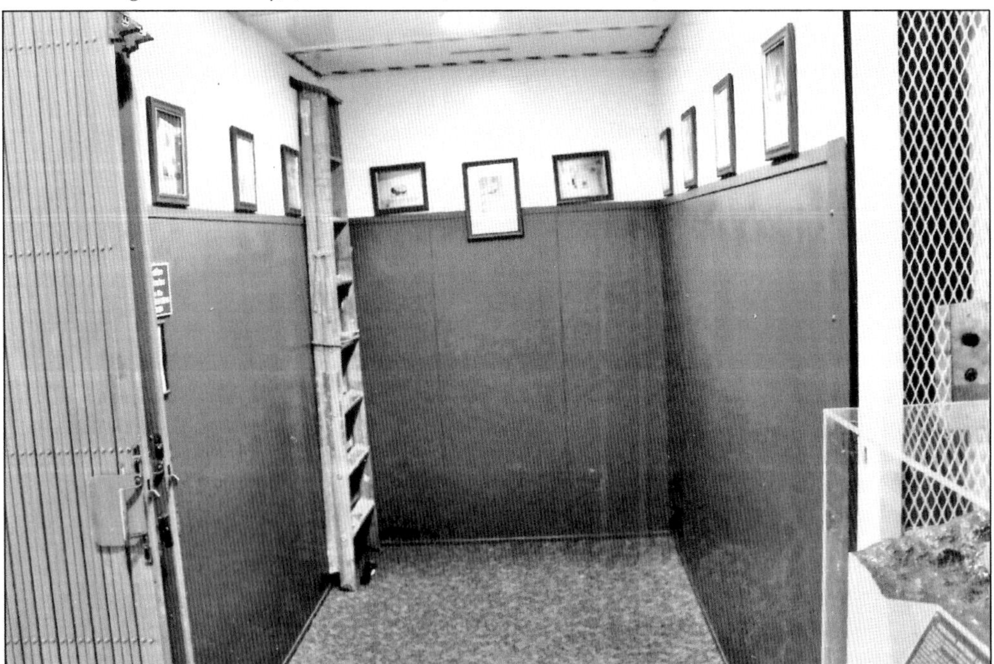

Shown is a standard freight elevator at the top of the shaft, adjacent to the security force control room, inside the LCSB. The elevator allows authorized personnel to reach the underground capsules. (Author's collection.)

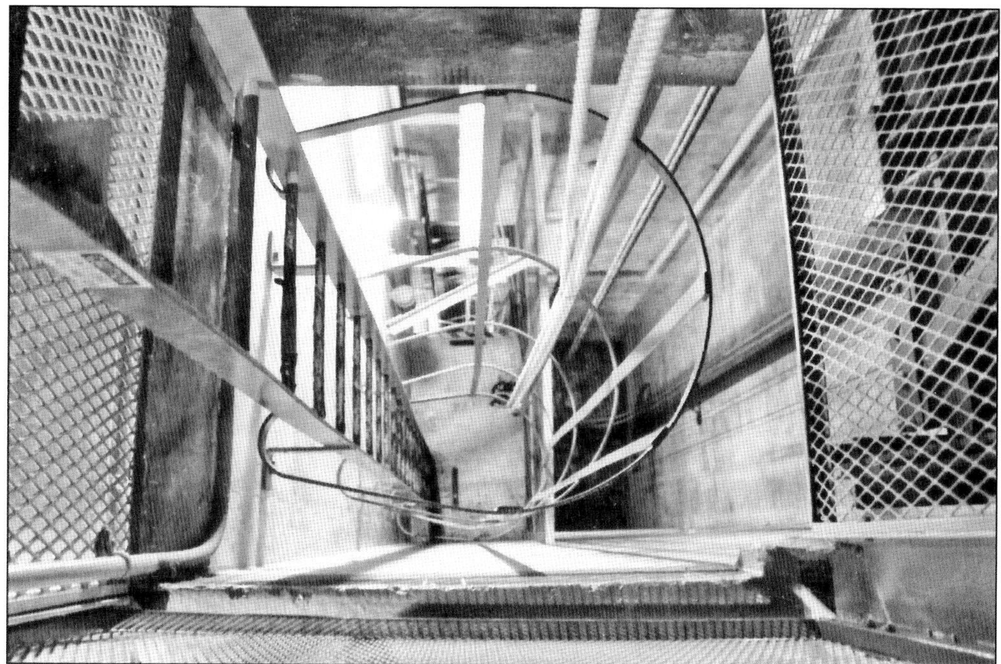

If the freight elevator malfunctioned, lost power to the electric motor, or was blocked due to ground movement from a nearby nuclear detonation, a caged ladder provided access to the underground capsules. The view down the caged steel ladder gives a perspective to the distant bottom of the elevator shaft to the left. (Author's collection.)

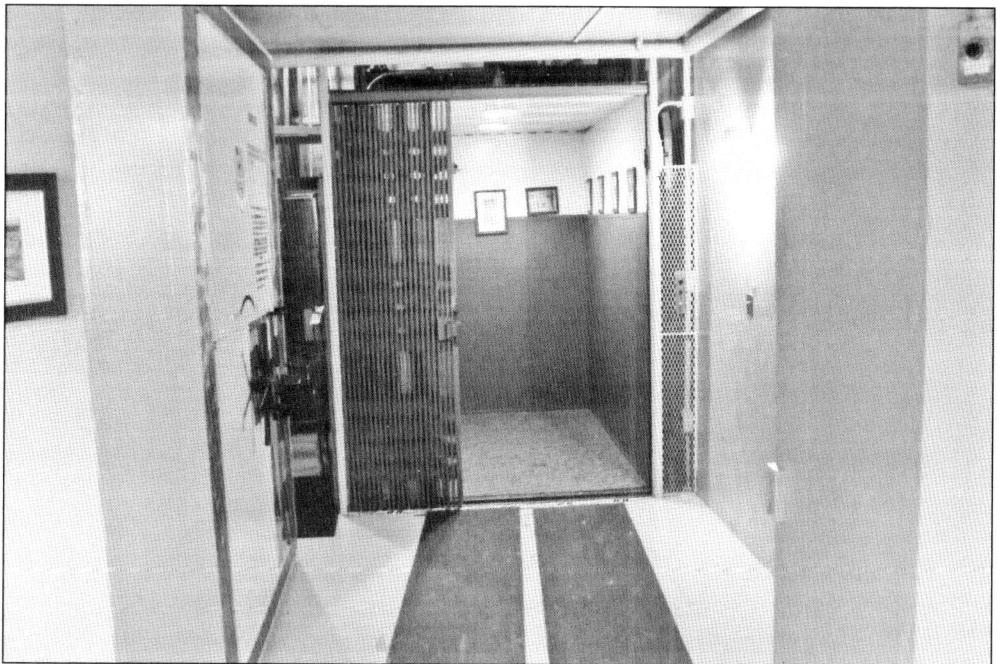

This is an interesting view looking back toward the freight elevator from the concrete vestibule at the bottom of the elevator shaft. To the left is the LCEB; to the right is the LCC. The thick concrete walls provide protection from potential nuclear detonations. (Author's collection.)

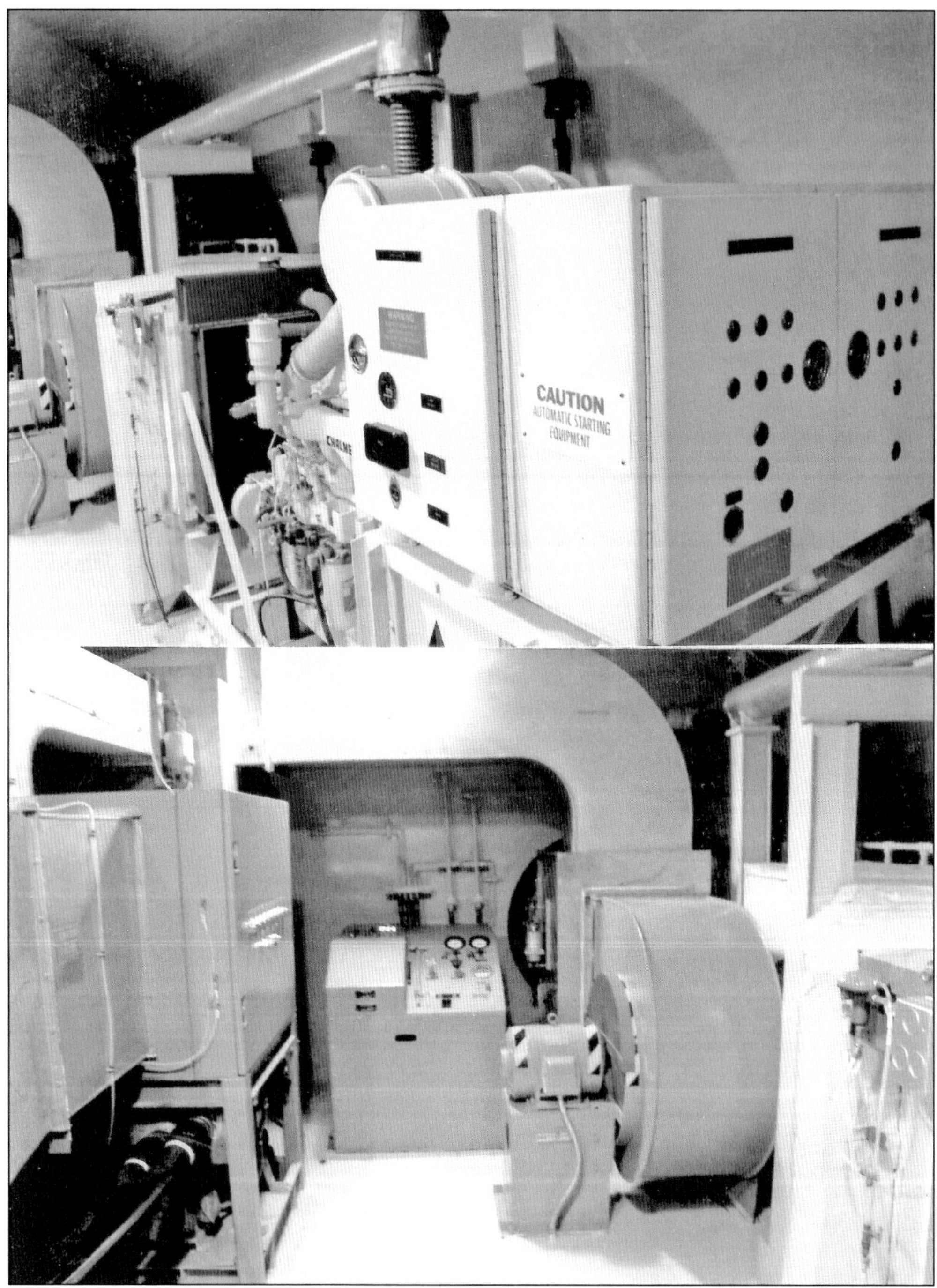

This photograph provides a close-up view of various equipment inside the LCEB. Internal electric generators and air handlers support the LCC at the opposite end of the concrete tunnel. (Author's collection.)

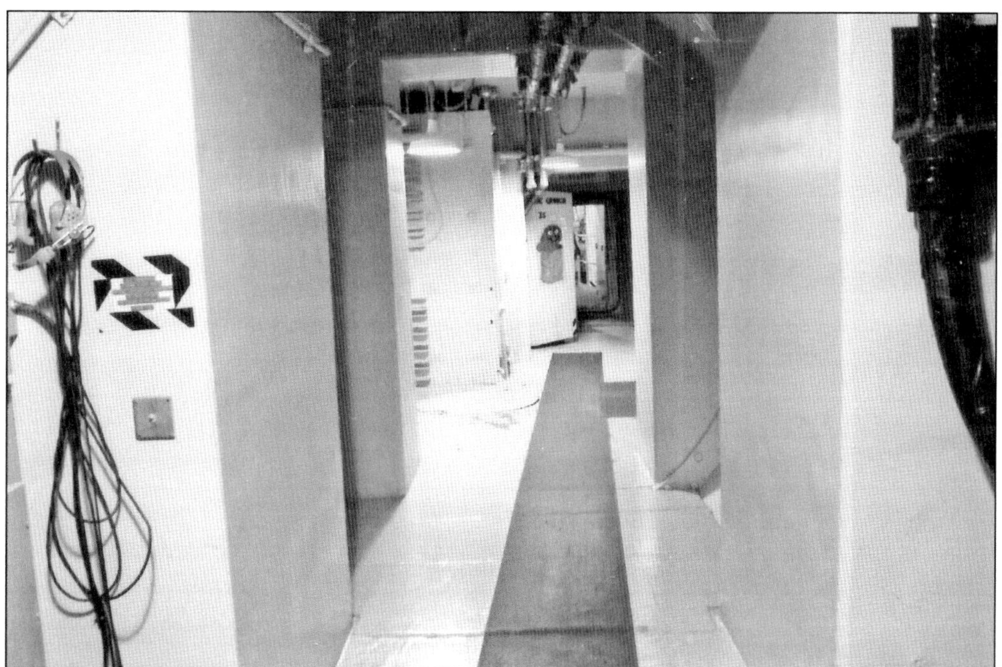

When one turns around inside the LCEB, the view toward the LCC shows how bomb-resistant the underground facility was built. (Author's collection.)

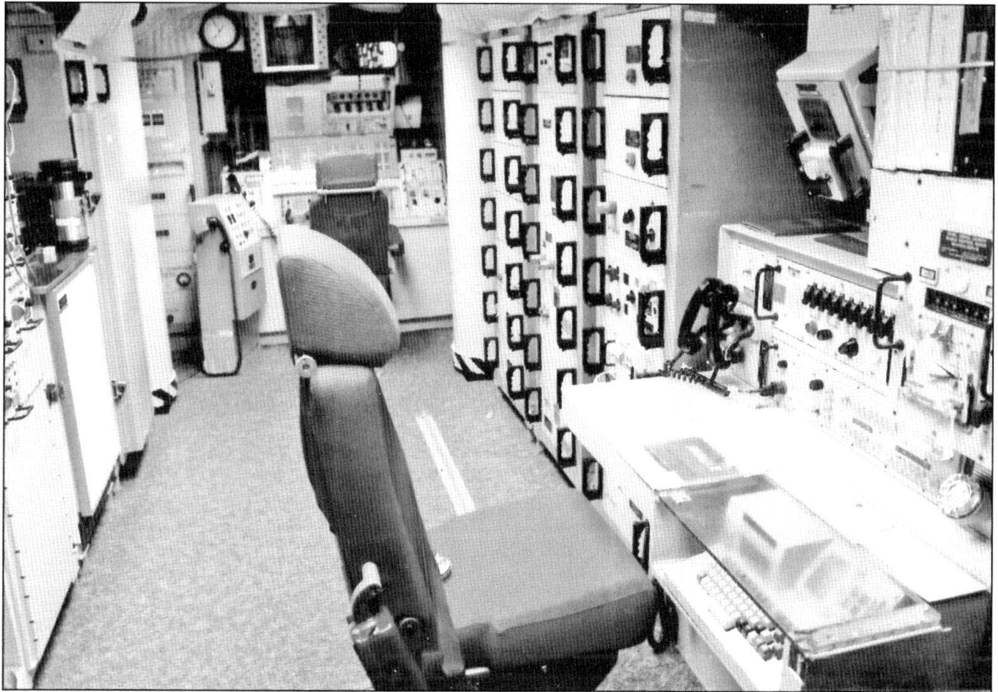

This photograph provides a look inside the LCC. In the foreground is the position of the deputy missile combat crew commander (DMCCC), with the high-backed aircraft-style chair. In the background is the missile combat crew commander's position. Banks of communications equipment line the capsule. (Author's collection.)

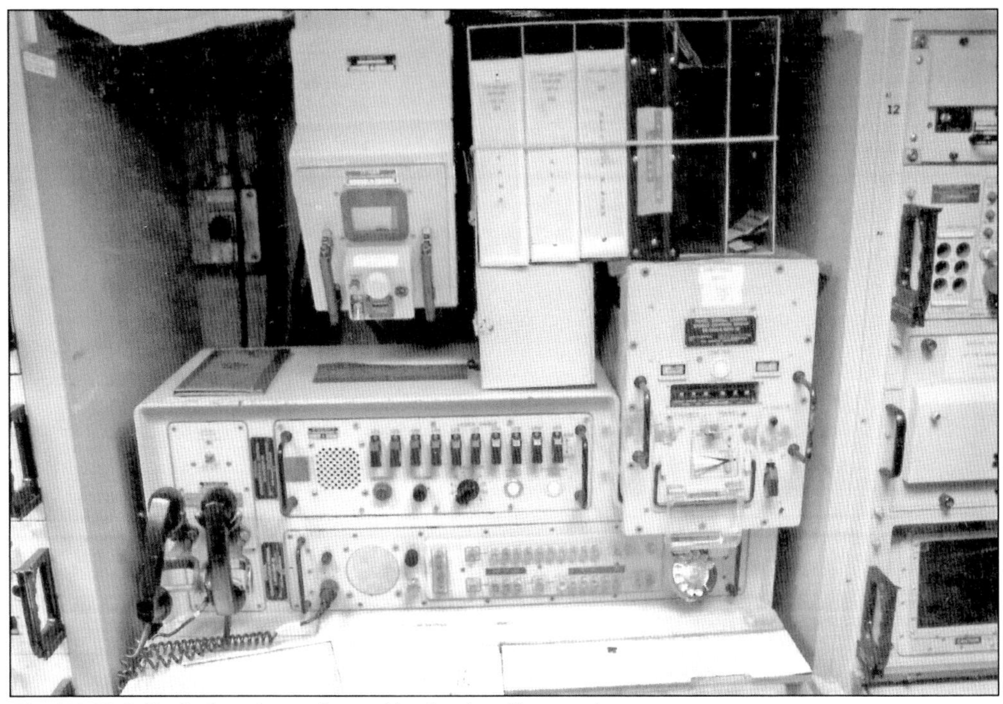

The DMCCC's desk is shown here. (Author's collection.)

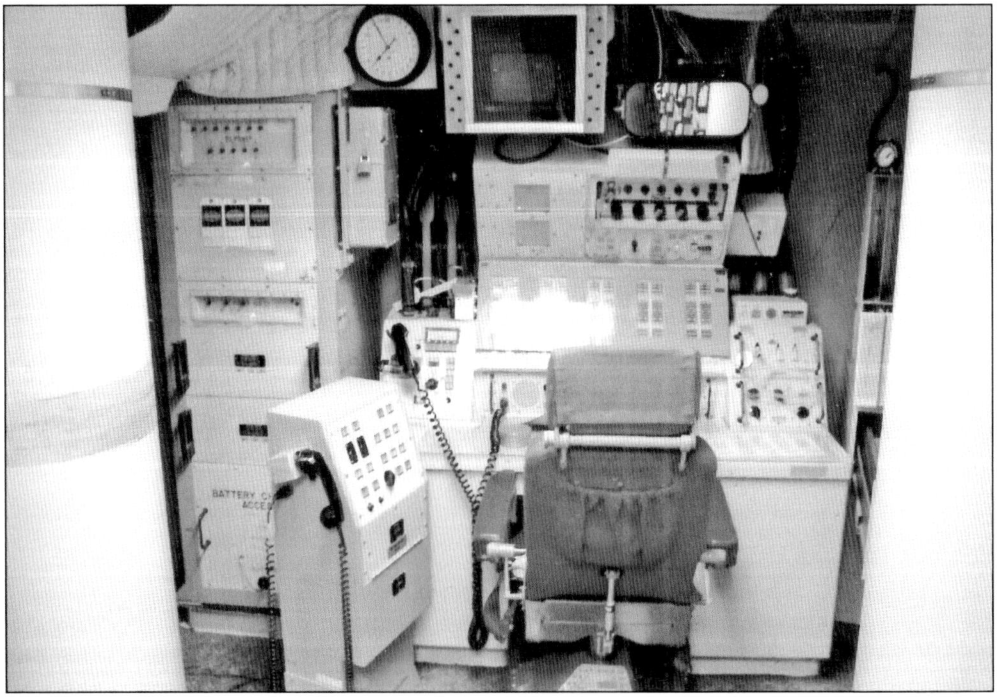

Also inside the LCC is the missile combat crew commander's position. (Author's collection.)

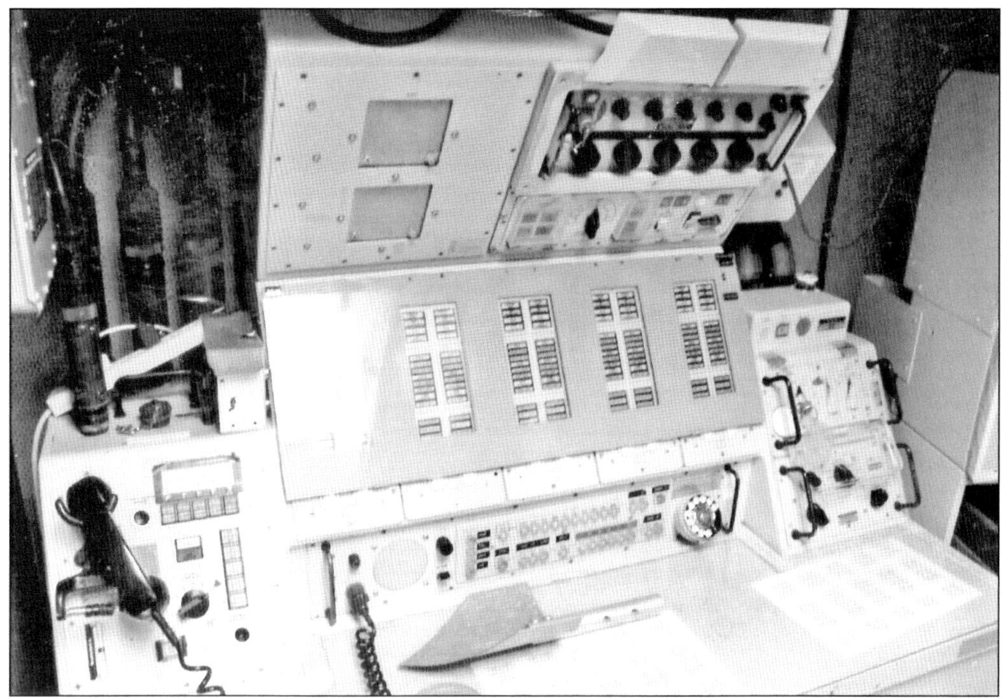

This close-up photograph of the missile combat crew commander's console shows the 10 missile status lights he is responsible for monitoring. (Author's collection.)

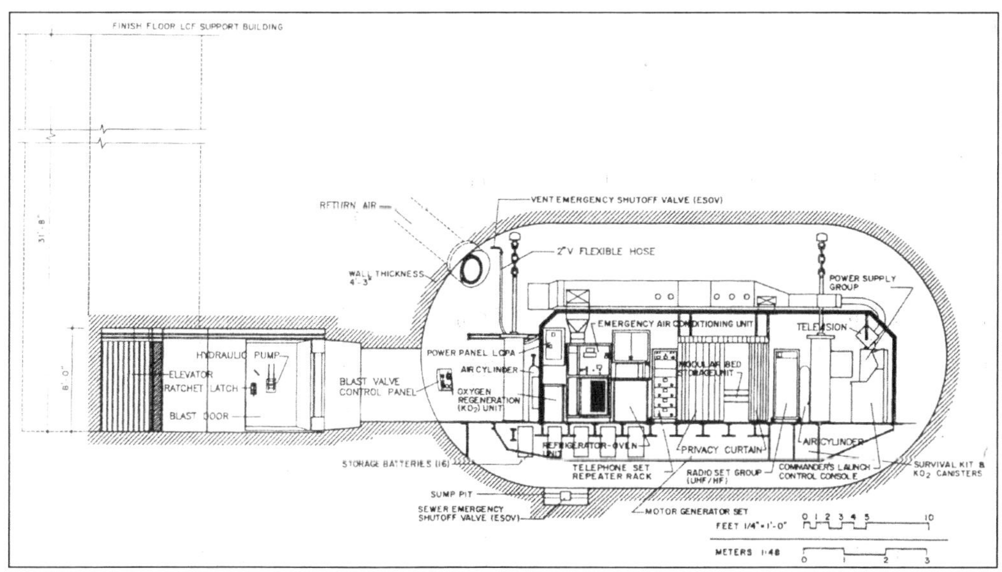

This engineering drawing of an LCC shows the standard layout used at all missile alert facilities. (Courtesy Whiteman Air Force Base, 509th Bomb Wing Historian Archives.)

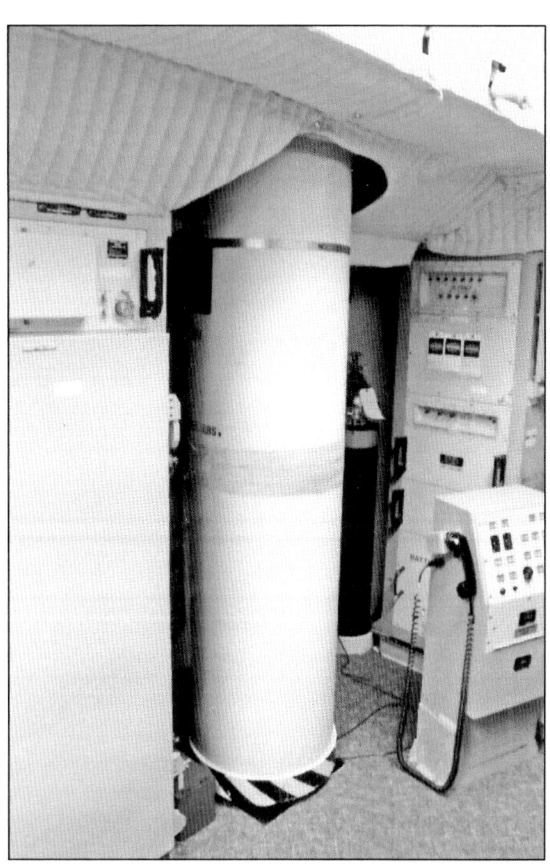

This is one of four shock suspension cylinders, which isolate the interior of the capsule from the walls to negate lateral movement from a nearby nuclear detonation or other ground movement. (Author's collection.)

The LCC is provided with a refrigerator and microwave oven for the missile officers on duty. (Author's collection.)

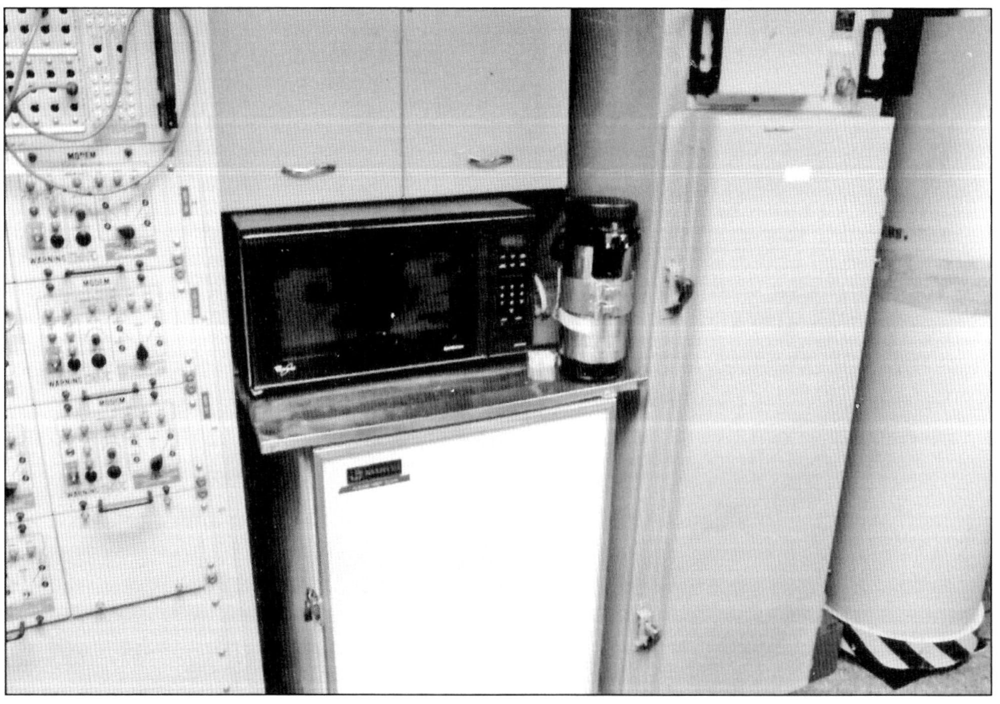

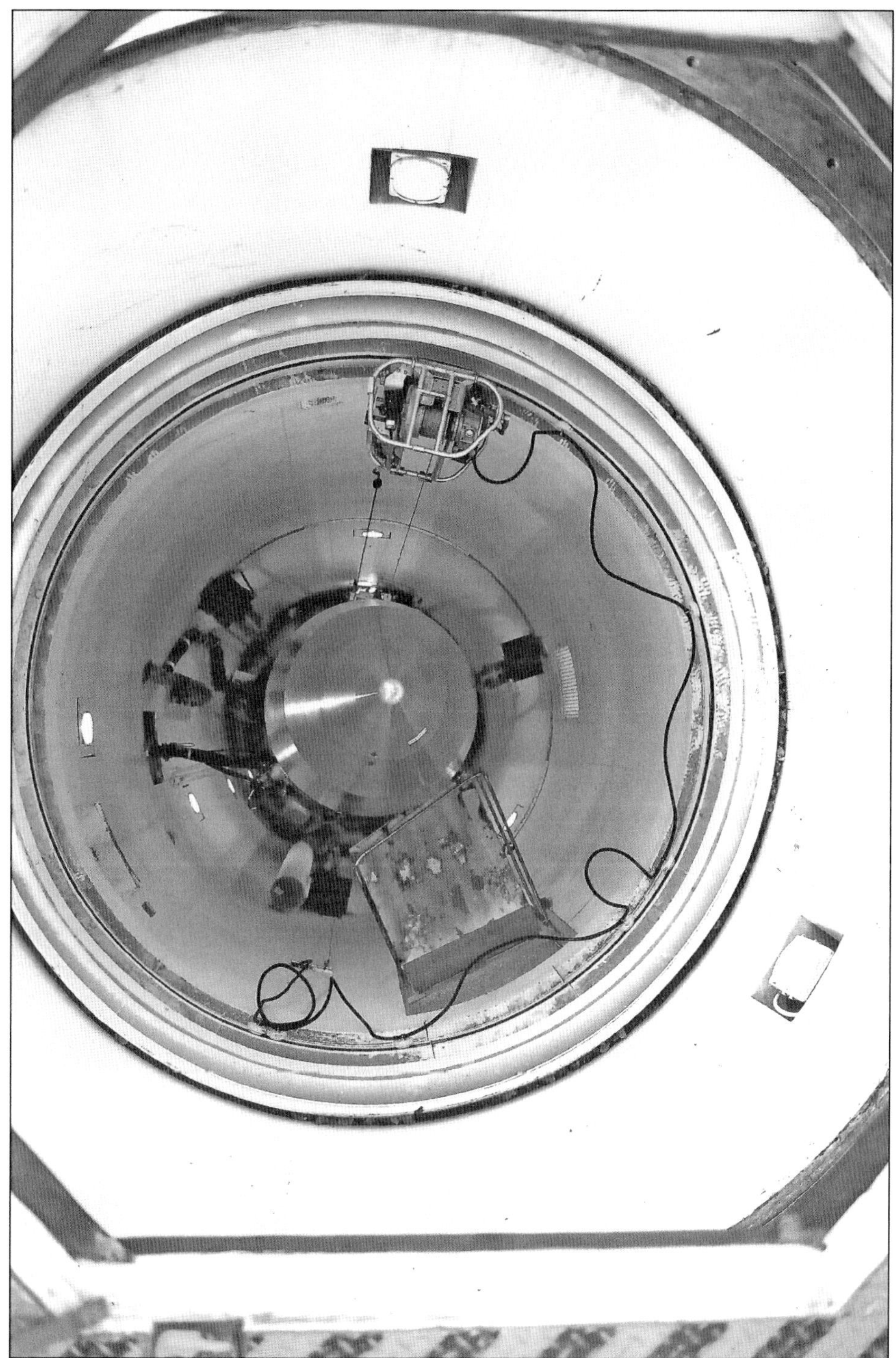

Shown is a Minuteman III ICBM inside its silo at the launch facility. A maintenance platform is lowered and available for personnel access. The missile's umbilical cables are attached to the missile for power, guidance information, and launch control. (Courtesy Minot Air Force Base, 351st Strategic Missile Wing Public Affairs.)

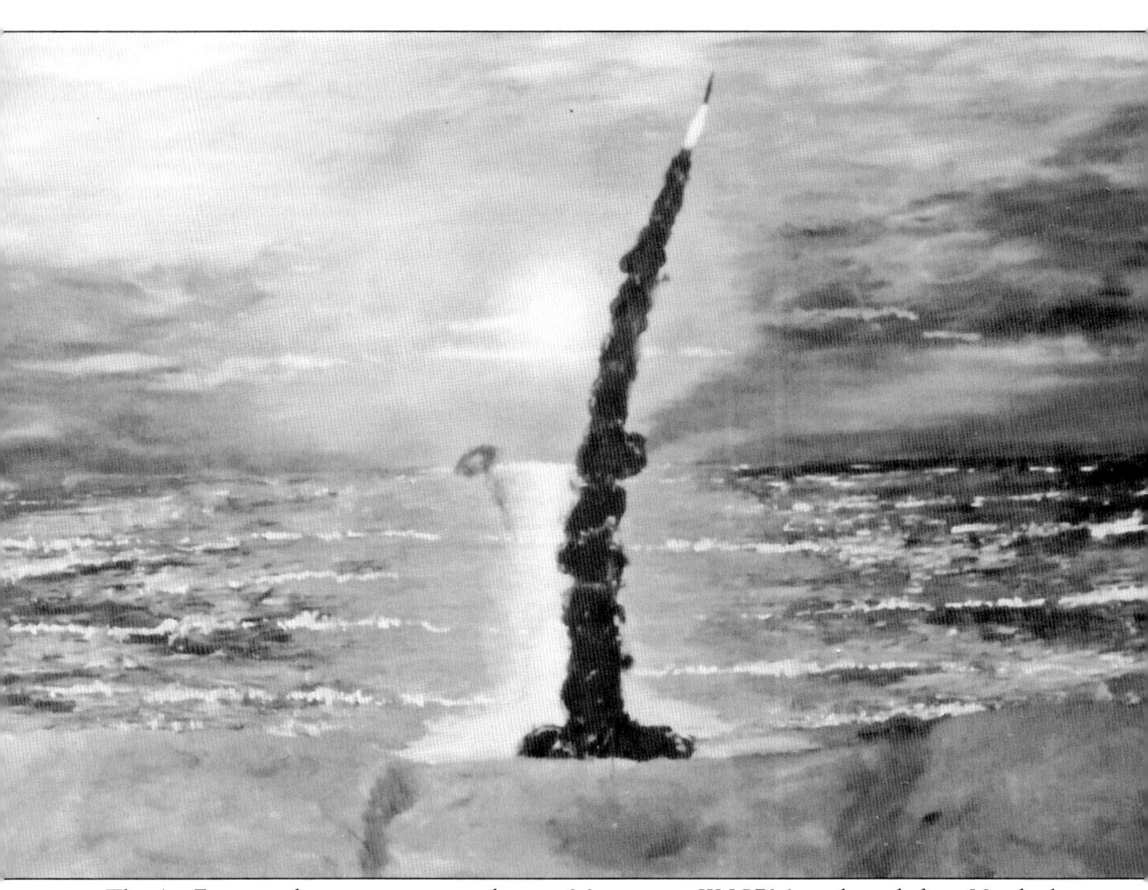

The Air Force used its art program to depict a Minuteman III ICBM test launch from Vandenberg Air Force Base, California. Many ICBM bases used these posters to line their headquarters and operations facilities. (Courtesy Whiteman Air Force Base, 509th Bomb Wing Public Affairs.)

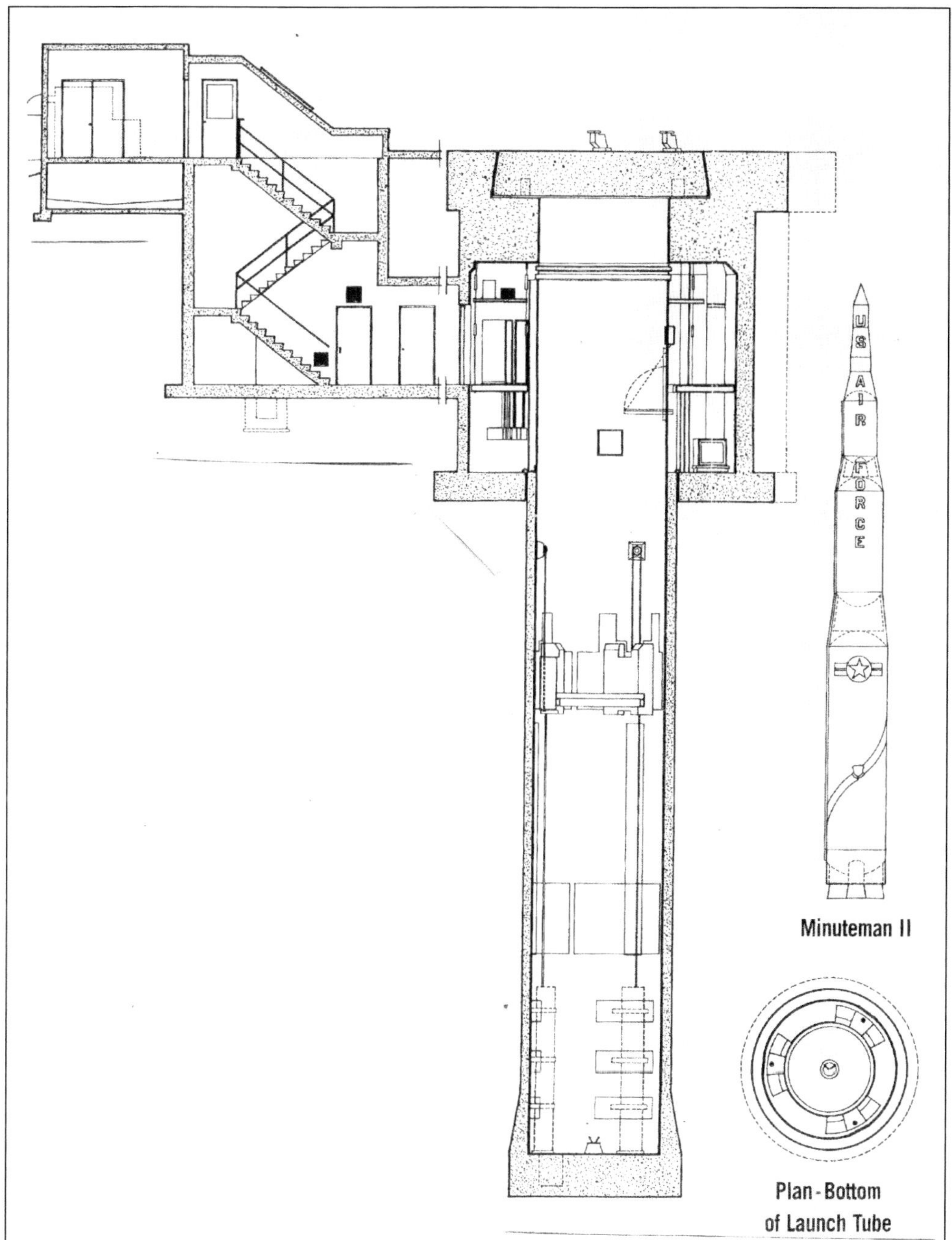

This is the former T-12 launch trainer on Whiteman Air Force Base, constructed to standard blueprints for missile bases. The trainer was destroyed to comply with START. (Courtesy Whiteman Air Force Base, 509th Bomb Wing Historian Archives.)

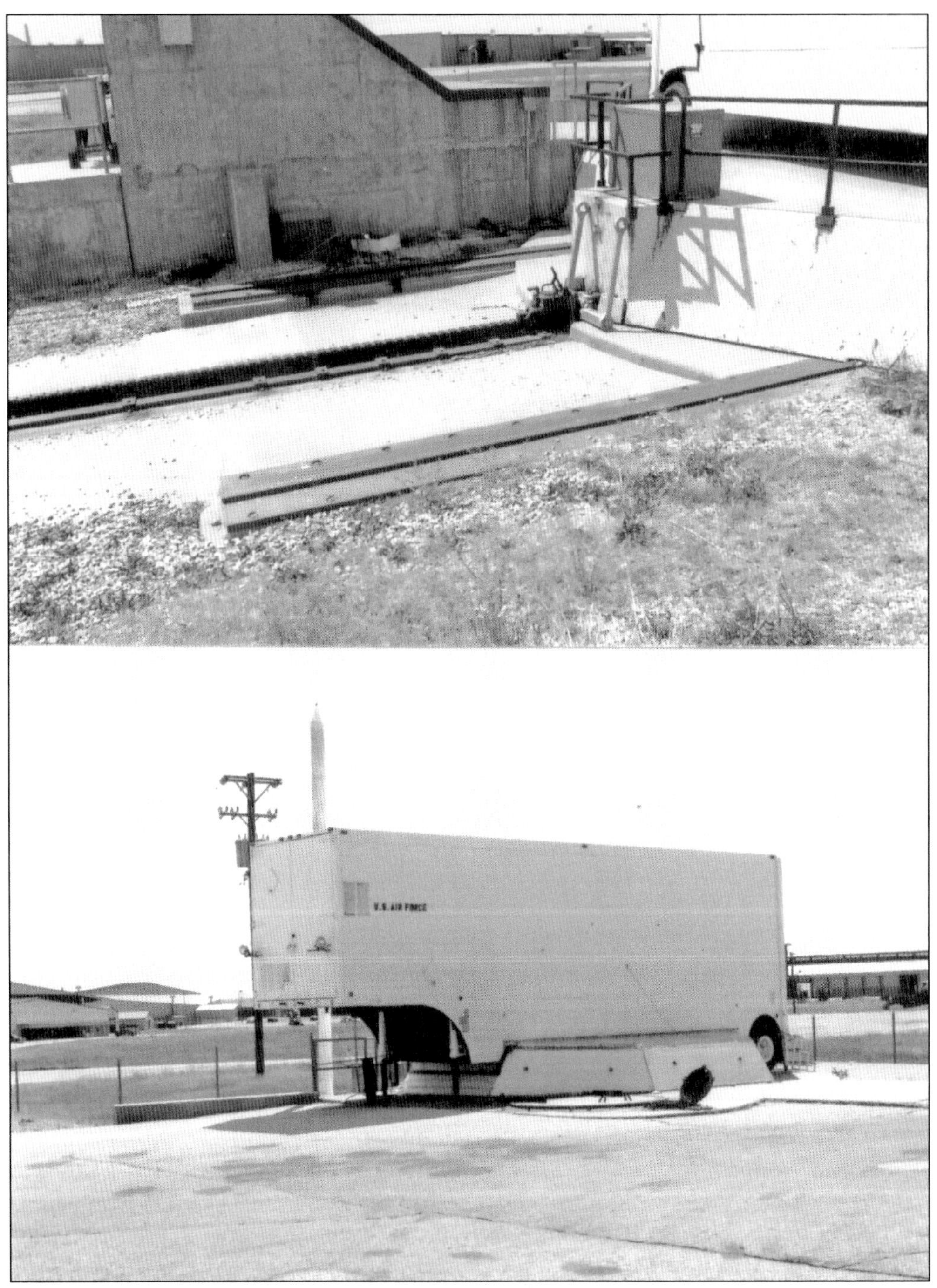

At the top of this photograph is the aboveground entrance to a surviving launch trainer on Ellsworth Air Force, now part of the South Dakota Air and Space Museum. At the bottom is a photograph of the trainer silo and an inert training Minuteman ICBM, covered with a missile payload transport trailer. (Author's collection.)

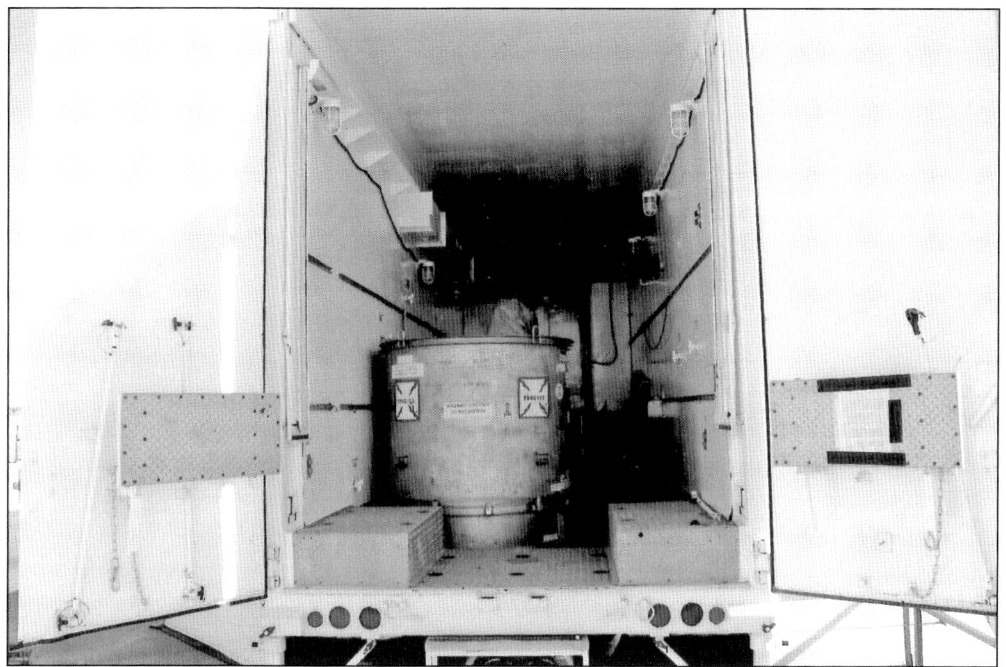

Cargo doors are open on the nuclear payload transport trailer on display at Ellsworth Air Force Base over the launch trainer's inert Minuteman II training missile. The round container held the removed guidance package and was provided with hookups for power to maintain the electric components of the guidance package. (Author's collection.)

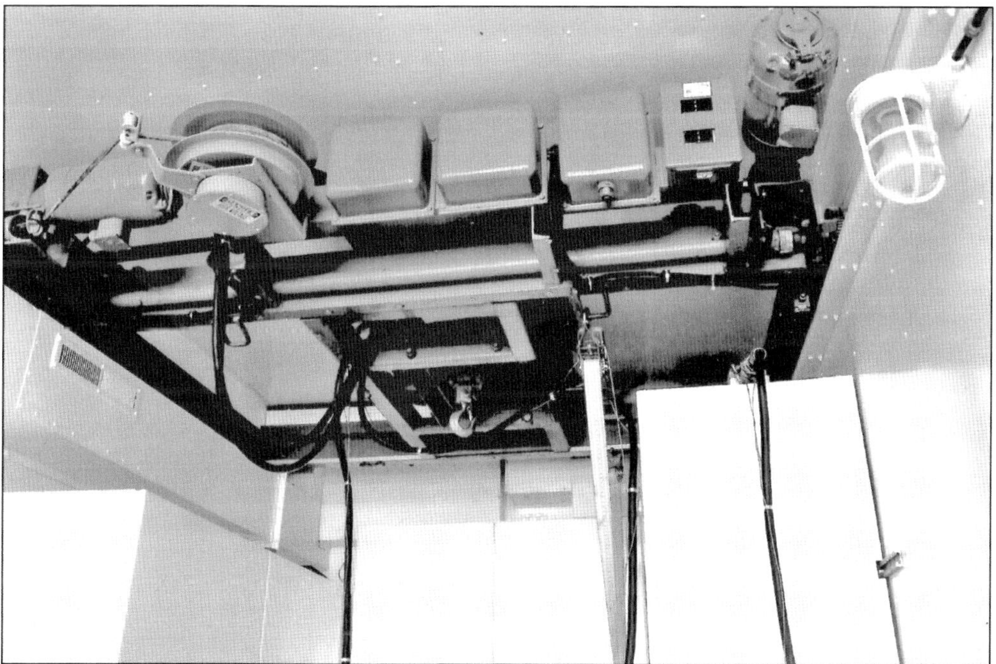

The nuclear payload transporter trailer was equipped with an overhead hoist to lower or raise the warhead and the missile guidance section. All operations were conducted inside an environmentally controlled atmosphere to protect the warhead and guidance package. (Author's collection.)

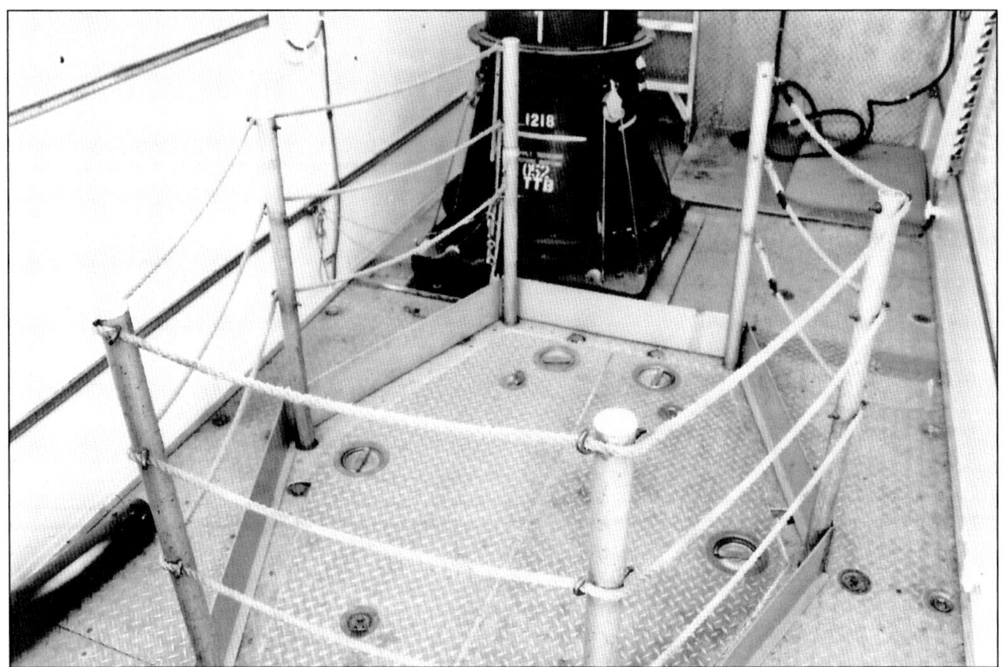

The steel floor of the nuclear payload transport trailer was equipped with a set of double doors that, when opened along with the launcher closure, allowed access to the top of the Minuteman ICBM inside. The door opening is surrounded by steel posts with ropes to prevent accidental falls. (Author's collection.)

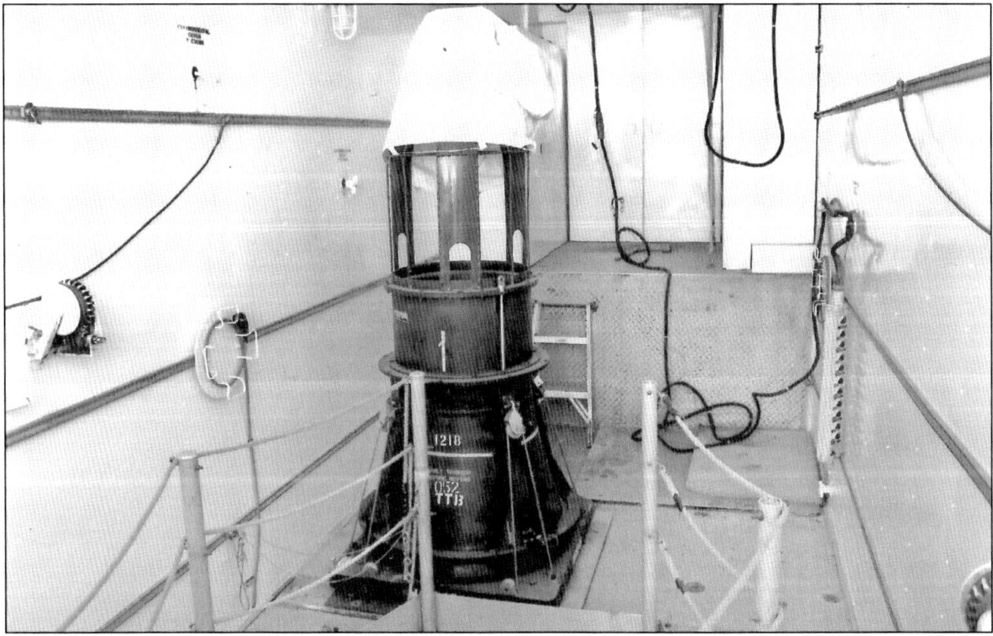

The nuclear payload transport trailer was equipped with a nuclear warhead cradle. The warhead was carefully secured inside the cradle to protect weapon when transported to and from a launch facility and during hoisting operations to lower the warhead onto the Minuteman ICBM or remove the warhead. (Author's collection.)

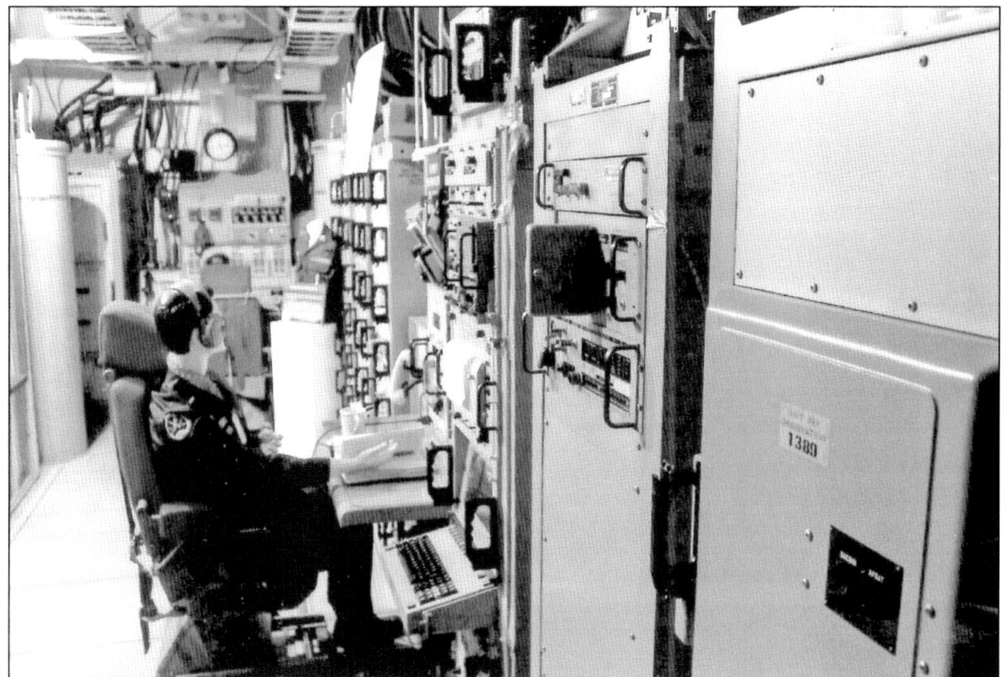

When the missile launch officers' trainer at Whiteman Air Force Base was deactivated, all equipment was removed. This equipment was retained at Ellsworth Air Force Base, transferred to the South Dakota Air and Space Museum, and re-created in its entirety with a glass wall to allow museum visitors to view the missile trainer. (Author's collection.)

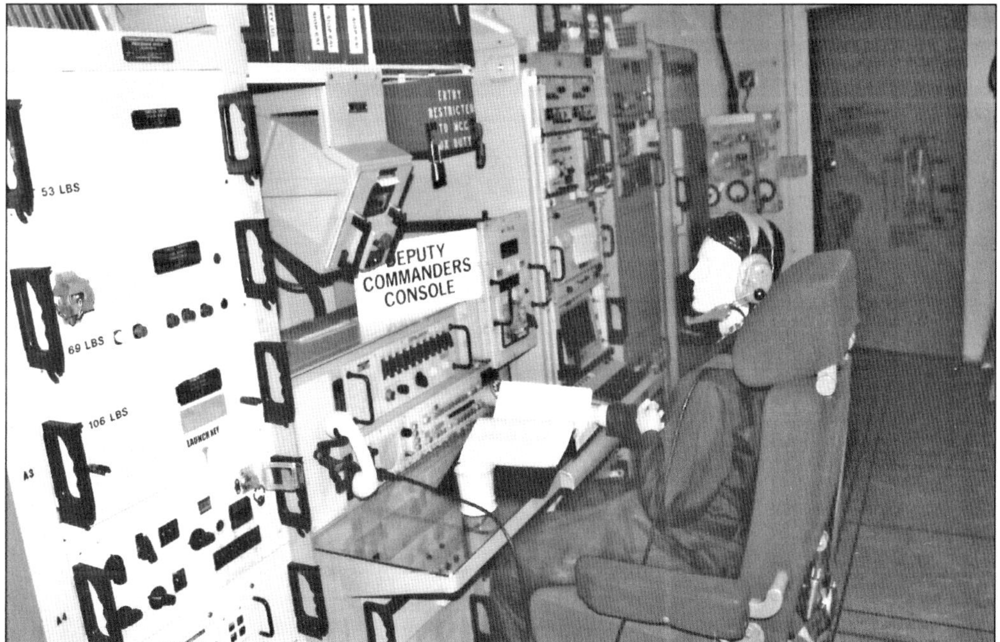

Pictured is the DMCCC's console, with the red box that contained the missile launch keys for the DMCCC and missile combat crew commander. Each has a key for the box, only opened under received message authorization. (Author's collection.)

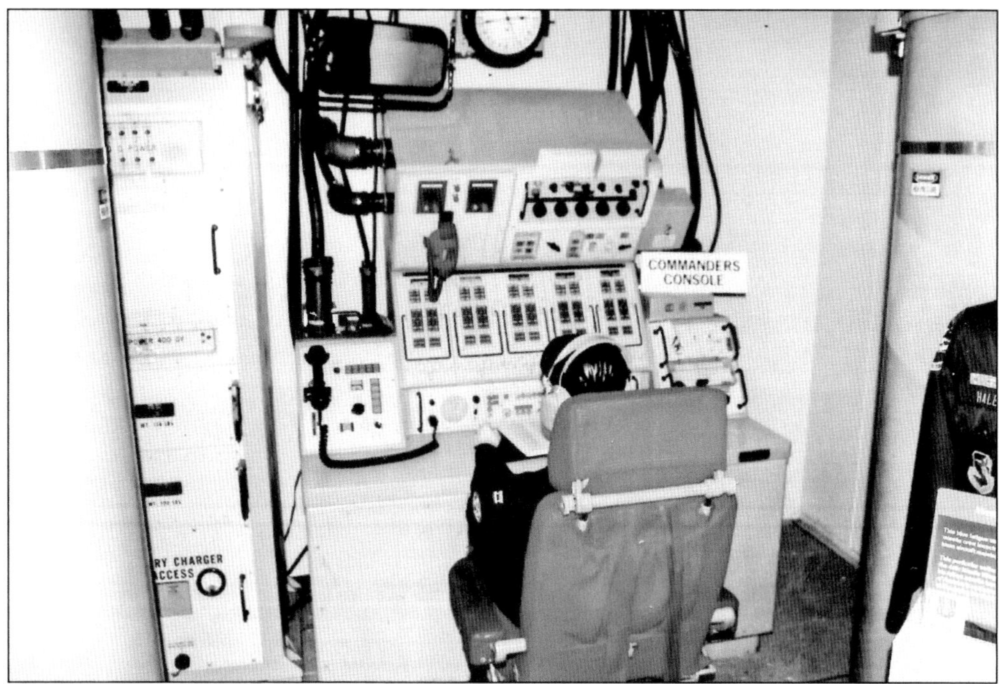

The missile combat crew commander's console inside the missile trainer is shown. The commander monitored 10 Minuteman II ICBMs from his flight and four other flights. If a launch order was received and authenticated, one single LCC could not launch its missiles without agreement from another LCC in the squadron. (Author's collection.)

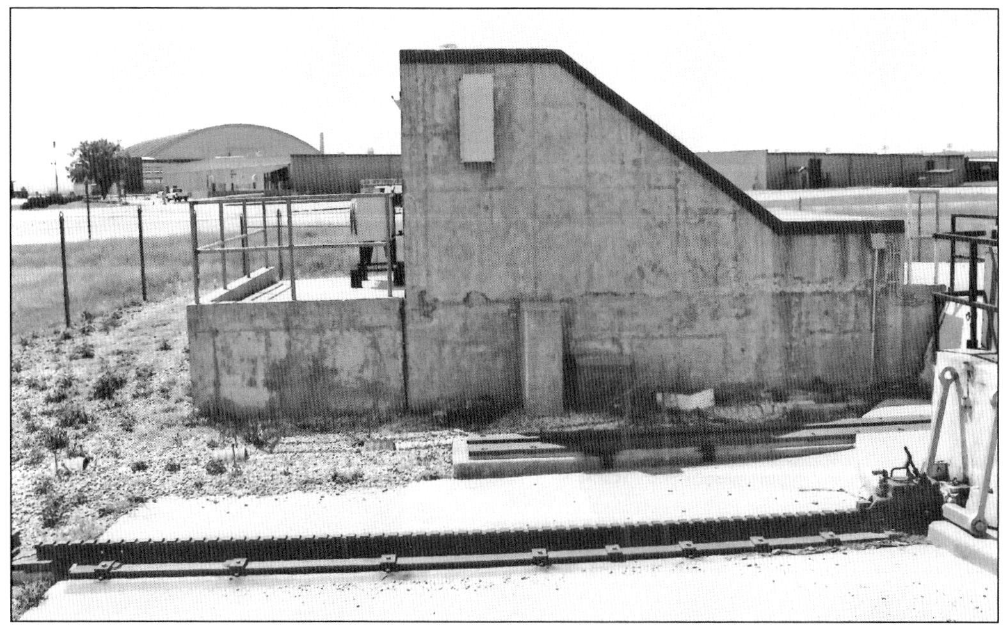
This is the entrance into the missile training facility on Ellsworth Air Force Base. The launch closure is opened on the heavy rails in the foreground. This facility provided training for missile maintenance personnel as well as security force personnel assigned to protect operations when entering the launch facility. (Author's collection.)

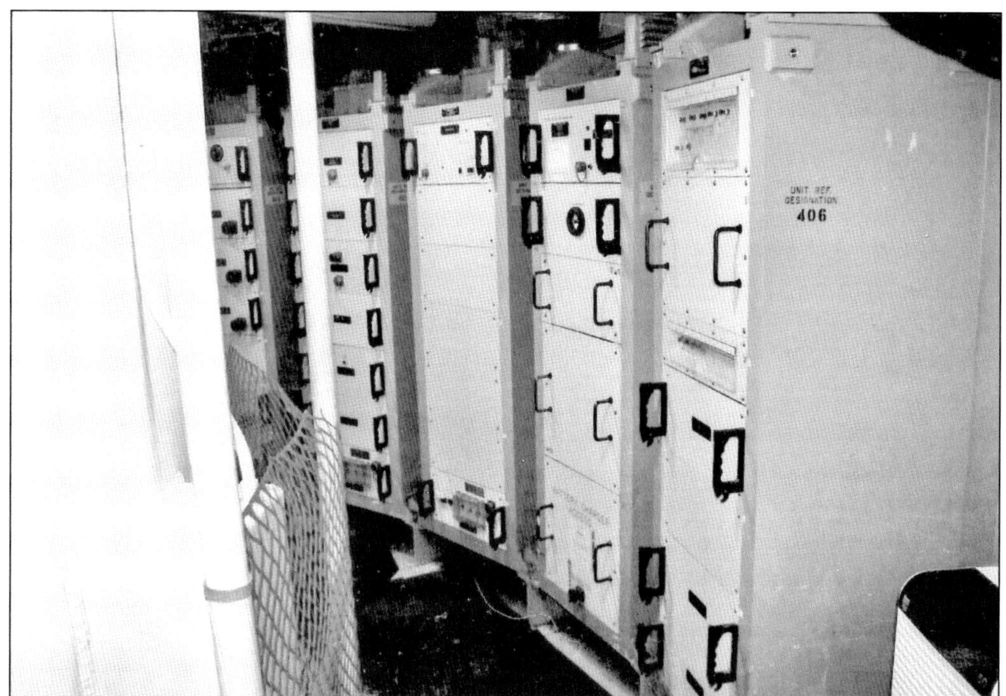

At the lower level of the missile trainer is the bank of electronics used to monitor the inert training missile to re-create that of an operational Minuteman ICBM at a launch facility. The inert training missile silo is to the left of this equipment. (Author's collection.)

An inert training Minuteman II ICBM is positioned inside the silo section of the missile trainer. All connections are as on an operational missile. The closed launcher closure door is visible above the warhead protective casing on the missile. The guidance section is the black section below the warhead section. (Author's collection.)

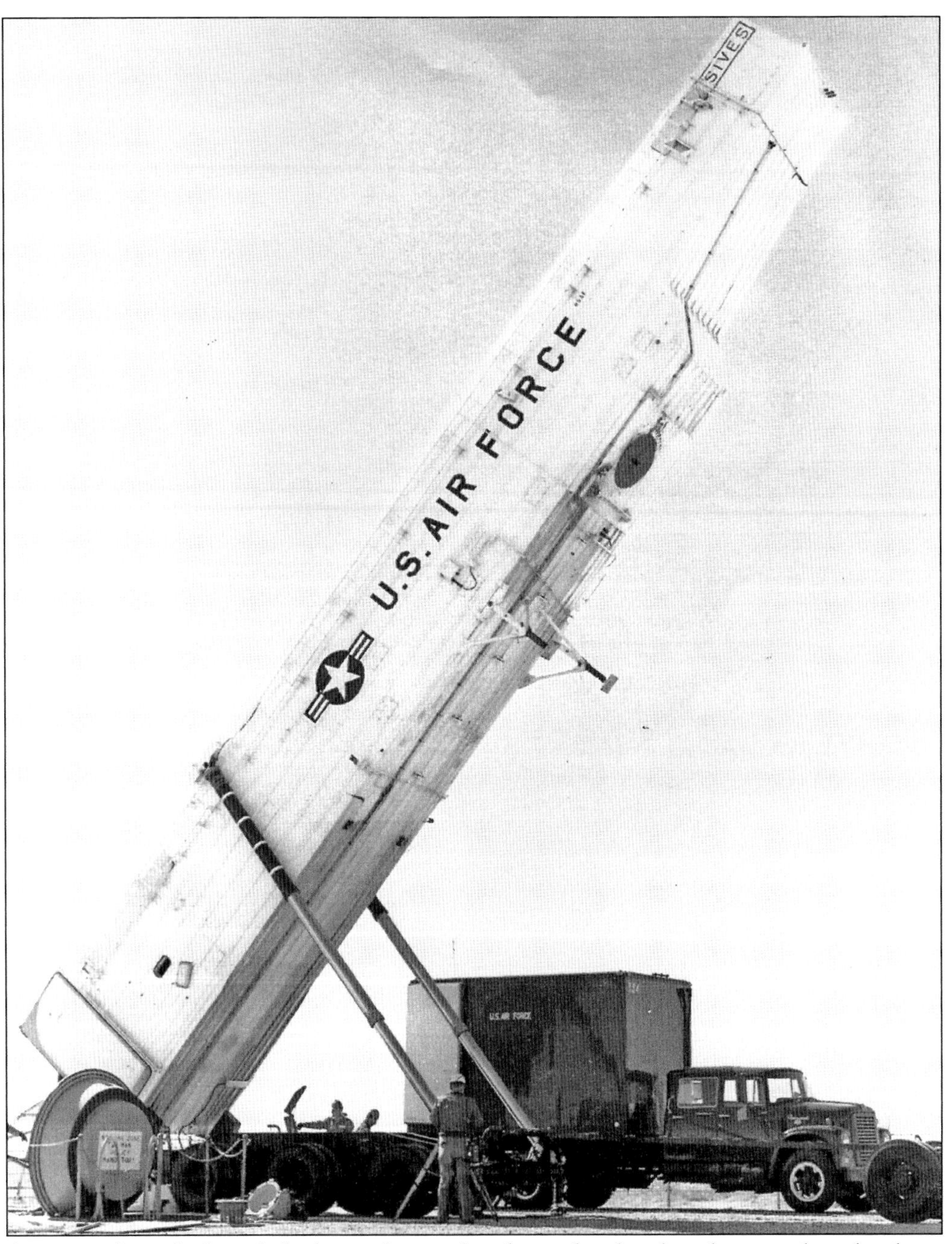

An open silo at the launch facility is shown after the warhead and guidance package has been removed in the deactivation process. The Boeing Minuteman Transporter-Erector (TE) was used to ferry missiles to and from the launch facility and raise them to 90 degrees (vertical). (Courtesy Whiteman Air Force Base, 509th Bomb Wing Public Affairs.)

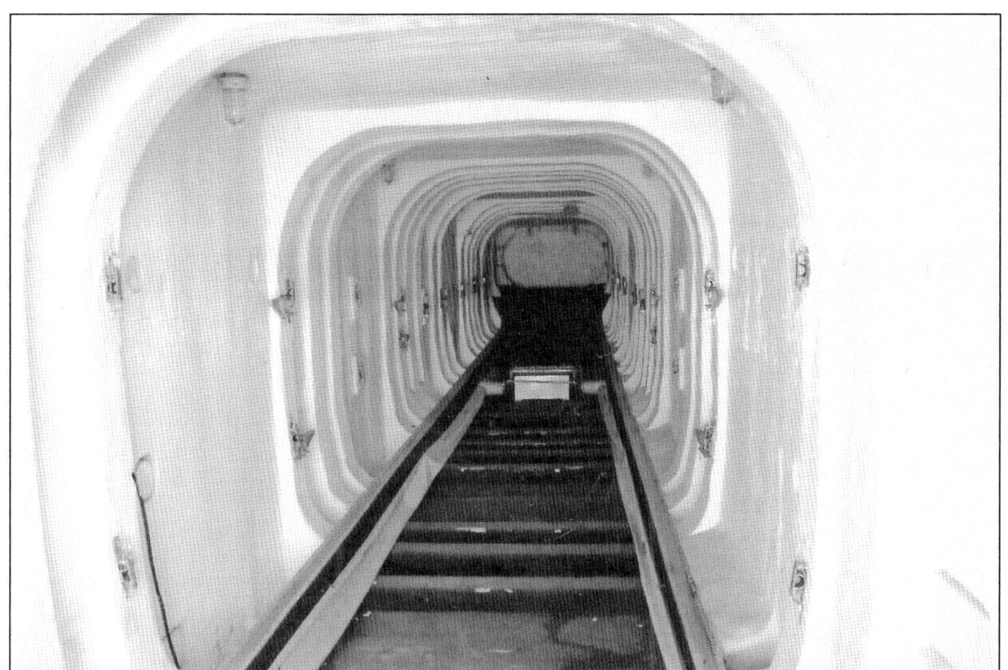

This Boeing TE is on display at Oscar-01 on Whiteman Air Force Base. This TE was built by Boeing in 1963 and remained functional with the 351st Strategic Missile Wing throughout most of its operational career. (Author's collection.)

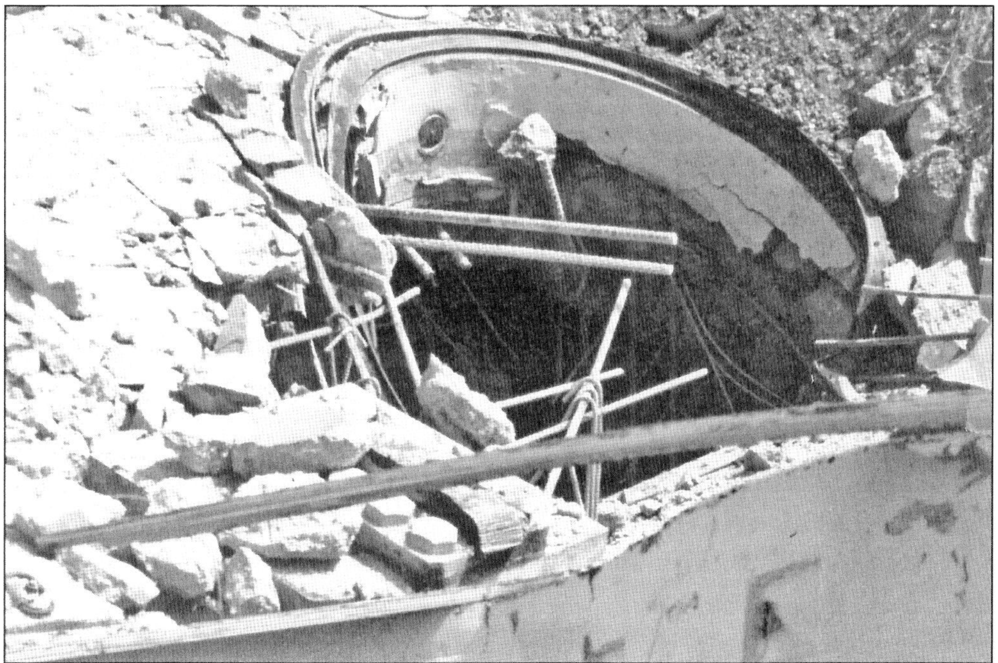

During the deactivation of the 150 launch facilities at Whiteman Air Force Base, 300 to 500 pounds of explosive were detonated to destroy the silo headworks after the launch closures had been opened on their rails. This is one of the Minuteman II launch facility silos destroyed at Ellsworth Air Force Base, South Dakota. Similar demolition was done at Whiteman. (Author's collection.)

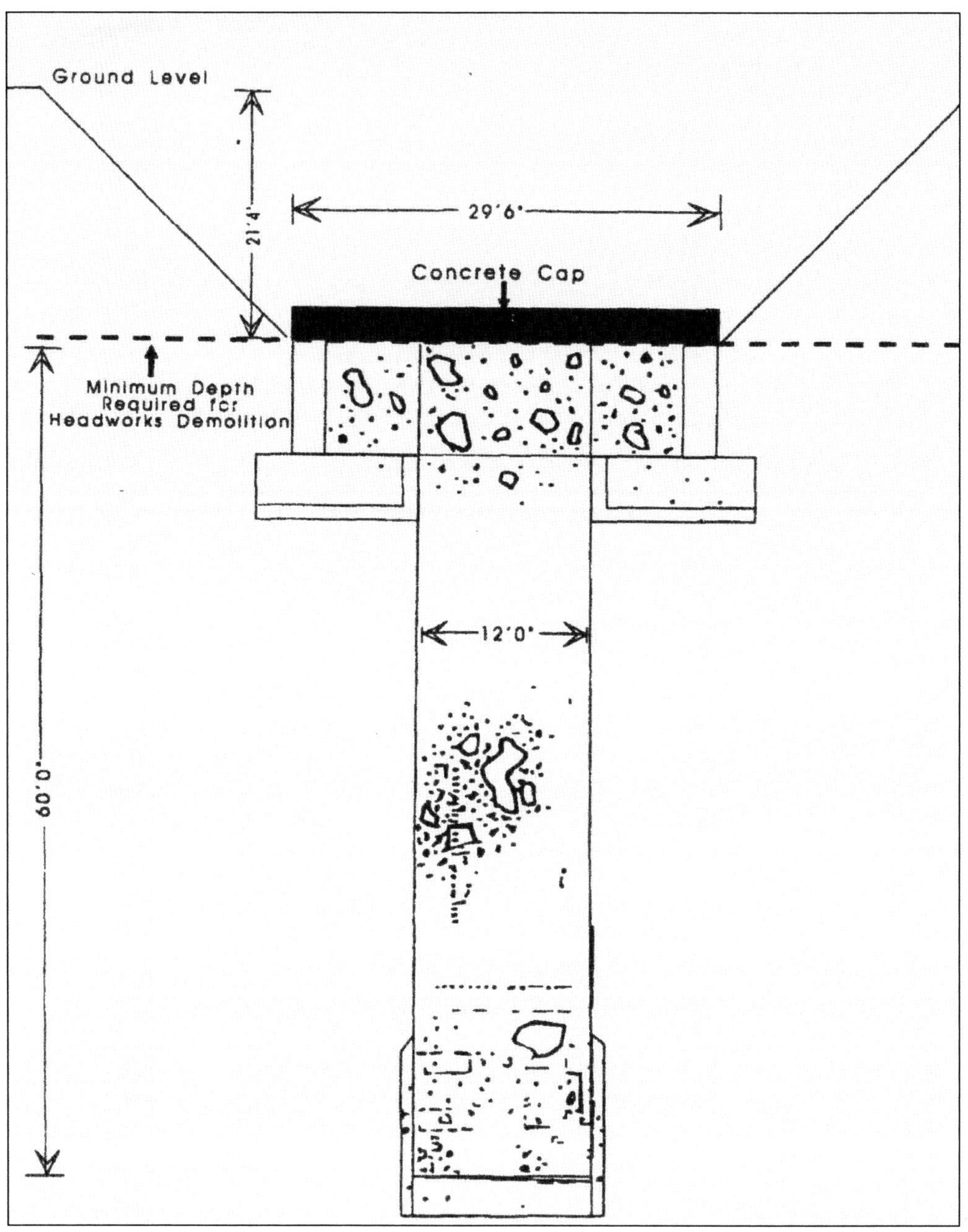

At each deactivated launch facility, the launch tube was filled with ruble from the exploded material, then covered by a thick concrete cap. (Courtesy Ellsworth Air Force Base, 28th Bomb Wing Historian Archives.)

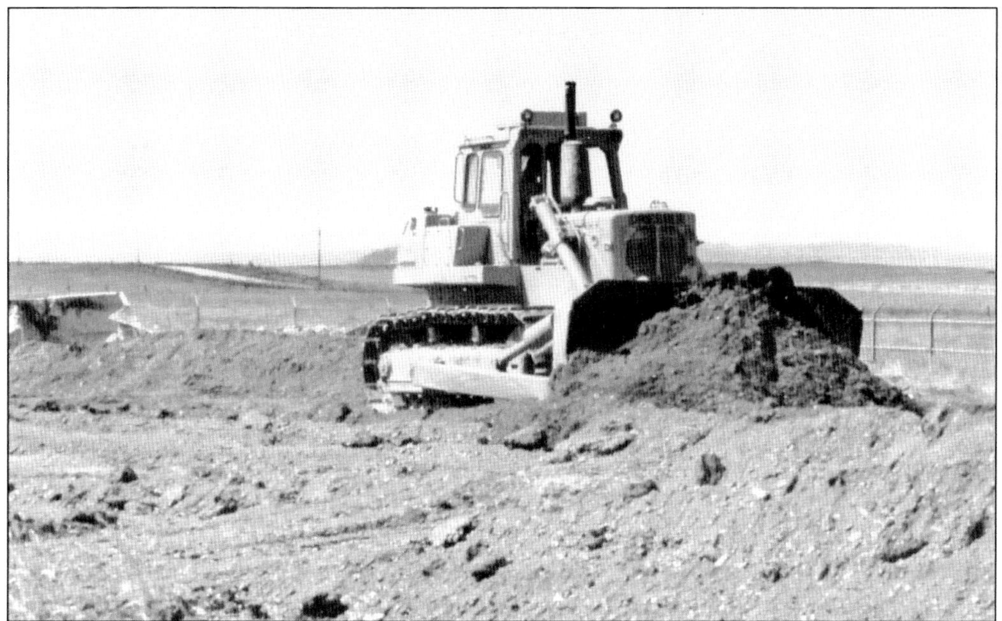

Civilian contractors came onto each launch facility site after the 90-day verification to fill in the silos and begin leveling the site. Bulldozers were used to return the site to surrounding grade level, usually leaving the chain-link fencing intact. The site was then offered for sale to the surrounding landowners or to the general public. (Author's collection.)

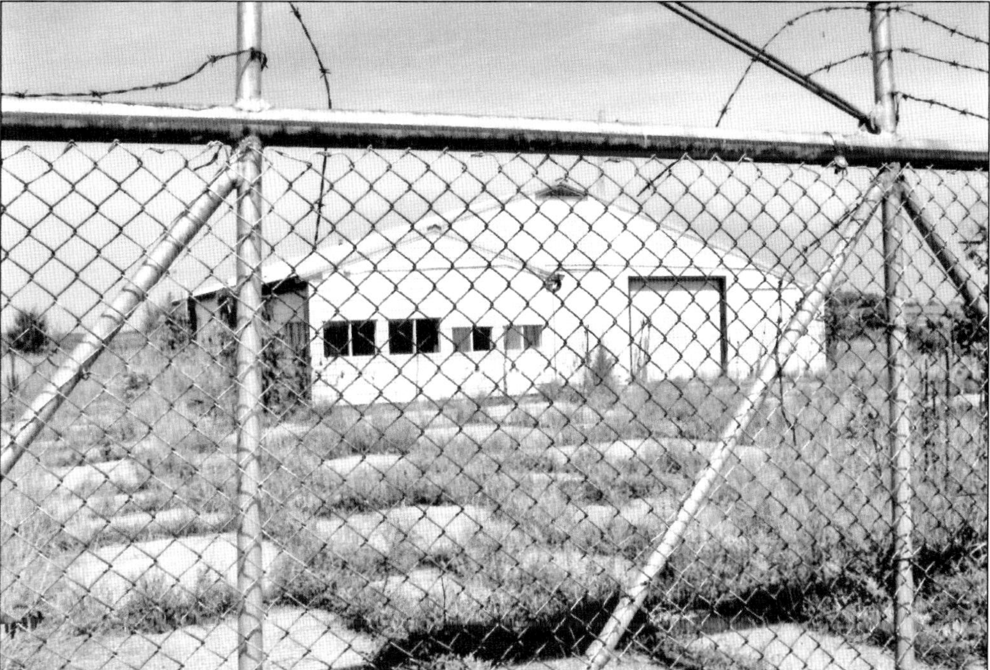

The LCSB Bravo-01 on Whiteman Air Force Base is northeast of the base and east of Highway 5, short of Interstate 70. The site was sold at auction. The building is not being used at this time, and the surrounding asphalt paving has deteriorated, with grass growing through the surface. (Author's collection.)

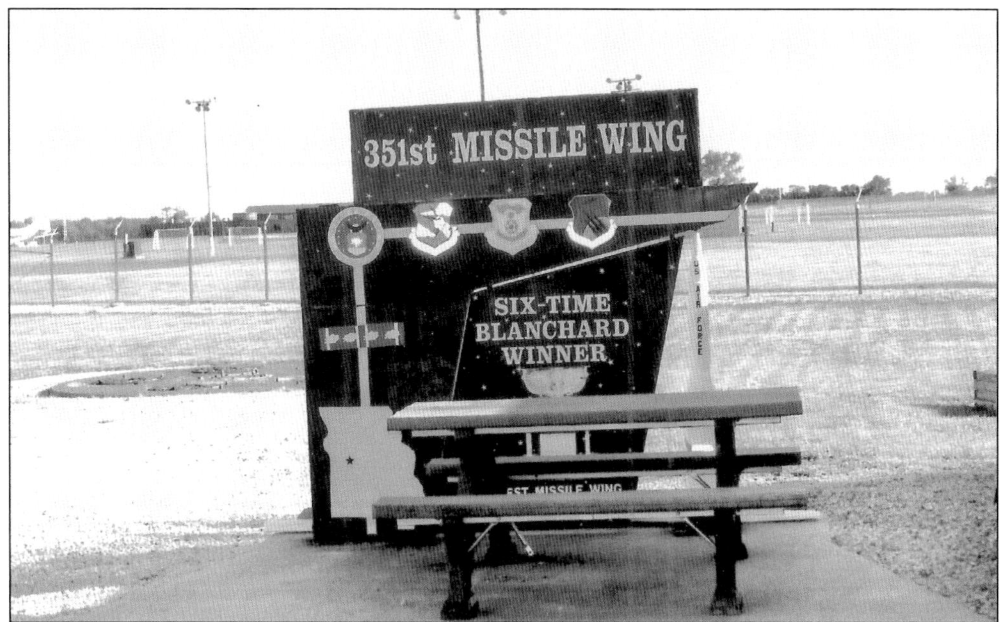

The Whiteman Air Force Base historian placed this 351st Strategic Missile Wing marker outside Oscar-01 on Whiteman Air Force Base. (Author's collection.)

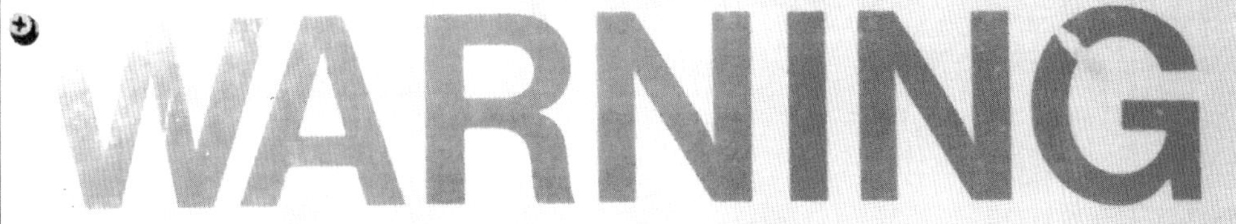

All launch facilities and LCSBs were enclosed by a security fence with metal signs attached to warn that no unauthorized entry was allowed. The author removed a weathered, worn sign from a launch facility site destroyed at Ellsworth Air Force Base. (Author's collection.)

Five

Weapons Storage Area, Conventional and Nuclear 1954–Present

SAC operations at Whiteman AFB required a weapons storage area (WSA) for handling and storing atomic weapons carried by the B-47E. Initially, the WSA was smaller than the current facility, consisting of a security force entry control point, a small assembly building, and 10 earth-covered explosive igloo storage bunkers, protected by a single security fence, with a manned guard tower in the middle of the igloos. Whiteman was assigned to SAC in 1951, with the construction of the WSA completed by March 1954, when the first B-47E landed on the base.

The Air Force uses weapons storage areas to place warheads in a holding facility for an indefinite period of time. Nuclear weapons are stored in secure, earth-covered igloo bunkers with a distinctive near-hemispherical appearance when viewed at ground level. The design philosophy behind the earth-covered ammunition storage igloos was for safety. In the event of an internal explosion, the explosive force of the blast would be directed upward through the roof of the magazine. The entire WSA has interspaced wood poles, similar to telephone poles, connected to each other with steel wire and with a top-to-ground lead to attract lightning from the igloos to a secure and safe grounding element. The poles and wires also function as an anti-helicopter screen to prevent aerial intrusion. High-intensity floodlights turn night into daylight for on-site security forces. An on-site guard tower, inside the original WSA, is 40 feet tall, with a glass-enclosed structure providing an unobstructed 360-degree view of the exclusion area. The structure's roof bristles with communications antennas. A steel walkway surrounds the structure, allowing security force to scan the areas below and use deadly force if necessary. Inside and around the exterior security fence, roving security forces patrol in Humvees. These are armed with .50-caliber, roof-mounted machine guns and a complement of armed security force personnel. These ground patrols add another layer of security to identify threats, respond to alarms, and visually inspect the igloos. Whiteman also has a K-9 detachment, and roving patrols with dogs are used. These security procedures protect the economic value of the top secret thermonuclear and advanced precision-guided conventional munitions. Whiteman is an active nuclear facility with the B-2, a START delivery system.

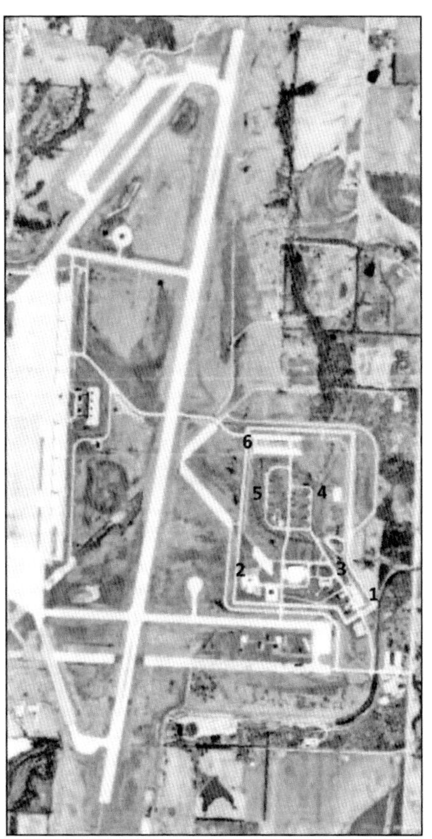

These numbers outline what is inside the weapons storage area: (1) security entry point; (2) missile assembly building; (3) weapons assembly building; (4) and (5) earth-covered bunkers; (6) large bunkers for storage of precision weapons. (Courtesy US Geological Survey, public aerial/satellite photograph.)

This photograph shows the security entry point, the only access point into the highly secured weapons storage area. There is no opportunity for direct passage of vehicles or personnel into the storage area. Identification is required, and that day's authorizations are checked and verified. (Author's collection.)

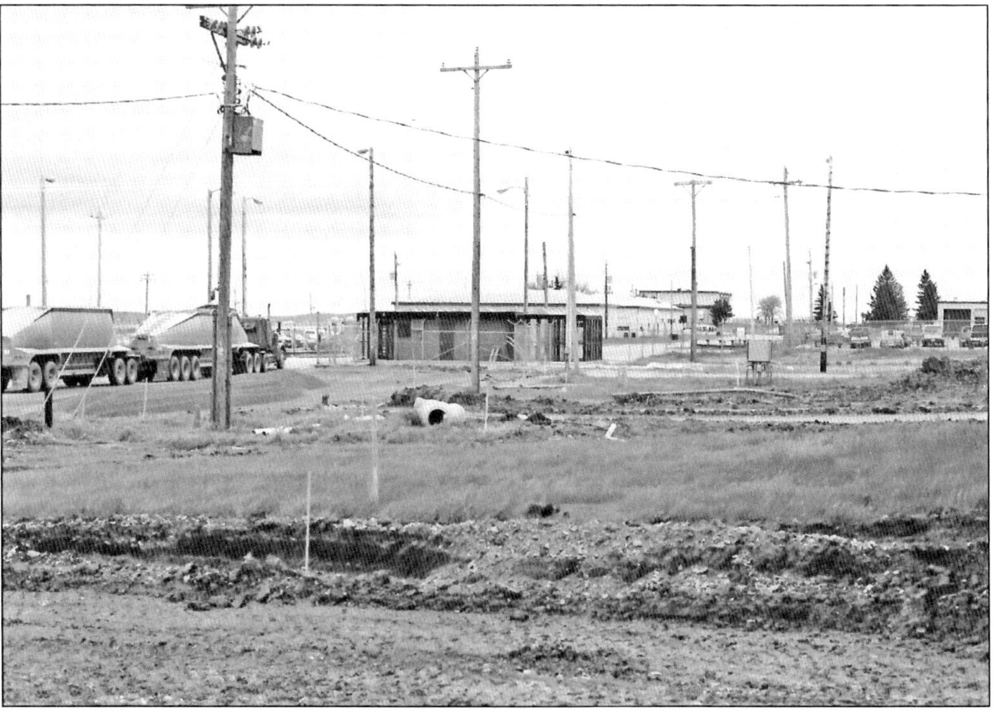

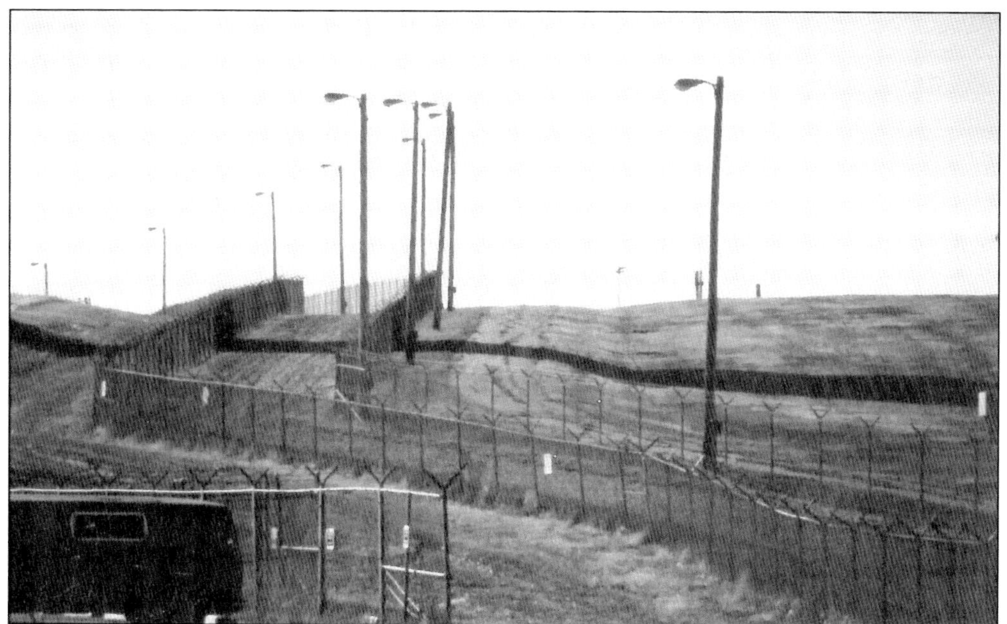
Air Force security of WSAs consists of a double security fence, patrol areas inside and outside, lighting, and motion sensors to warn of unauthorized intrusion. The deactivated nuclear weapons storage area at Ellsworth Air Force Base, South Dakota, is shown here. (Author's collection.)

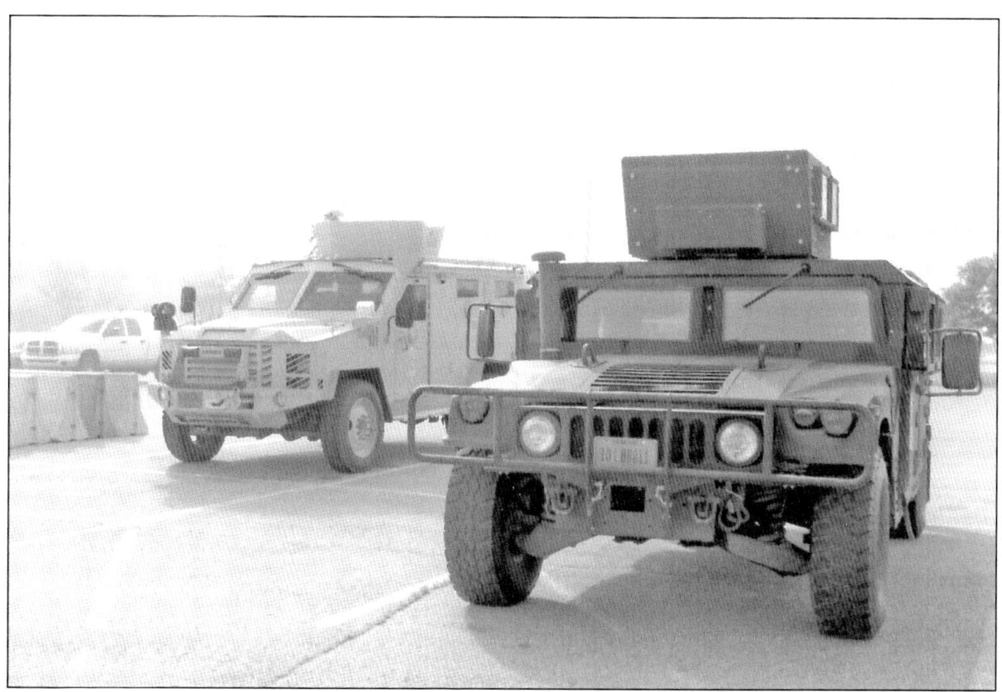
The vehicle to the right is a High Mobility Multi-Purpose Vehicle (HMMWV), used for internal base security and external and internal security force patrols at the WSA. The other vehicle is a called a Bearcat (ballistic enhanced armored, reinforced vehicle) used for Minuteman III ICBM force security. (Author's collection.)

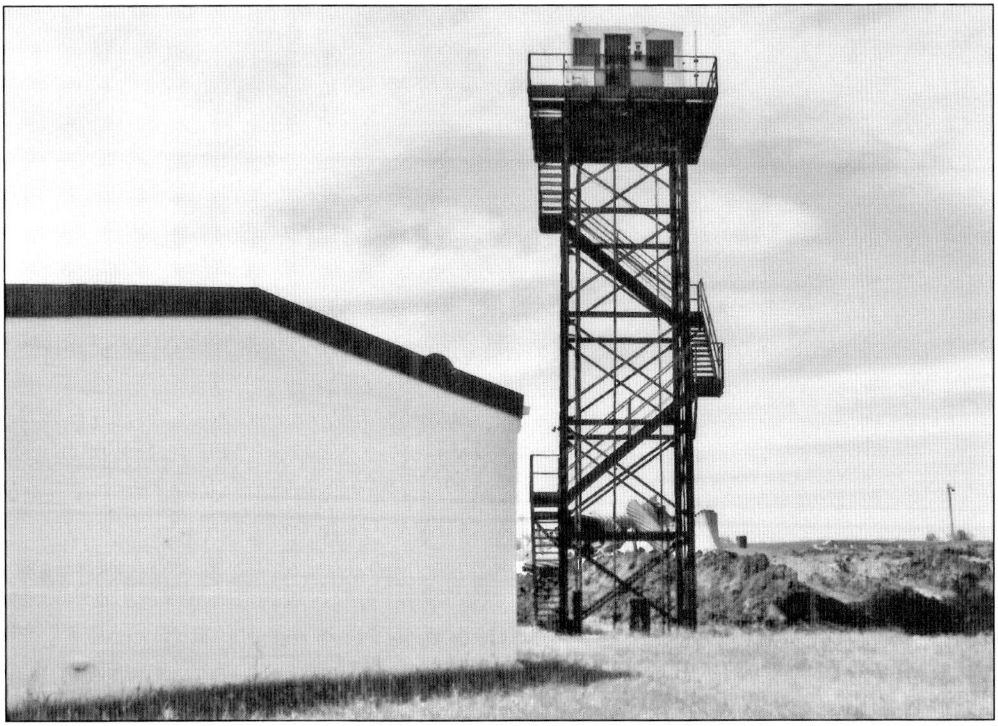

Pictured is a standard Air Force security tower in a WSA. Security force personnel climbed the steel tower on the external stairs to the top, where a steel platform provided a 360-degree view of the storage complex. This tower remained intact until June 2014 during the site demolition to meet compliance with START. (Author's collection.)

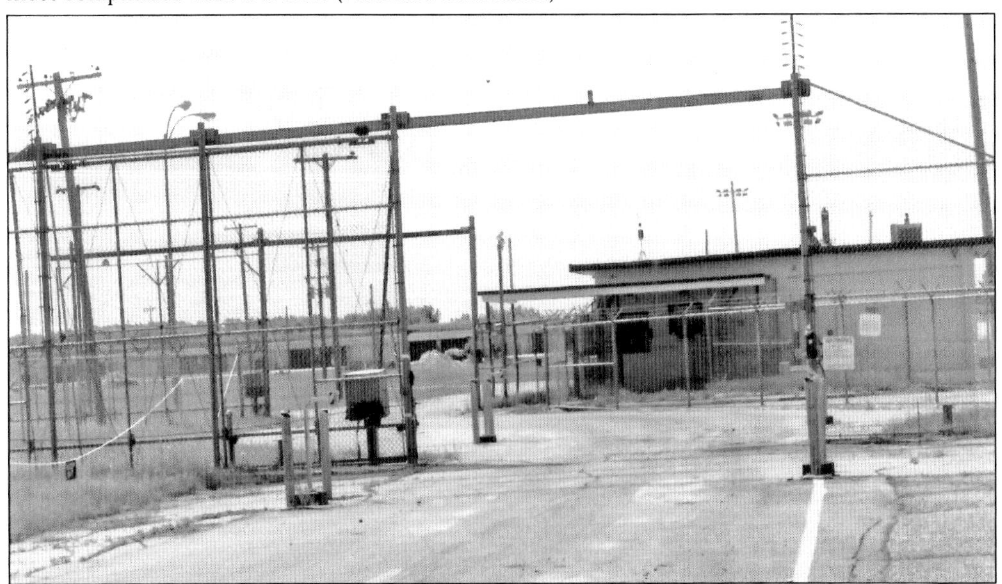

Pictured is the entry into the former Grand Forks Air Force Base, North Dakota, WSA. The sliding double gates are open to allow contractors into the facility to destroy the earth-covered concrete bunker to comply with START. The same security structure is at Whiteman Air Force Base's active WSA. (Author's collection.)

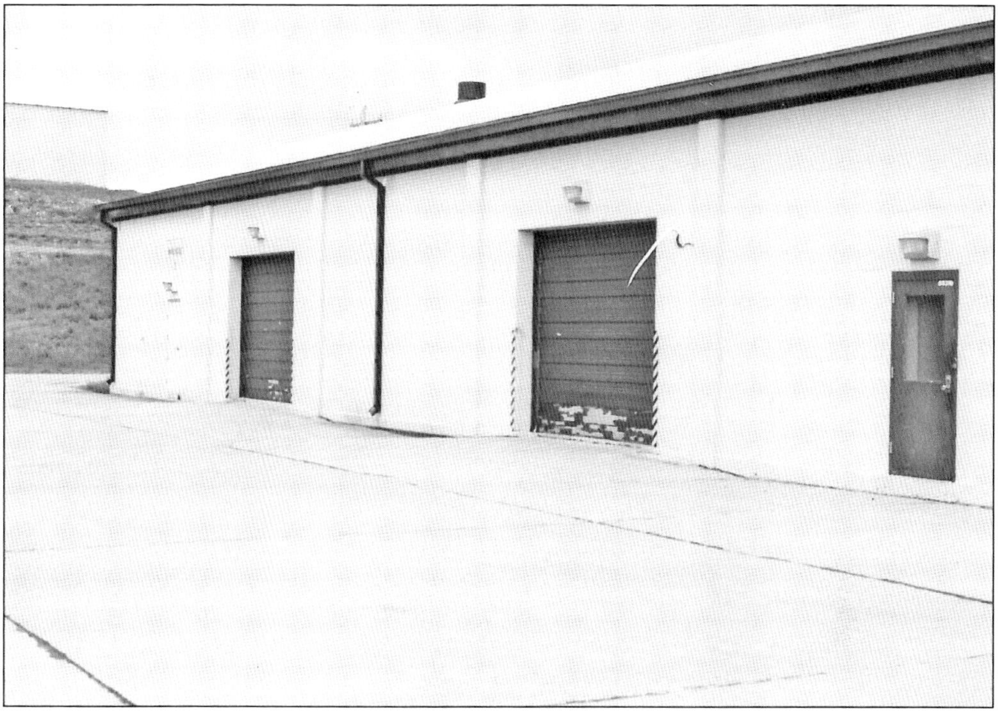

This missile assembly building is built to standard plans across Air Force bases, with rollup doors on each side to allow trucks with trailers to drive in and out. This building is on Ellsworth Air Force Base, South Dakota. (Author's collection.)

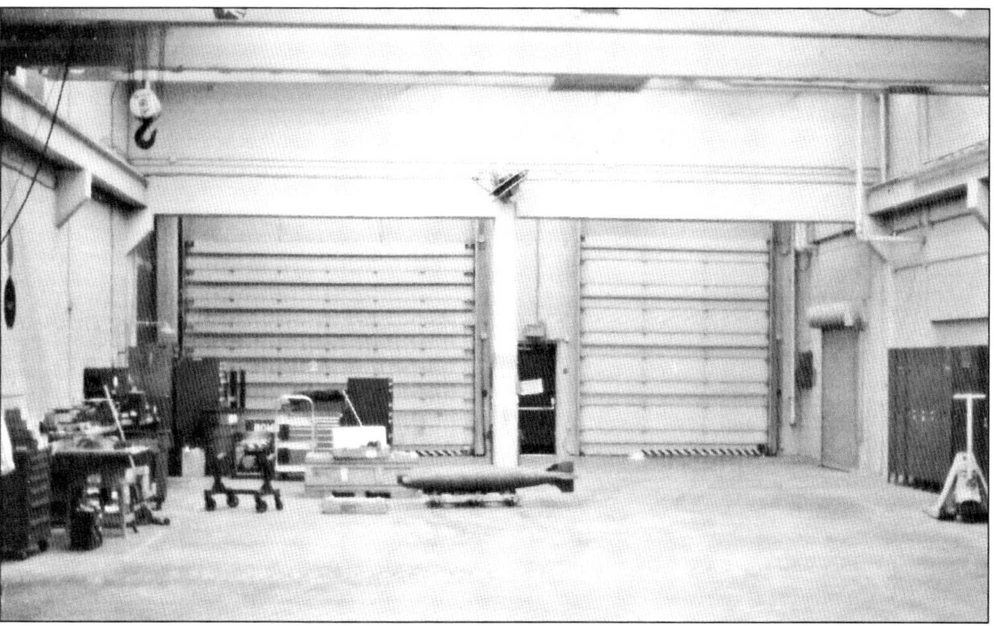

This photograph shows the interior of missile assembly building on Ellsworth Air Force Base, South Dakota. One set of the drive-through-capable doors is visible in the background. The heavy-duty overhead crane is hung on beams to lift Cold War weapons and, now, precision nuclear and conventional weapons. (Author's collection.)

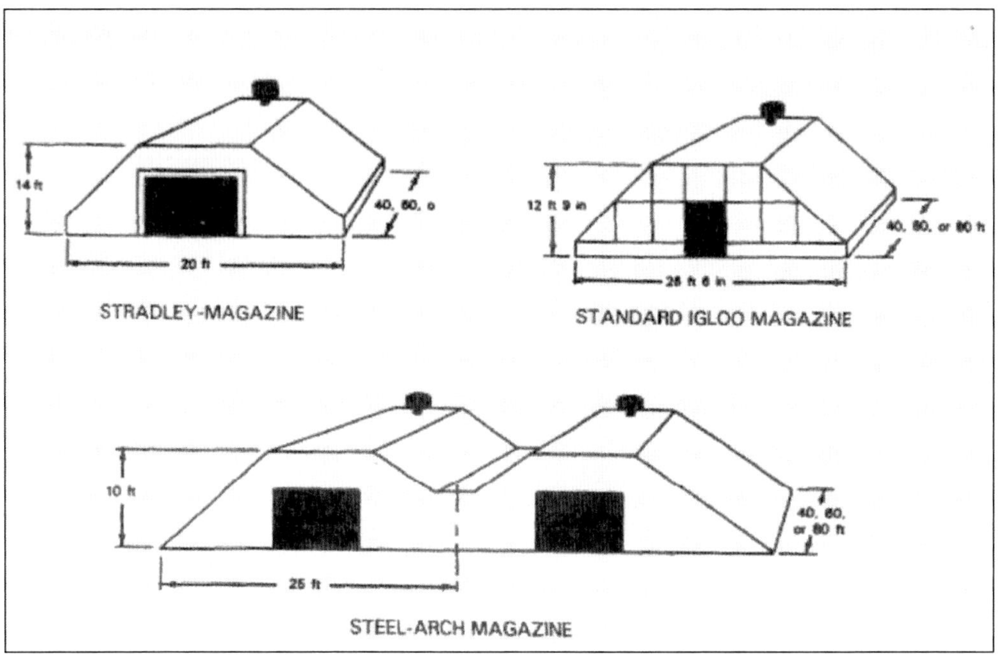

These drawings are of standardized Air Force earth-covered munitions storage buildings used at active WSAs. (Author's collection.)

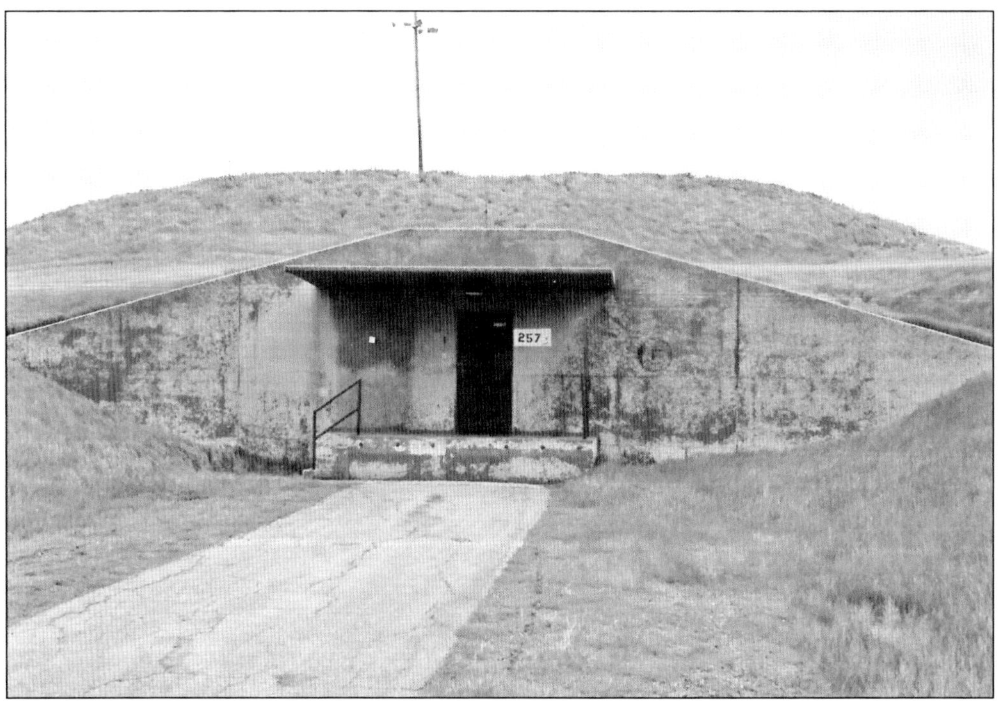

This a standard Air Force single earth-covered munitions storage bunker, used to store nuclear or conventional weapons. The front access drive leads to a loading dock, which is at truck level for unloading and loading operations, and vault security door, covered with earth for blast protection from a nearby bunker blowing up. (Author's collection.)

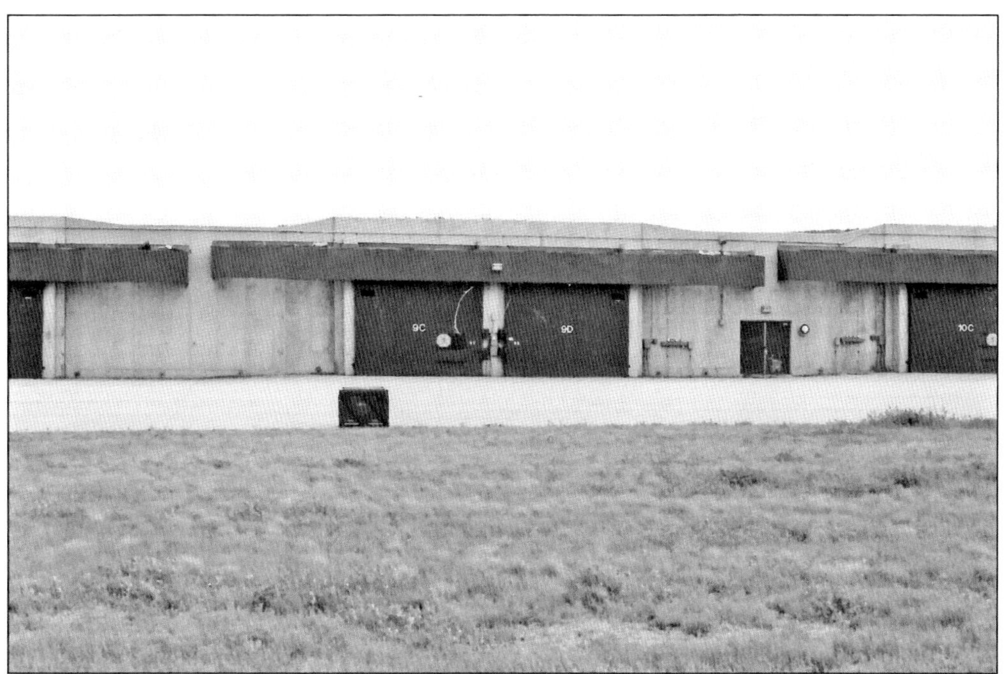

These igloos were constructed in the weapons storage area to store the modern precision-guided munitions carried by the B-2. These were built at Ellsworth Air Force Base and are similar to those on Whiteman Air Force Base. (Author's collection.)

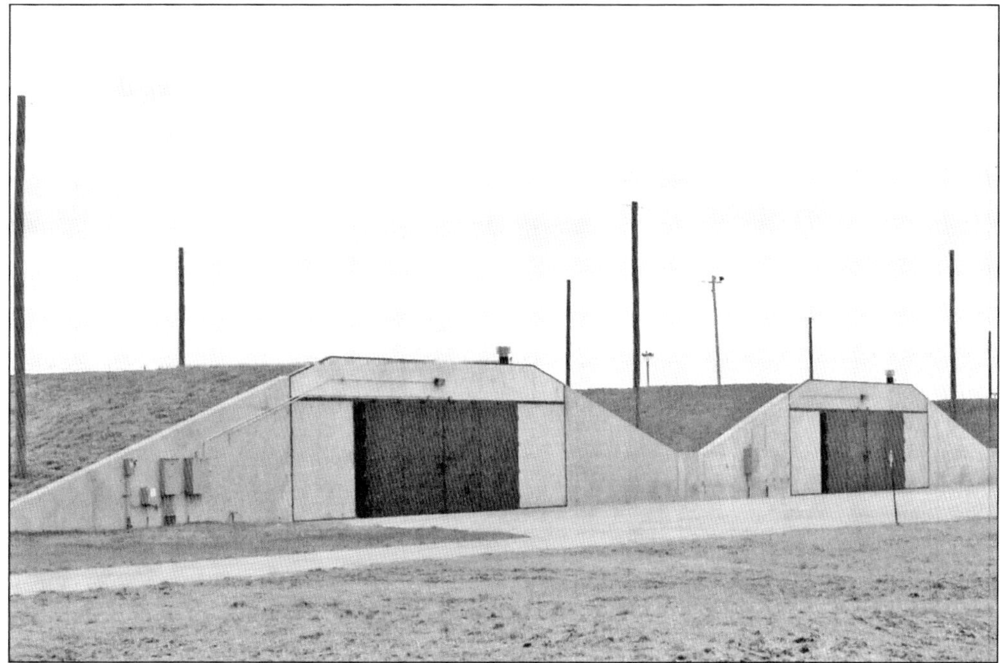

At the north end of the weapons storage area is a row of steel-arched magazines. The front concrete walls show the slope of the earth-covered sides and the minimal earth-covered tops of the bunkers. The sliding steel entry doors are large enough to allow access to the interior. (Courtesy Whiteman Air Force Base, 509th Bomb Wing Public Affairs.)

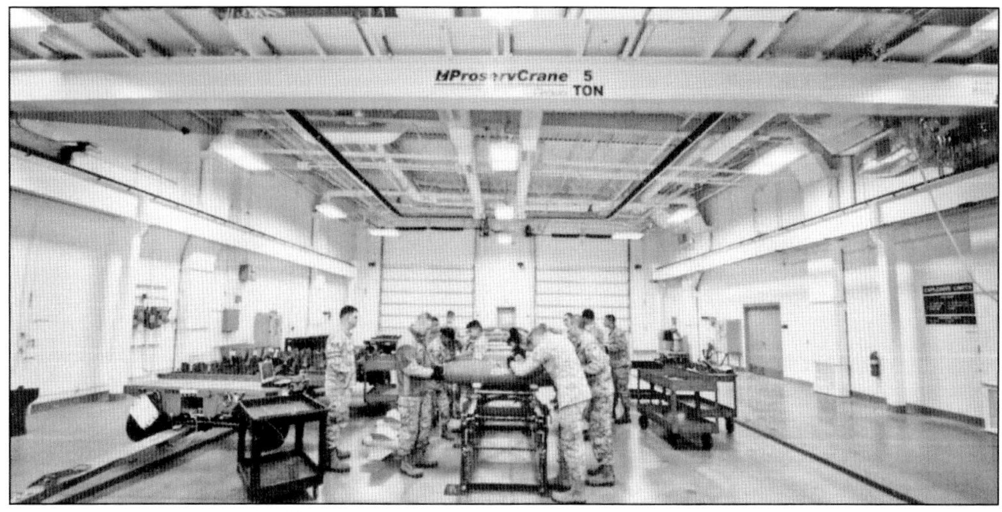

The munitions assembly building is equipped to add guidance packages and electronics to munitions to meet the planned mission for the aircraft assigned to the base in a controlled environment. (Courtesy US Air Force.)

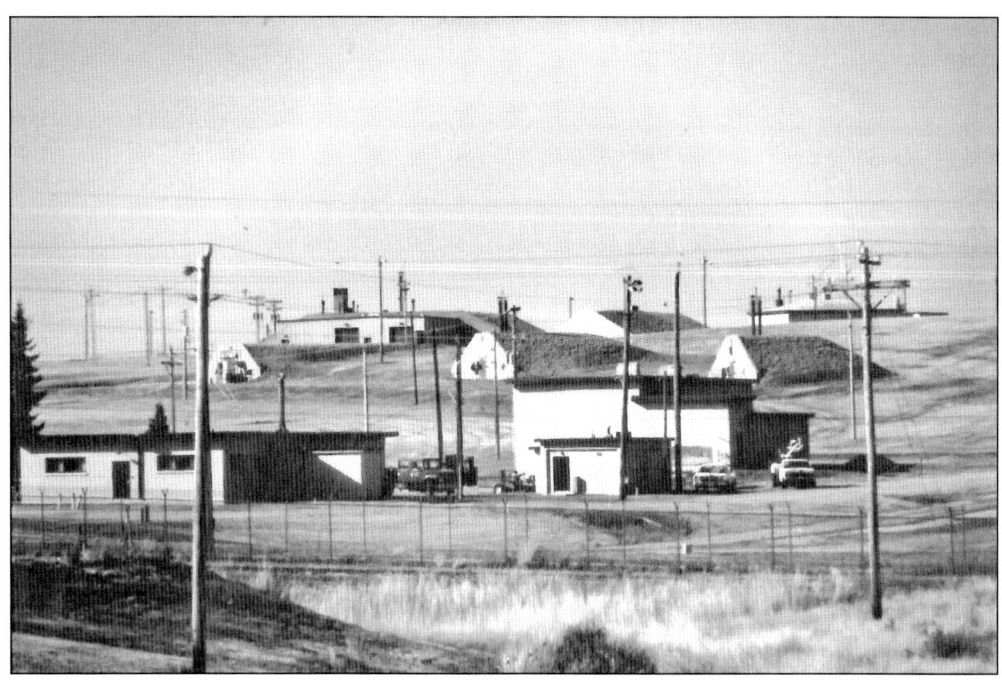

The storage igloos were spread out inside the storage area to ensure that an accidental explosion inside one igloo did not ignite other igloos. This photograph of the Ellsworth Air Force Base munitions storage area shows the spacing between the munitions storage igloos as at Whiteman Air Force Base. (Author's collection.)

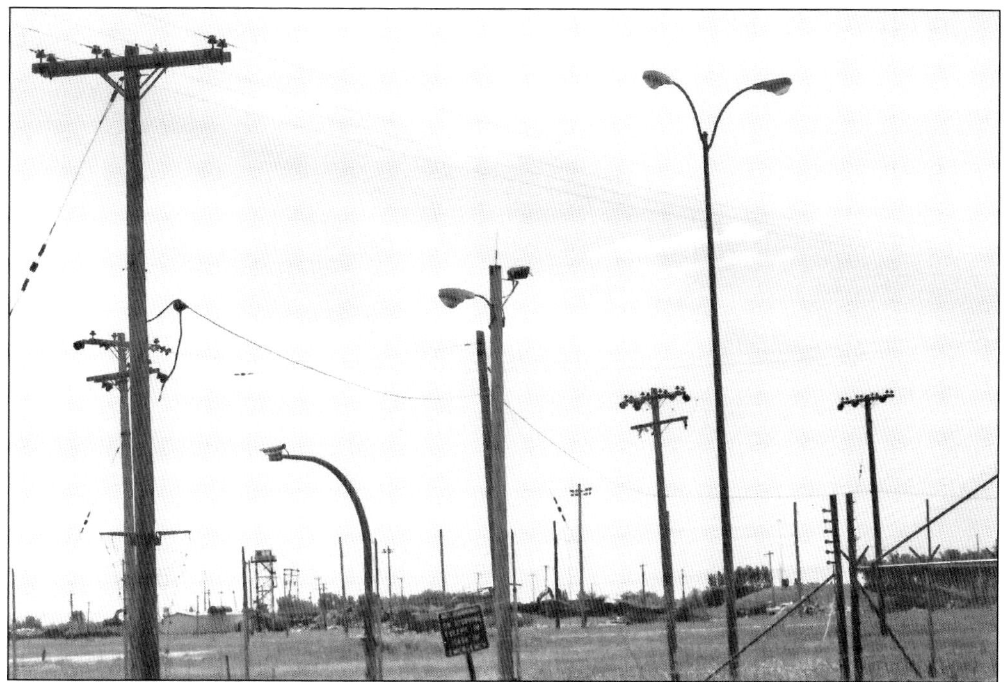

The photograph provides a close-up view of the inside the deactivated Grand Forks Air Force Base weapons storage area, showing the security lights and poles serving as anti-helicopter intrusion obstacles as at the Whiteman munitions complex. (Author's collection.)

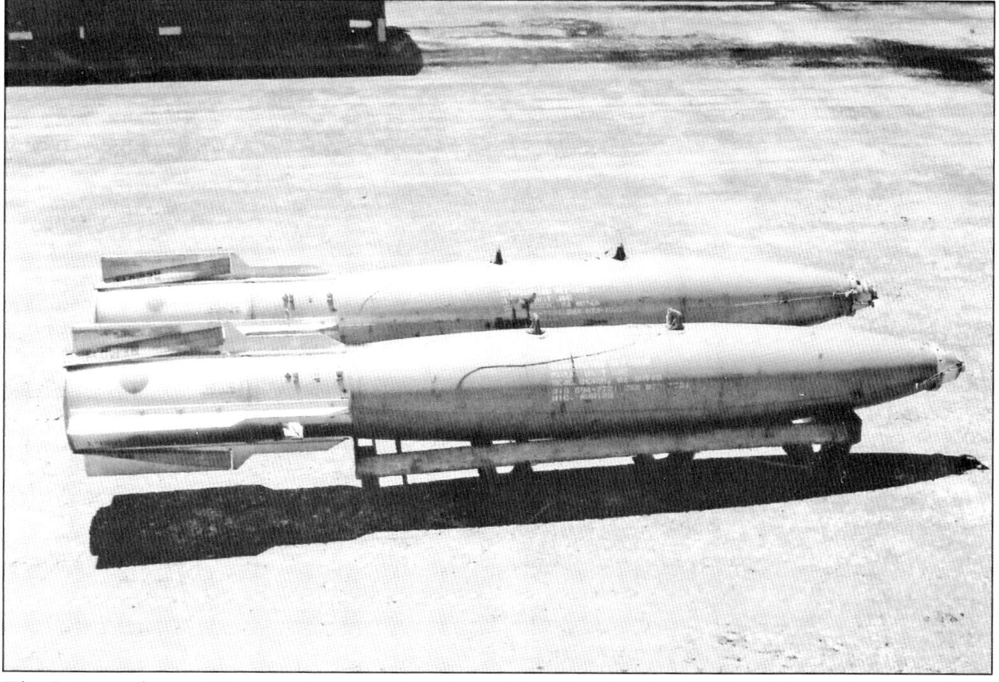

The B-2 can drop a 750-pound conventional munition fitted with a GPS tail fin guidance package to limit damage to collateral targets surrounding the primary target. (Courtesy Dyess Air Force Base, 7th Bomb Wing Public Affairs.)

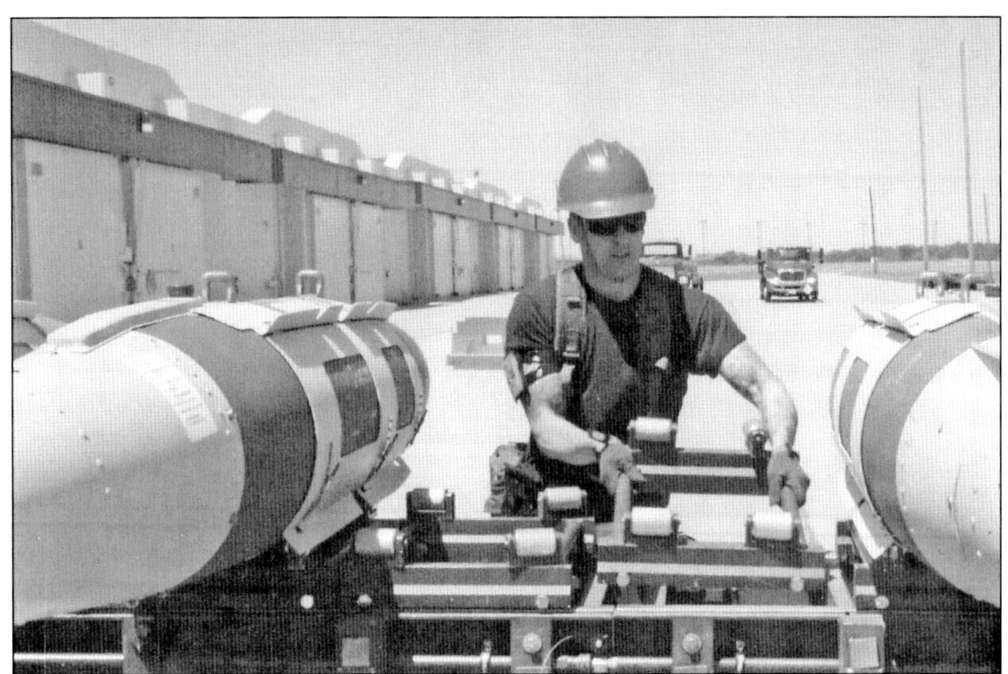

The B-2 is able to accurately deliver the 2,000-pound MK-84 Joint Defense Air Munition (JDAM) within feet of its intended target on the ground, creating massive destruction. These are training JDAMs loaded on a munitions trailer. (Courtesy Dyess Air Force Base, 7th Bomb Wing Public Affairs.)

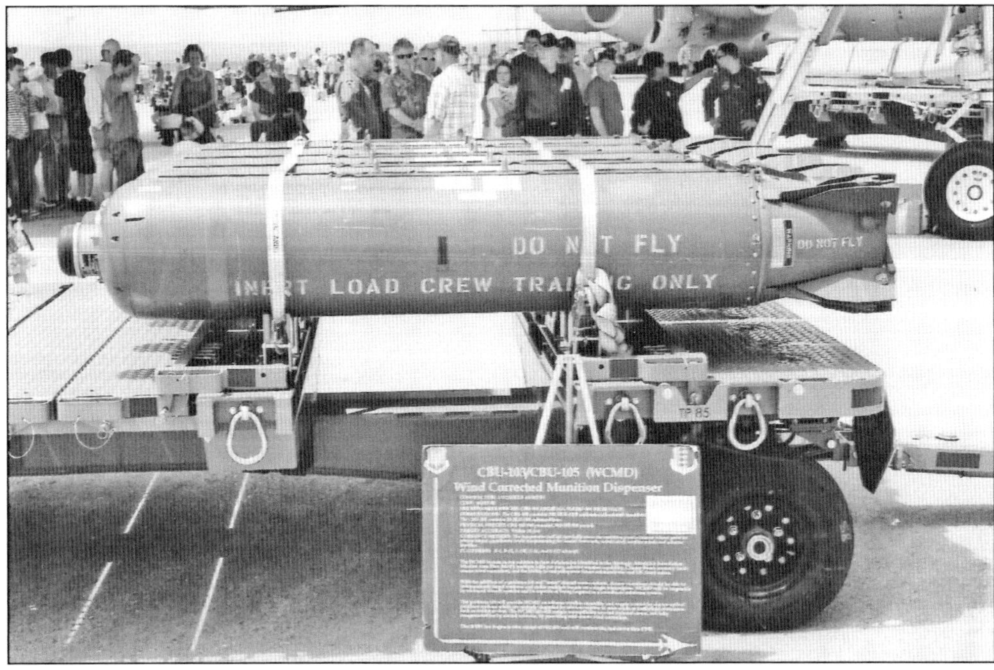

For safety, inert training munitions are used, with security, handling, and loading into the B-2 comparable to armed munitions. The CBU-103/CBU-105 Wind Corrected Munitions Dispensers are loaded on a munitions trailer for display at an open house on Ellsworth Air Force Base, South Dakota. (Author's collection.)

Six

509th Bomb Wing, Northrop B-2 Spirit Stealth Bomber 1993–Present

The 509th BW became operational on July 1, 1993, and became the host unit on Whiteman AFB. On July 20, the wing received its first operational aircraft in three years, the Northrup T-38 Talon, complete with a B-2-style gray paint scheme and marked with WM tail code. On December 17, the first operational B-2 Spirit, the *Spirit of Missouri*, landed at Whiteman on the 49th anniversary of the 509th CG.

The B-2 is a multirole bomber capable of delivering conventional or nuclear munitions. Its low-observable stealth characteristics give the B-2 a unique ability to penetrate sophisticated enemy air defenses, threatening that nation's most valued military installations. This gives the United States an effective worldwide retaliation combat force. Whiteman is the only B-2 base, clustering 19 of the Air Force's 20 B-2s at one location for reasons of economics, mission response, logistics, and support. Northrop Aircraft built 21 B-2s: one crashed and was destroyed, and one is assigned to Edwards Flight Test Center, California, with depot maintenance at Oklahoma City Logistics Center, Tinker AFB, Oklahoma.

The selection process for B-2 pilots is arduous due to the limited number of available pilot authorizations within the 509th BW. The prospective pilot's Air Force Flight Record must be clean with no flight safety infractions for initial consideration. Once they are accepted, the training program for the new B-2 pilots lasts six months. The pilots must learn everything about the B-2, including takeoff, weather flying operations, weapon releases, aircraft tactics, range, aerial refueling, payload options, stealth characteristics, and tactical implementation. B-2 pilots fly one mission each week, requiring one day prior of mission planning and mission review.

Whiteman AFB includes the Missouri Air National Guard's 131st Bomb Wing, whose personnel also support and fly the stealth bomber. The 131st BW was assigned to Whiteman on October 4, 2008, becoming fully operational in August 2013. Members of the 131st BW work and fly side by side with members of the 509th BW.

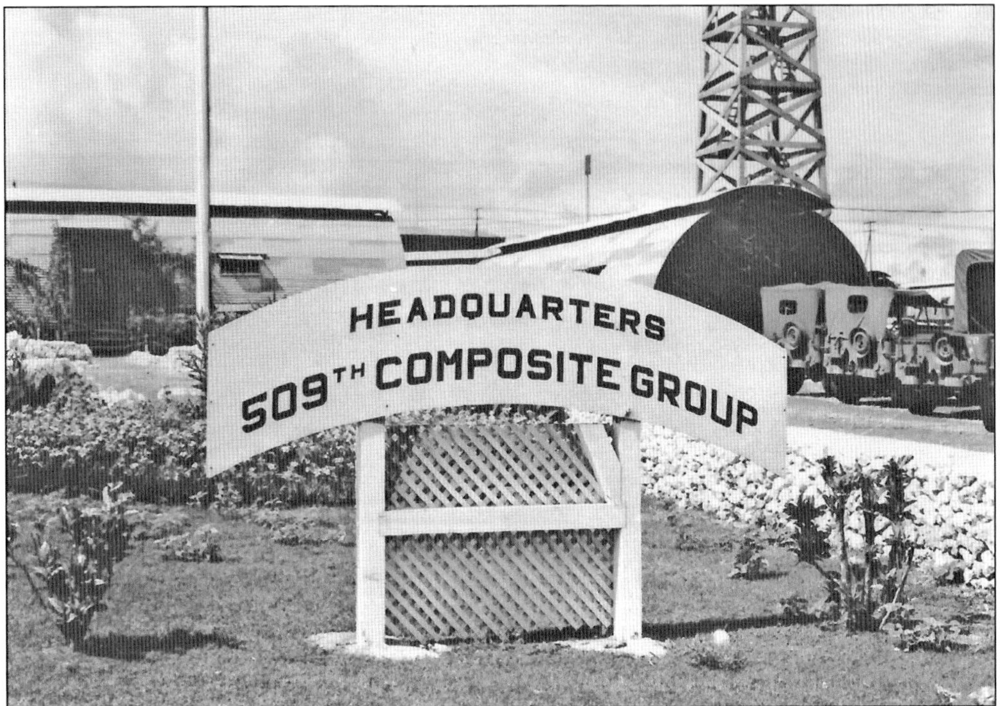

This is a photograph of the World War II 509th Composite Group on North Field, Tinian Island. The author's father, a member of the 135th US Naval Construction Battalion, worked on building the various metal Quonset huts for the bomb group. (Author's collection.)

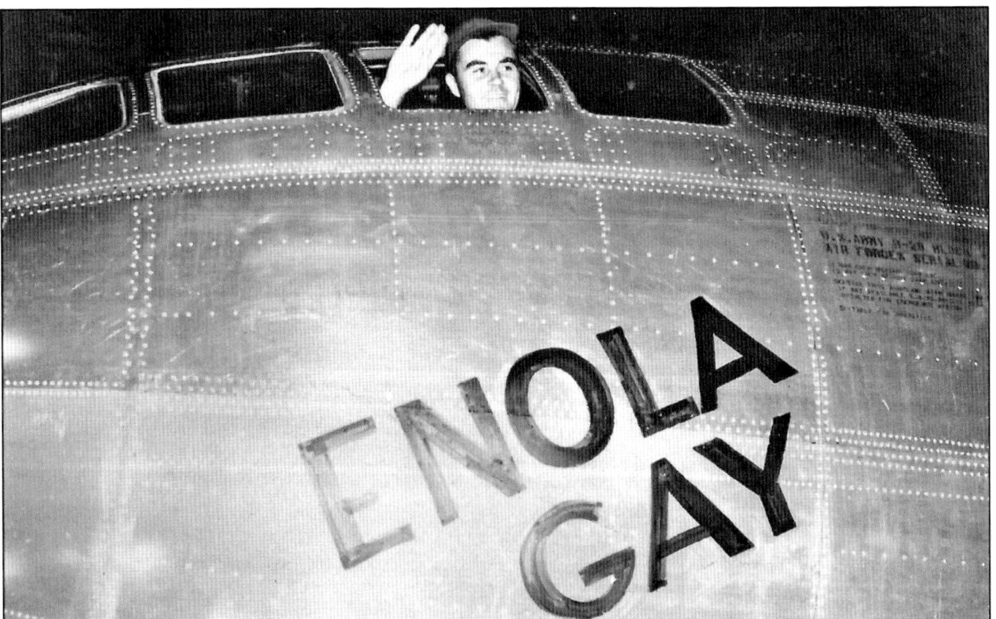

Col. Paul Tibbets leans out the window of the B-29 Superfortress on North Field, Tinian Island, on the morning of August 6, 1945, prior to takeoff with an atomic bomb, eventually to be released on the Japanese city of Hiroshima. (Courtesy John Vandervoort, World War II 509th Composite Group photographer.)

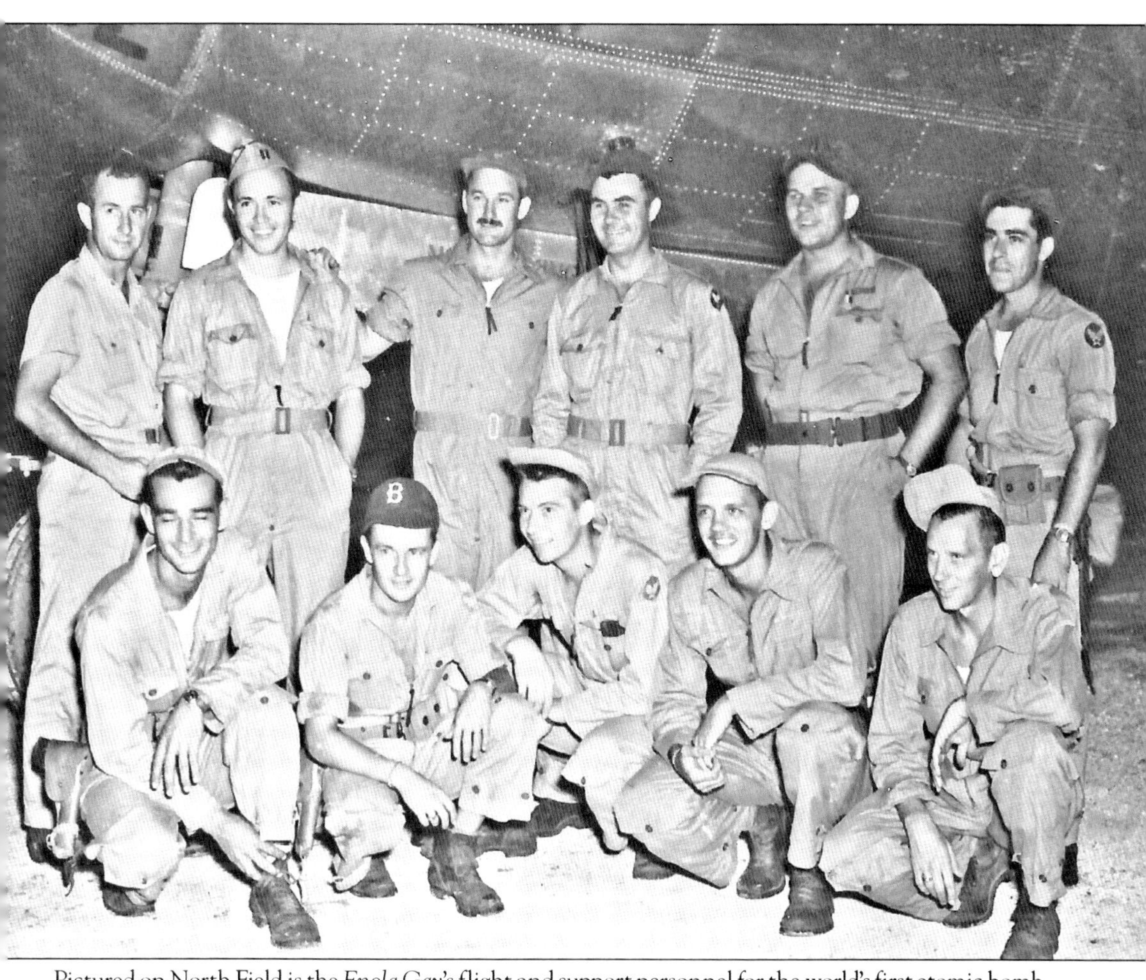

Pictured on North Field is the *Enola Gay*'s flight and support personnel for the world's first atomic bomb mission. (Courtesy John Vandervoort, World War II 509th Composite Group photographer.)

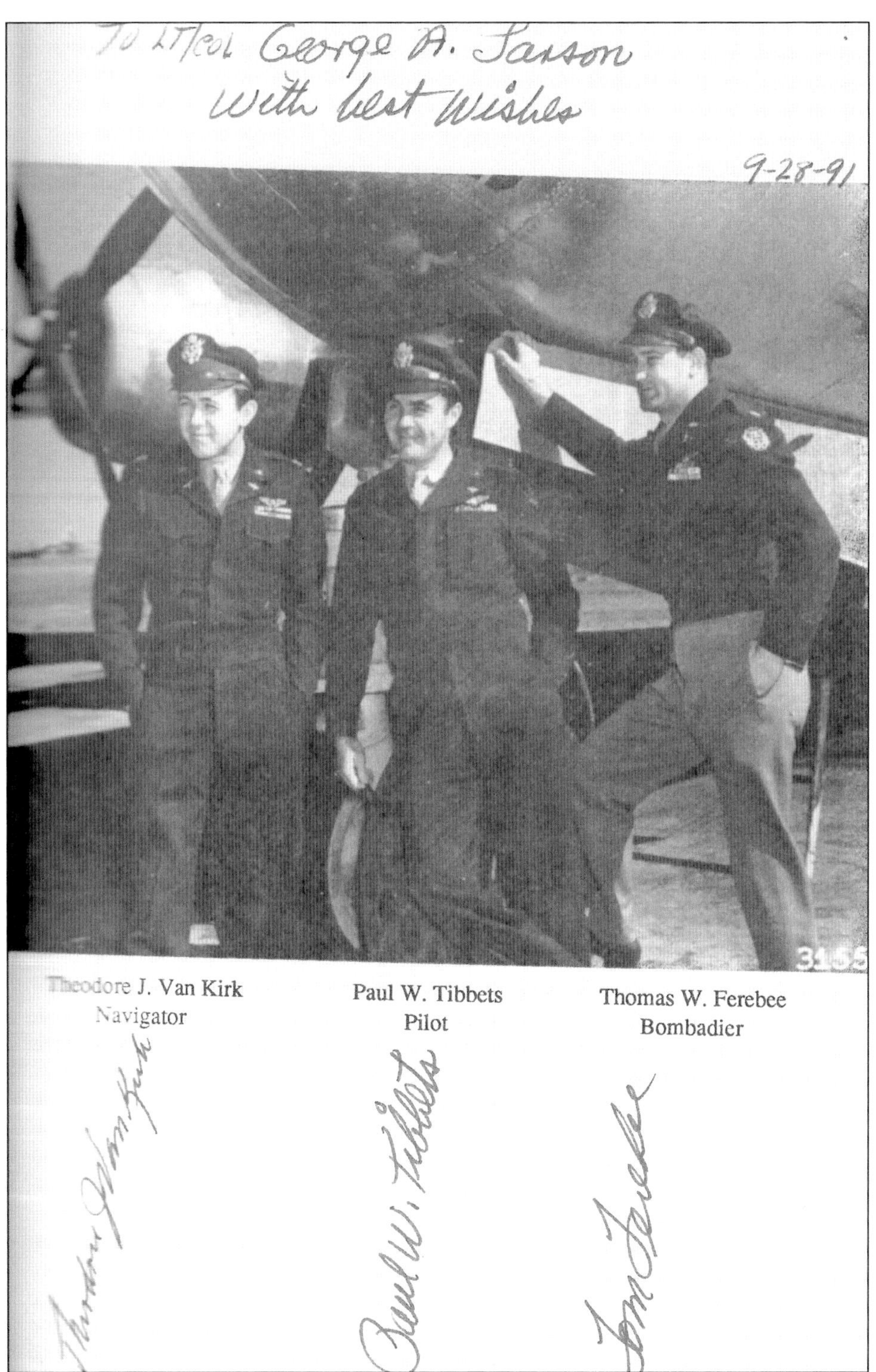

The author's photograph of the three crew members in front of the *Enola Gay* was signed by these World War II B-29 crew members when they were at the Strategic Air Command Museum in Bellevue, Nebraska. (Author's collection.)

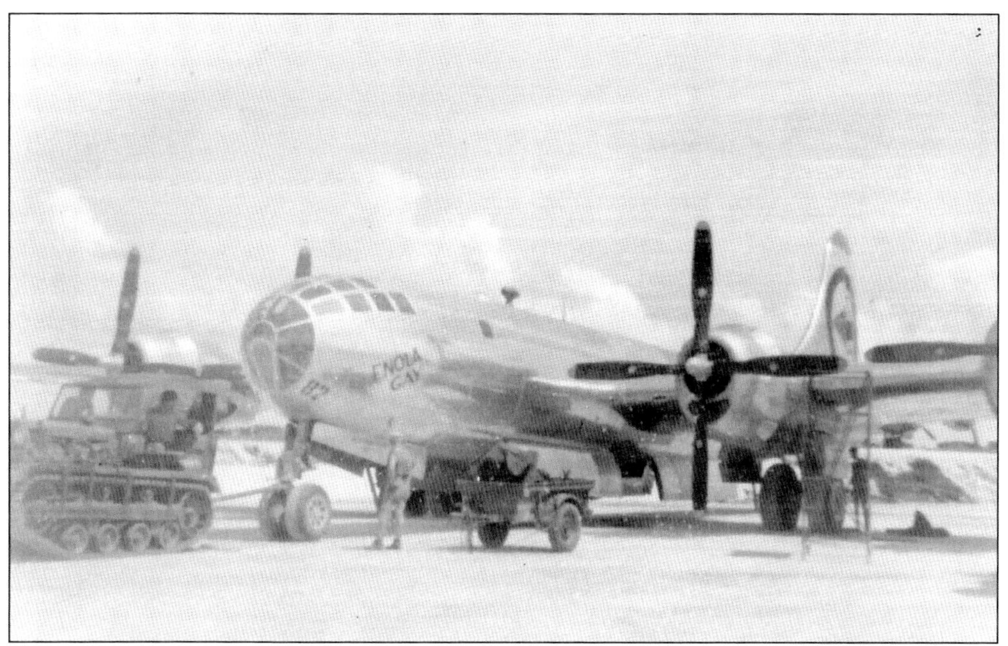

After the *Enola Gay* landed back on North Field, a tracked tow tractor is moving the B-29 on its parking apron. (Courtesy John Vandervoort, World War II 509th Composite Group photographer.)

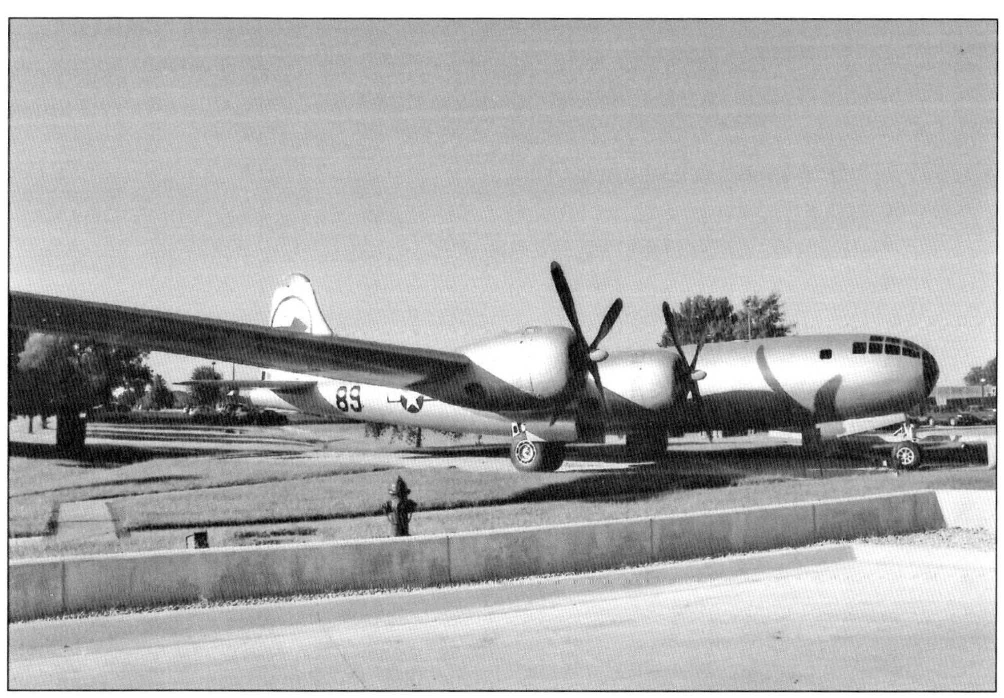

A restored Boeing B-29 Superfortress is in the Whiteman Air Force Base Air Park. The World War II *Enola Gay* is on display at the National Air and Space Museum. (Author's collection.)

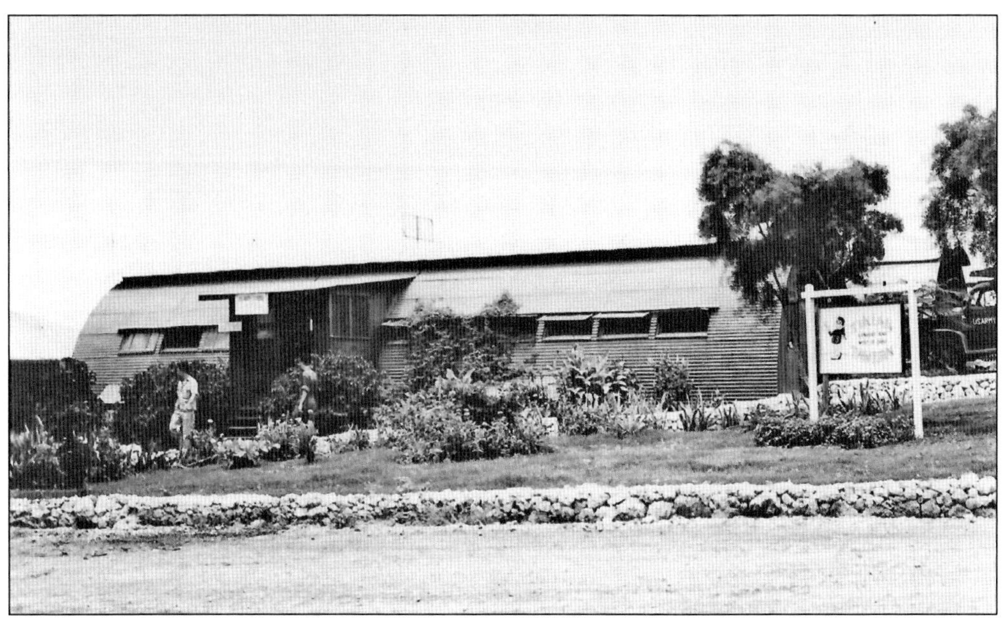

Shown is one of the Quonset huts built by the 135th US Naval Construction Battalion (Seabees), which the author's father took part in, on Tinian Island for the 509th Composite Group. They could be built quickly and adapted to whatever function or operation was needed by the group for its two atomic bomb missions against Japan. (Author's collection.)

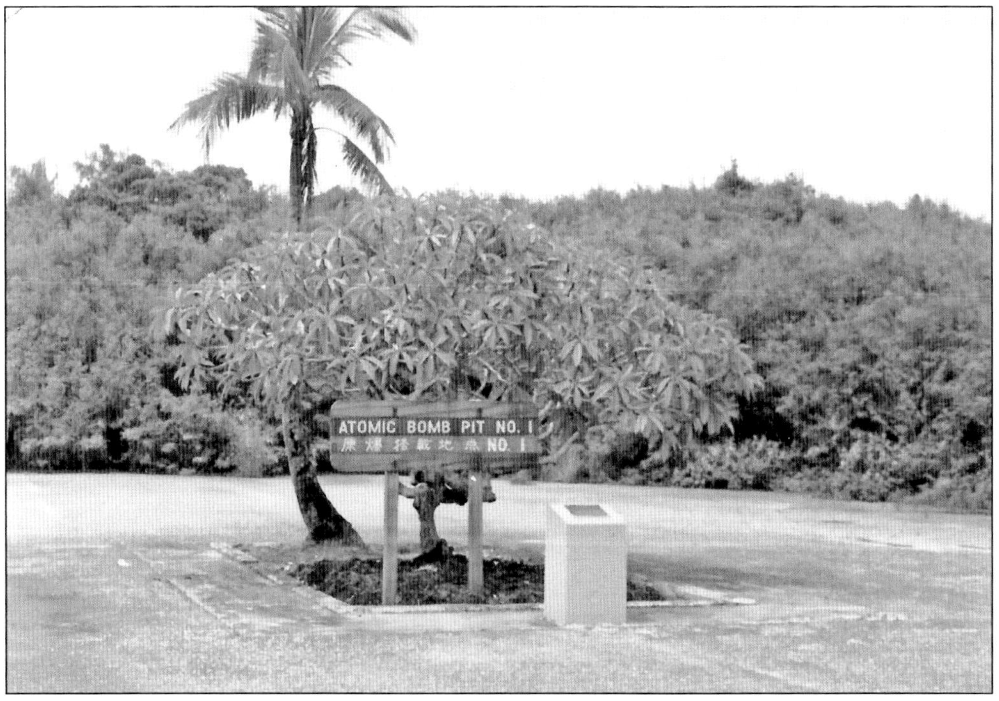

Two special atomic bomb loading pits were built off the northwest edge of runway number four, which the author's father help build, driving a road grader. He was pulled to help dig and construct the two bomb loading pits to be used by the 509th Composite Group. The bomb bay pits have been enclosed to protect them. (Author's collection.)

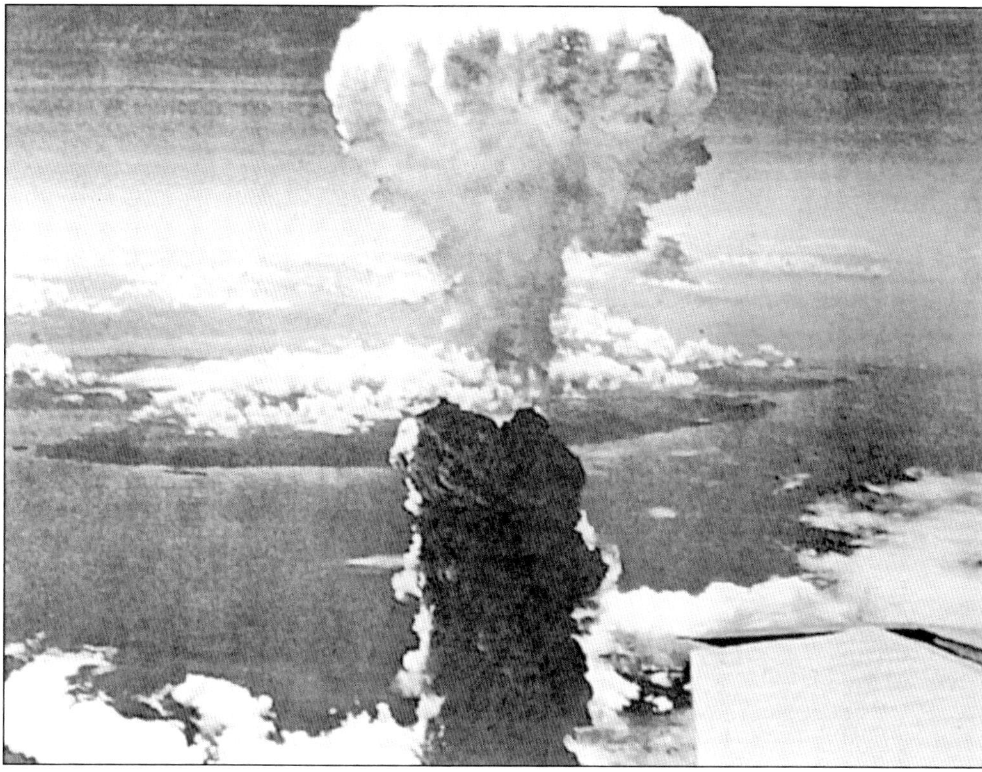

The *Enola Gay* dropped a uranium, gun-type atomic bomb on the city of Hiroshima, resulting in a ground destruction equivalent to 20,000 pounds of TNT. The mushroom cloud rose to a height of 20,000 feet over the city. (Courtesy John Vandervoort, World War II 509th Composite Group photographer.)

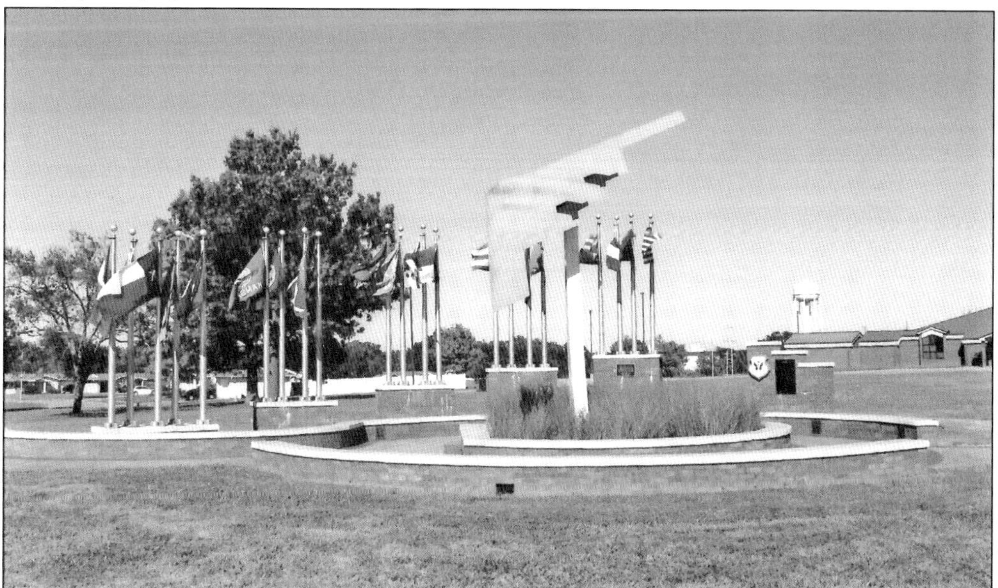

Inside Whiteman Air Force Base is a display of the 509th Bomb Wing's B-2 mounted on a pedestal, around which are 21 state flags, one for each named B-2. (Author's collection.)

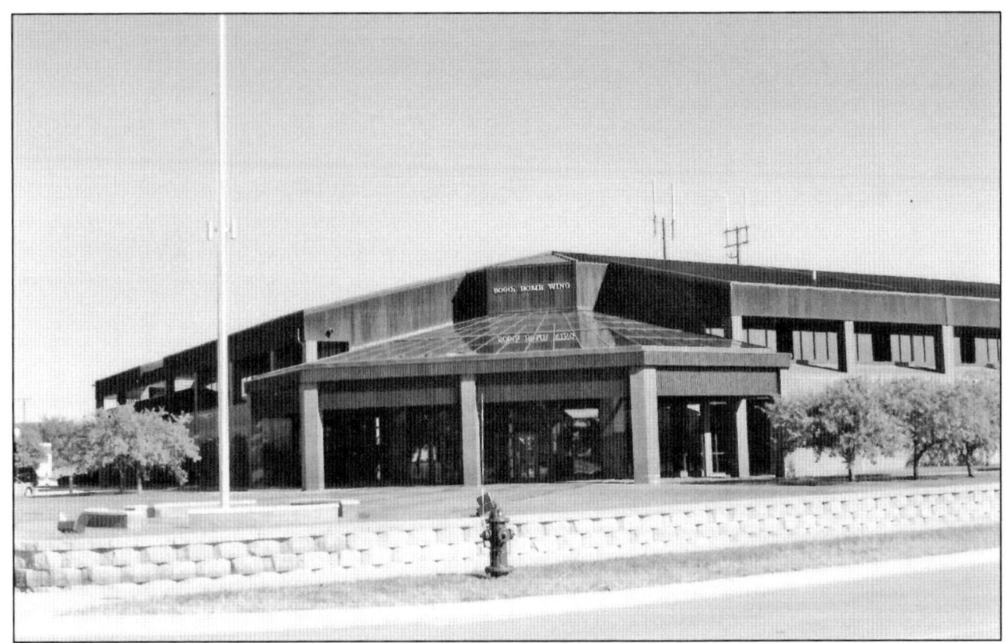

This photograph shows the 509th Bomb Wing Headquarters on Whiteman Air Force Base. The author had the opportunity when on Tinian to walk on the site where the World War II 509th Composite Group's headquarters Quonset hut had been built. The author's father remembered raising the walls on that building. (Author's collection.)

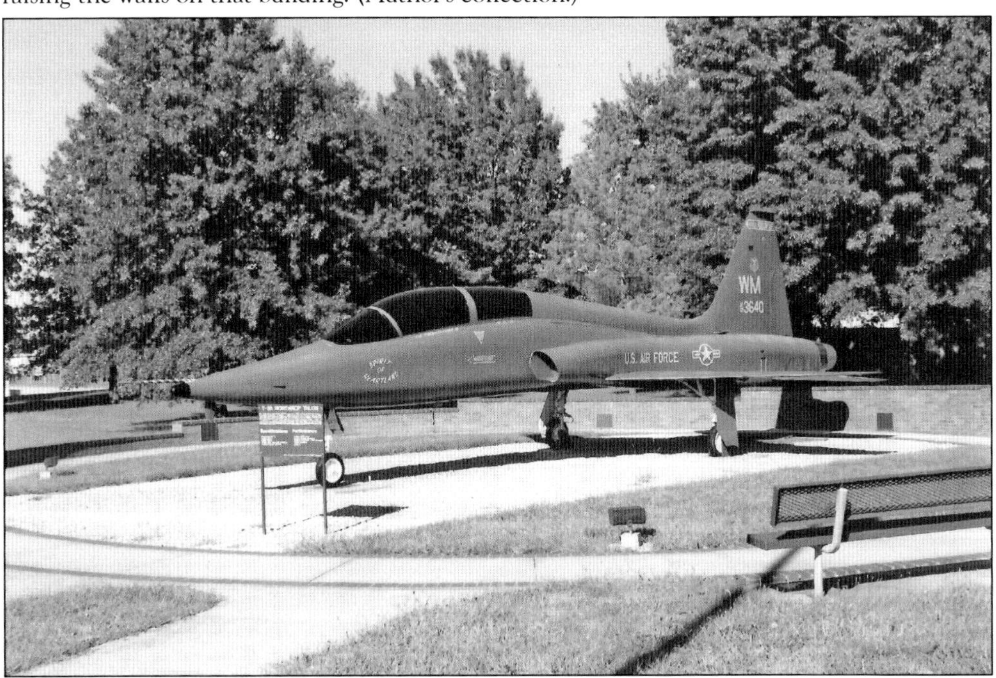

The T-38 was the first aircraft assigned to the 509th Bomb Wing on Whiteman Air Force Base on July 20, 1993. The T-38 companion training program, 394th Combat Training Squadron, provides a low-cost substitute for B-2 stealth pilots to maintain airmanship. The aircraft is on display at Whiteman Air Force Base Air Park. (Author's collection.)

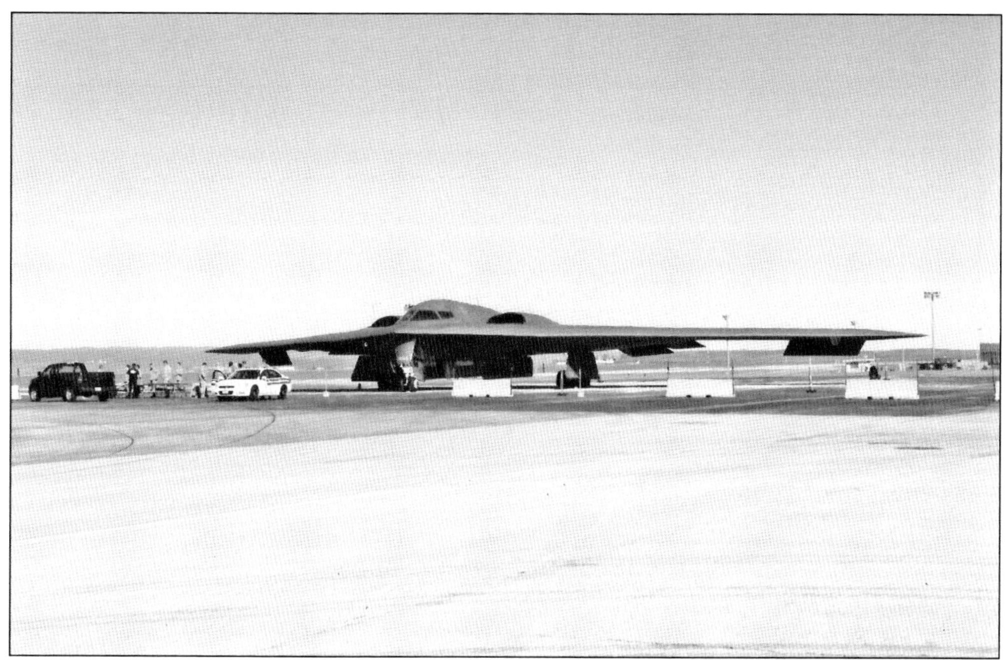

One of the nation's stealth bombers, *Spirit of Alaska*, is on Ellsworth Air Force Base for an air show display. The aircraft was segregated from other aircraft and guarded by the security force, but photographs were allowed. (Author's collection.)

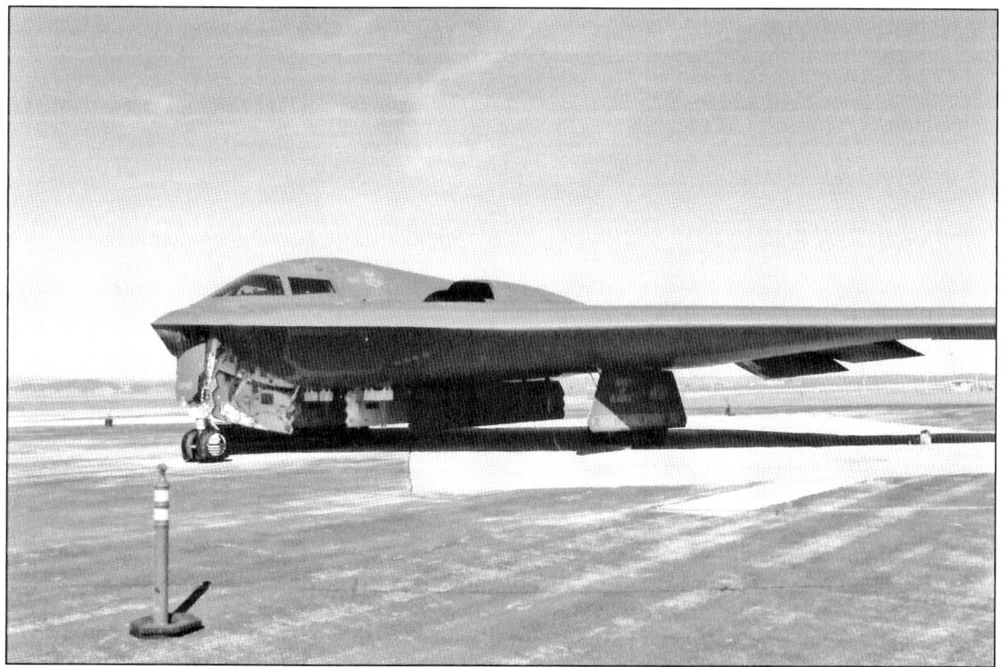

This is a close-up side photograph of the *Spirit of Alaska* on Ellsworth Air Force Base. The aircraft is clean, designed to minimally reflect radar, creating a nearly invisible airborne radar signature. (Author's collection.)

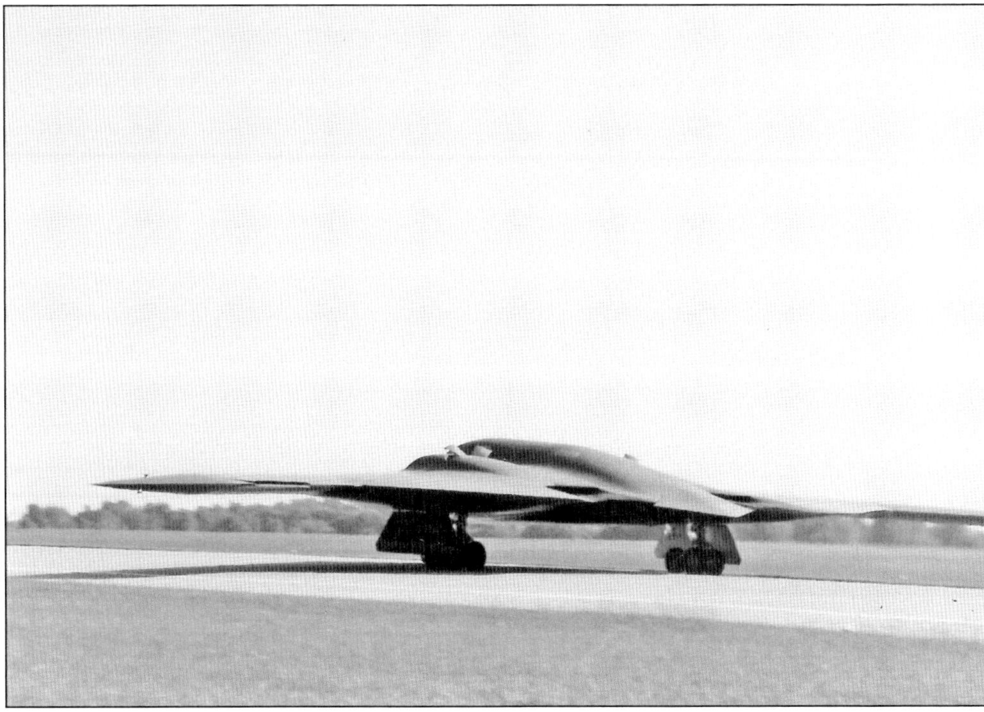

A B-2 takes off from Ellsworth Air Force Base after the airshow, showing the unique rear view of the aircraft. (Author's collection.)

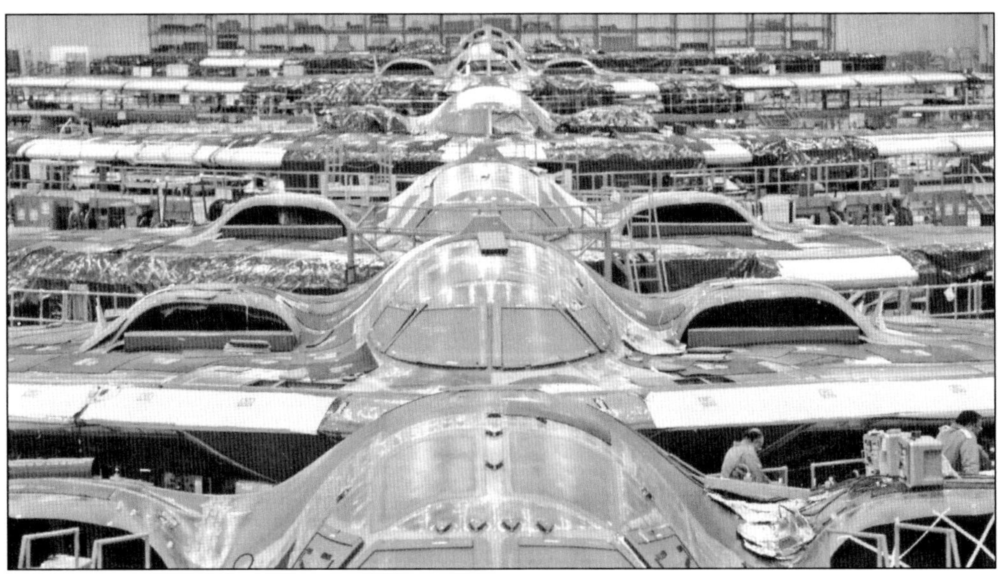

This an unclassified view of the Northrop B-2 production line at Hawthorne, California. The B-2 in the foreground is the *Spirit of Mississippi.* (Courtesy Northrop Grumman Aircraft Corporation.)

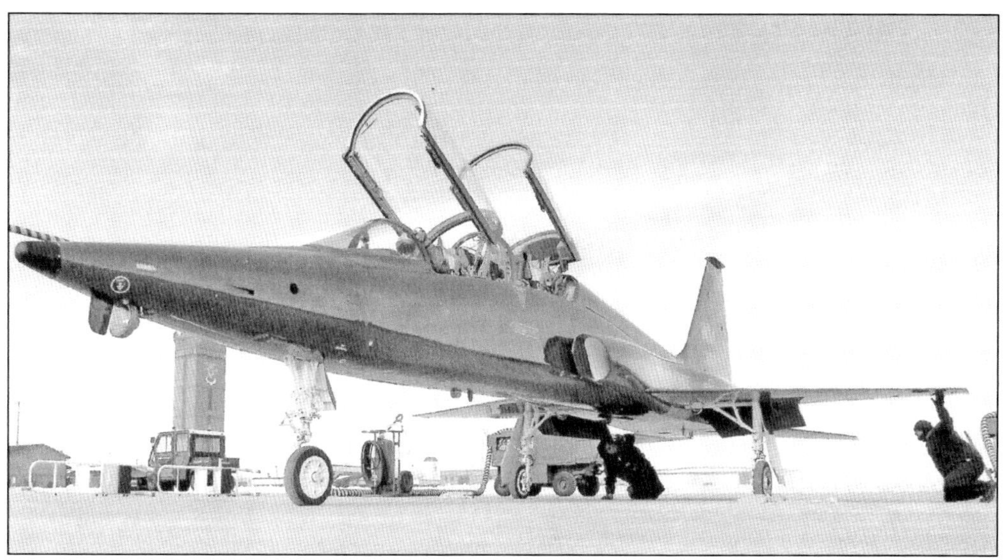

The close-up view of a gray-painted T-38 Talon on the Whiteman Air Force Base flight line shows the slim fuselage of the aircraft. These aircraft provide flying time for B-2 pilots to maintain proficiency in the B-2, following flight profiles of the bomber. (Courtesy Whiteman Air Force Base, 509th Bomb Wing Public Affairs.)

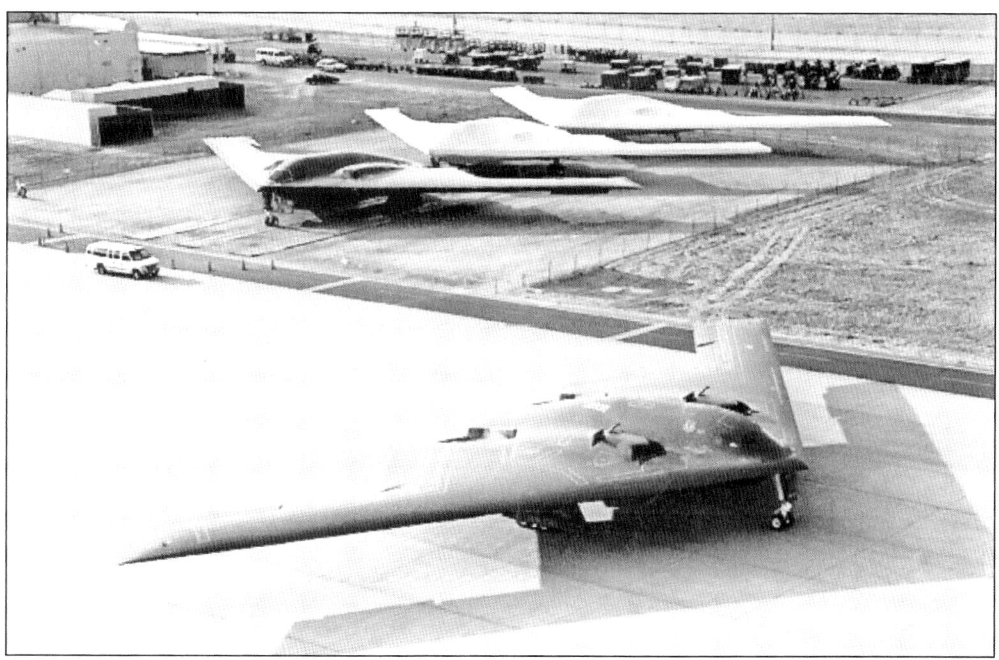

This photograph shows B-2 stealth bombers in front of Northrop Grumman's Air Force Plant at Palmdale, California. The foreground B-2, aircraft number 88-0330, the *Spirit of California*, is on the taxiway. (Courtesy Northrop Grumman.)

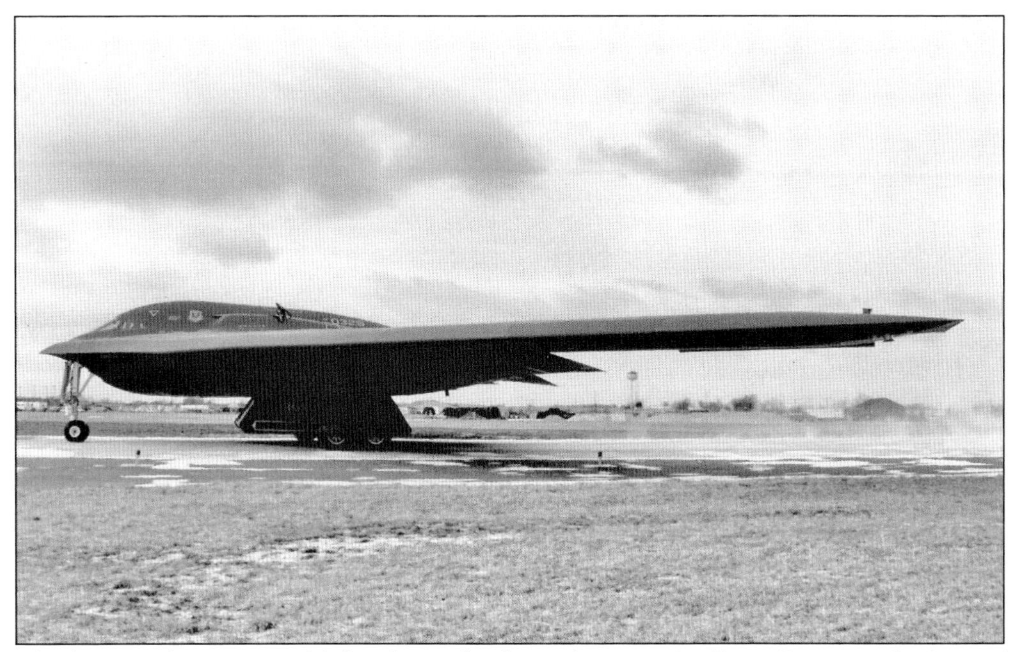

The first Northrop B-2 stealth bomber to land at Whiteman Air Force Base was the *Spirit of Louisiana*, aircraft number 88-0329, on December 17, 1993. There was light snow on Whiteman Air Force Base when the aircraft landed. (Courtesy Whiteman Air Force Base, 509th Bomb Wing Public Affairs.)

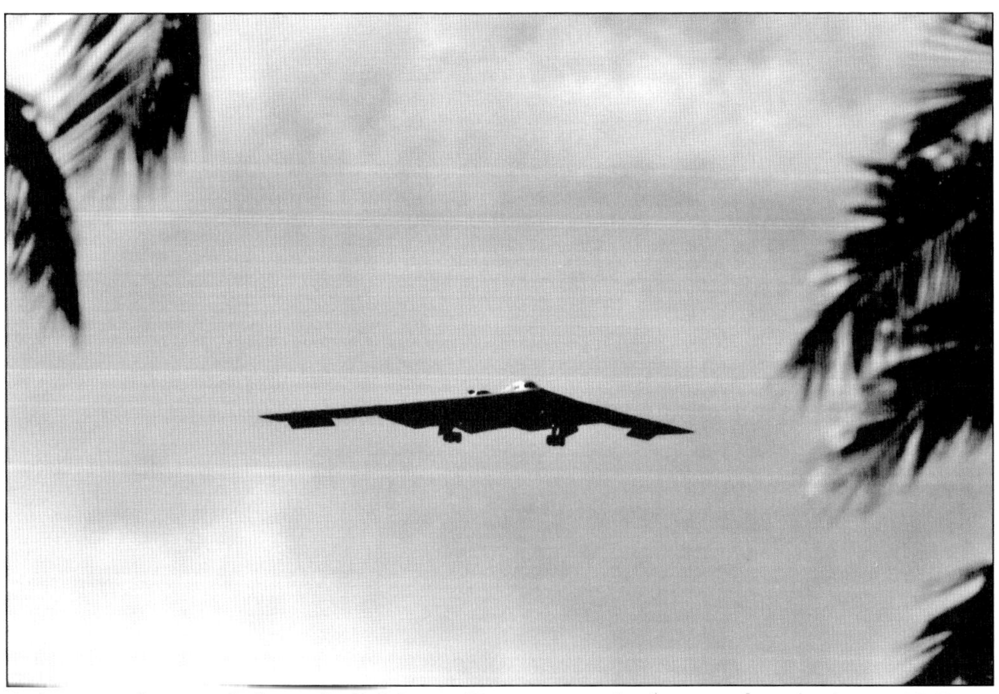

A dramatic photograph shows the B-2 *Spirit of Louisiana* on final approach at Andersen Air Force Base, Guam. (Courtesy Whiteman Air Force Base, 509th Bomb Wing Public Affairs.)

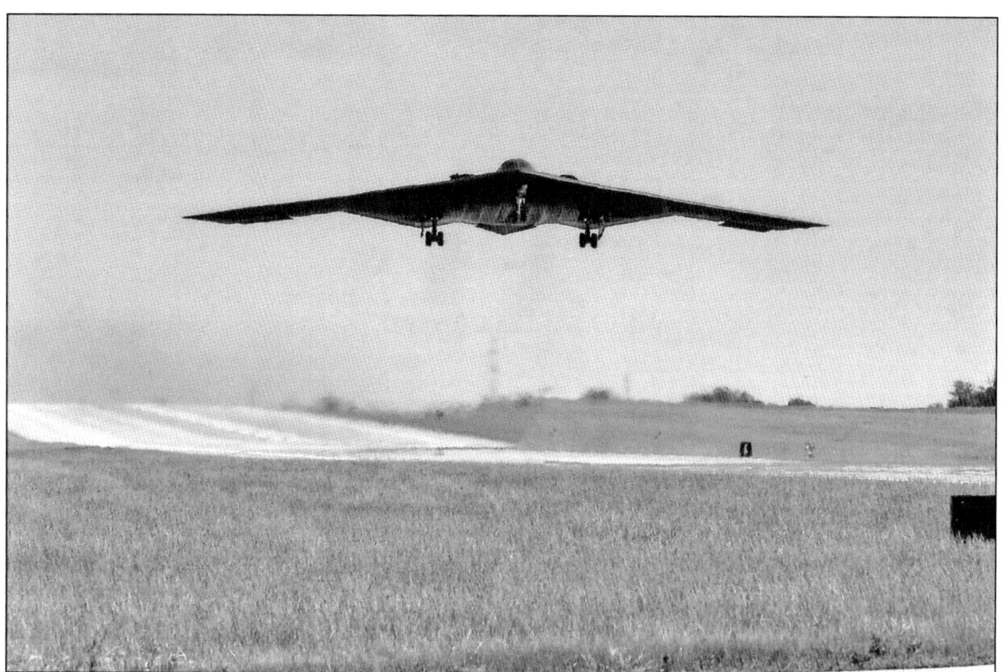

A B-2 stealth bomber takes off from Whiteman Air Force Base on a training sortie. (Courtesy Whiteman Air Force Base, 509th Bomb Wing Public Affairs.)

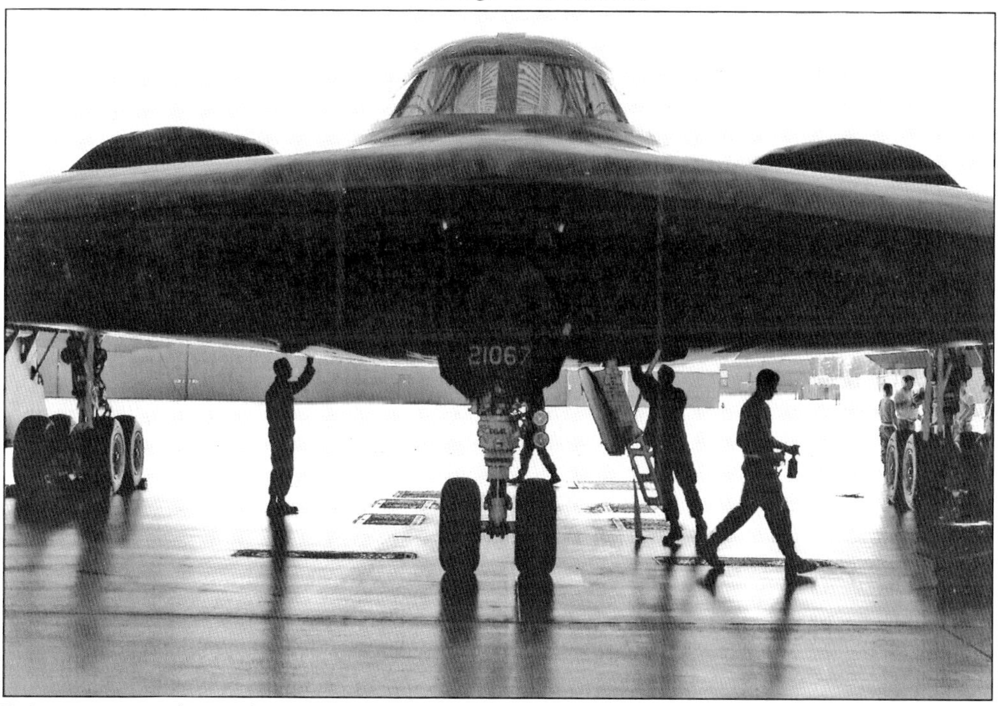

B-2 maintainers (ground crew personnel) perform detailed maintenance checklists on an aircraft in its hangar. This is the *Spirit of Arizona*, aircraft number 82-1067. The two crewmen are inspecting the underside of the wing. (Courtesy Whiteman Air Force Base, 509th Bomb Wing Public Affairs.)

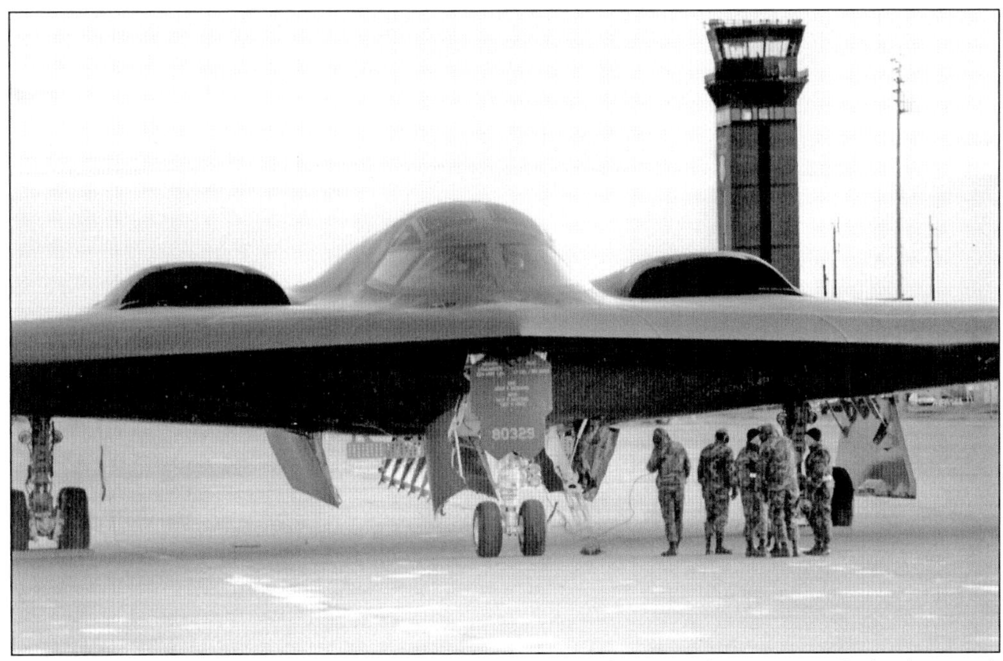

This B-2 is on the Whiteman Air Force Base flight line. The control tower is in the background; from there, tower personnel monitor all flight and ground activity on the base to maintain safe operations. The B-2's weapons bays are open for preflight inspection by the ground crew. (Courtesy Whiteman Air Force Base, 509th Bomb Wing Public Affairs.)

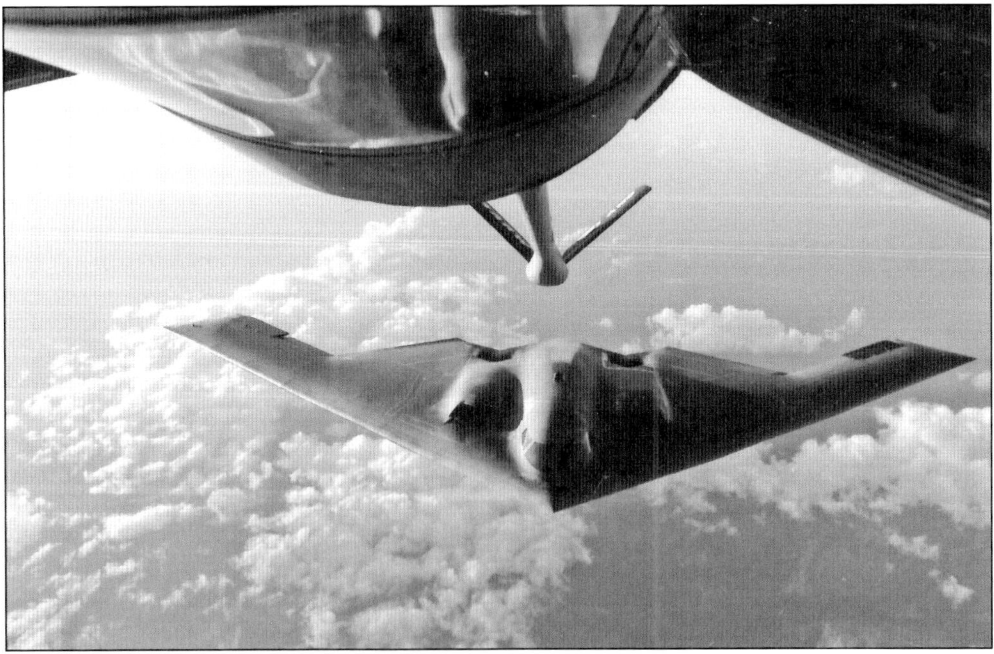

A B-2 is approaching a Boeing KC-135R Stratotanker for refueling as part of a training sortie. The black rectangle on top of the fuselage is the open refueling receptacle. The tanker boom operator lowers the flying boom to allow the B-2 to make contact for refueling to begin. (Courtesy Whiteman Air Force Base, 509th Bomb Wing Public Affairs.)

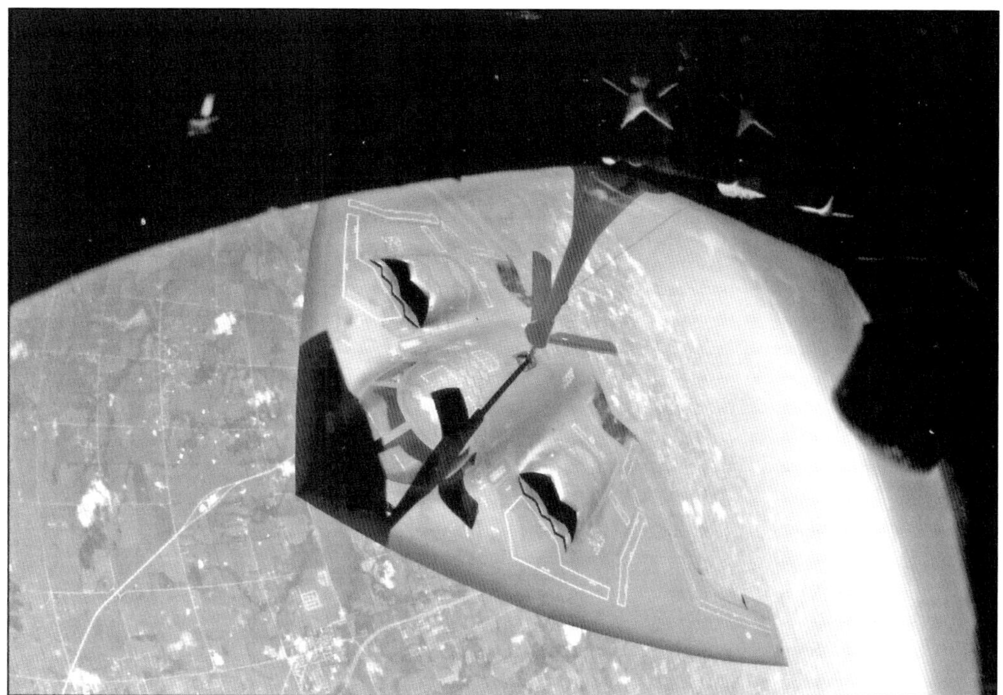

A B-2 is in contact with an airborne tanker to take on fuel. The refueling receptacle is visible behind the cockpit, between the two engine air intakes. When refueling is complete, the boom operator initiates a break of contact. (Courtesy Whiteman Air Force Base, 509th Bomb Wing Public Affairs.)

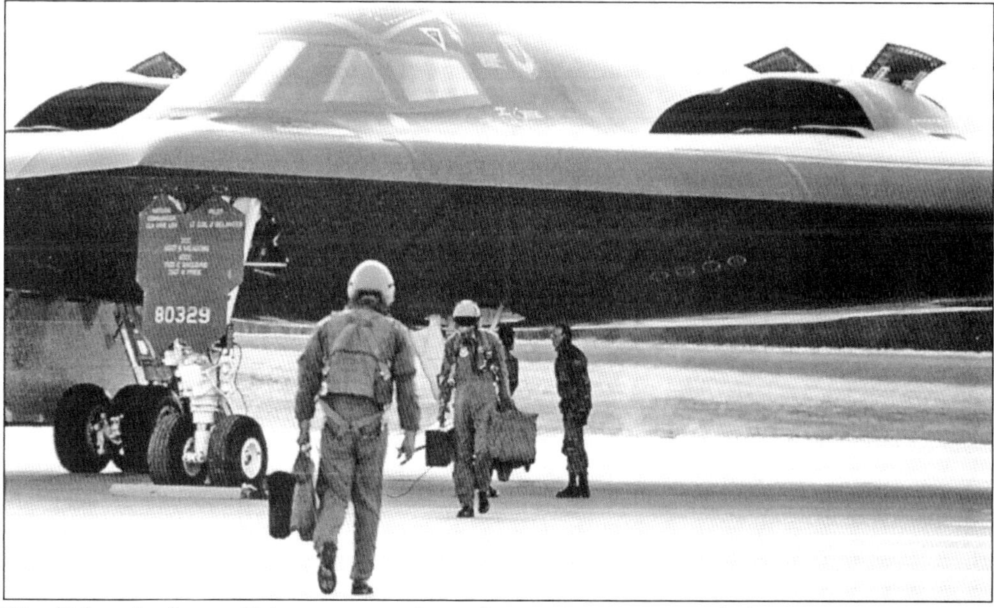

This B-2 is the *Spirit of Missouri*, aircraft number 88-0329. Two B-2 flight crew members are in the process of performing a "hot turnaround." The front flight crew member is approaching the aircraft, and the approaching flight crew member has completed the required training sortie. (Courtesy Northrop Grumman.)

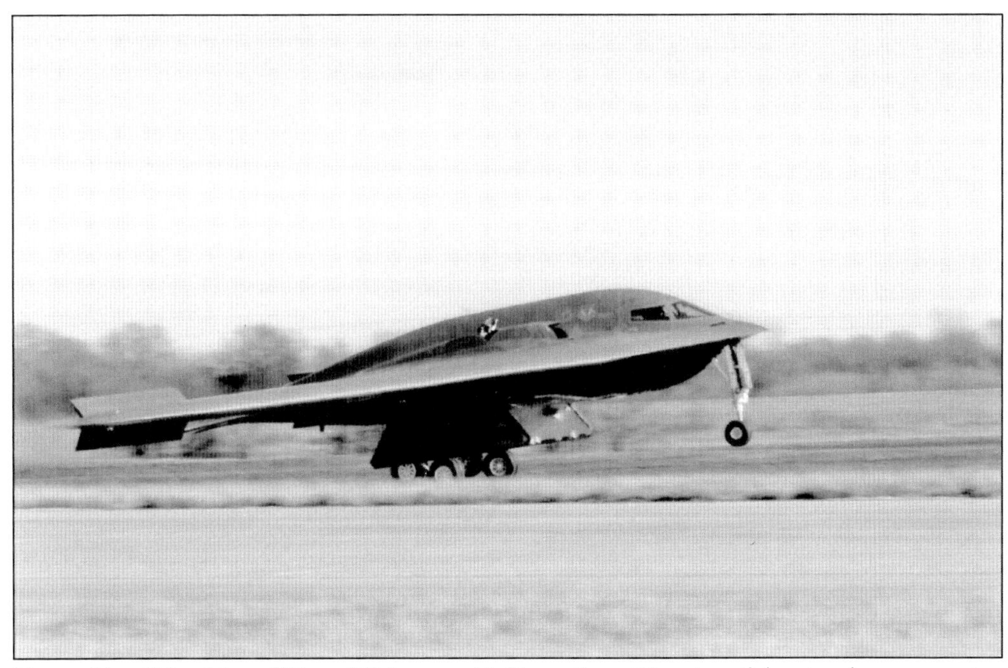

Pictured is a B-2 taking off from Whiteman Air Force Base. The aircraft has just begun rotation off the runway—the nose wheel comes off the runway creating a proper angle of attack for the transition to an airborne flight profile. (Courtesy Whiteman Air Force Base, 509th Bomb Wing Public Affairs.)

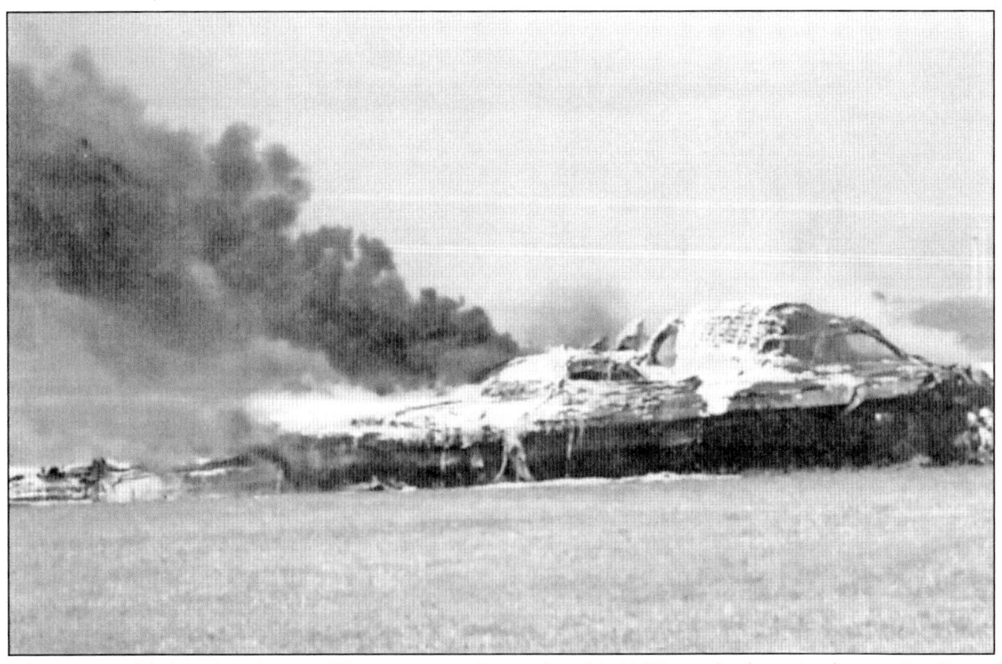

The B-2 stealth bomber *Spirit of Kansas*, aircraft number 89-0127, crashed on Andersen Air Force Base, Guam, during takeoff on February 23, 2008. An Air Force Accident Investigation Report indicated the crash was due to malfunctioning sensors. (Courtesy Pacific Air Force, Andersen Air Force Base, 36th Wing Public Affairs.)

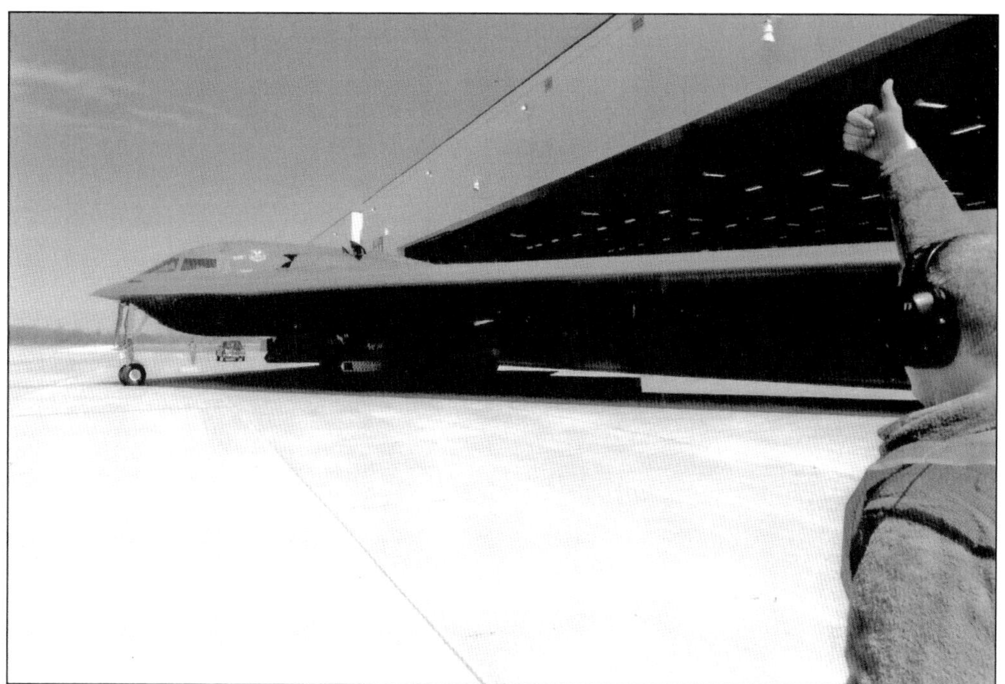

This B-2 is the *Spirit of New York*, aircraft number 82-1068. The aircraft is assigned to Edwards Air Force Base as a test platform. Air Force planners estimate that the B-2 has an operational life expectancy of 40,000 hours, with one loss expected every 10 years. (Courtesy Whiteman Air Force Base, 509th Bomb Wing Public Affairs.)

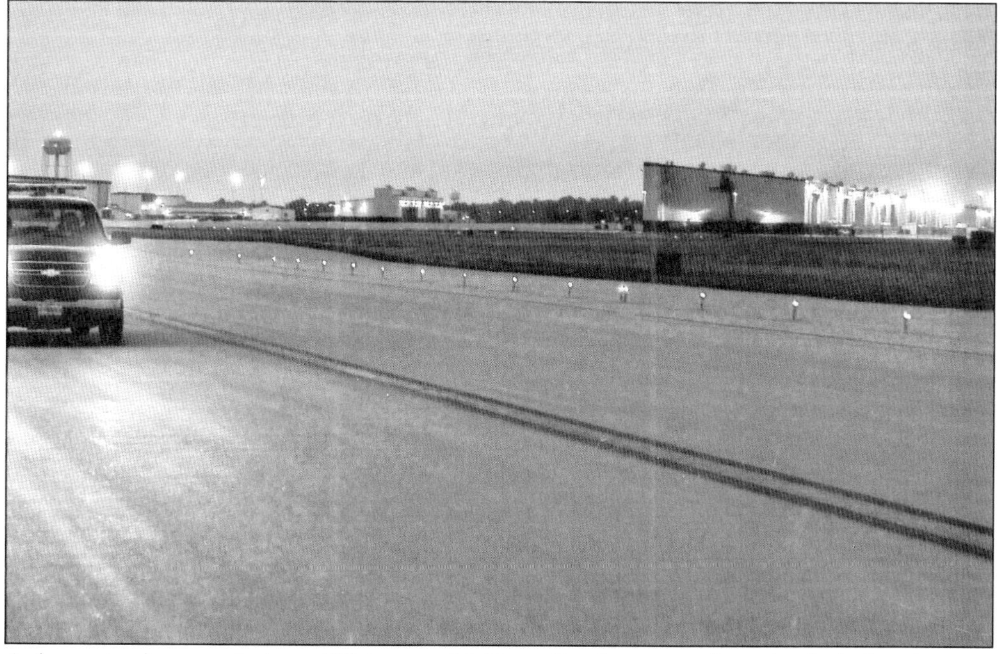

A dramatic photograph shows Whiteman Air Force Base's taxiway from the flight line hangars onto the runway at night. B-2 hangars are lit up, providing a nighttime look at the flight line. (Courtesy Whiteman Air Force Base, 509th Bomb Wing Public Affairs.)

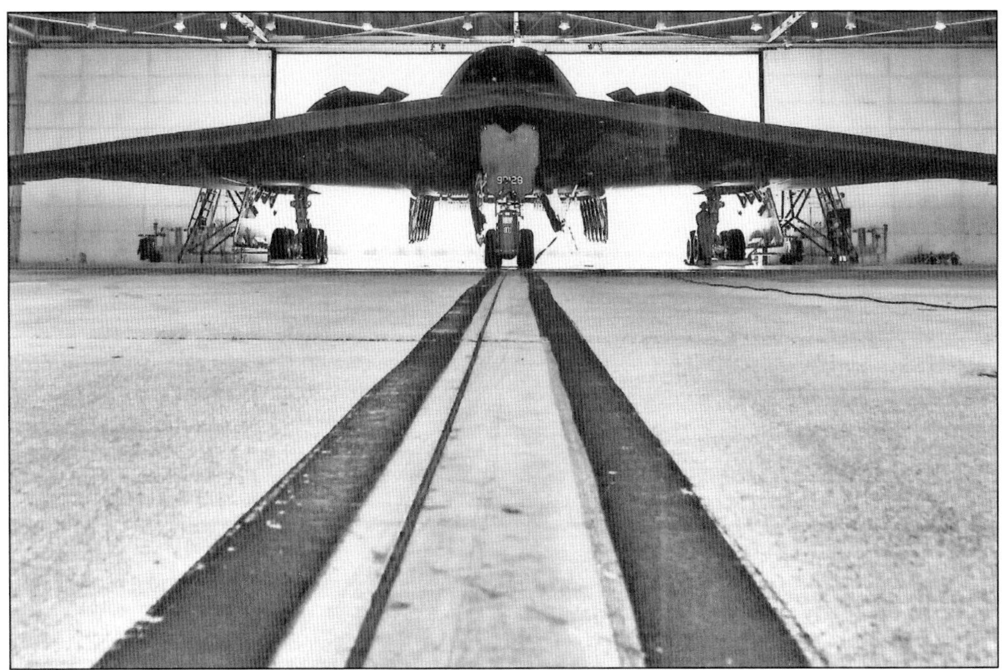

This B-2, the *Spirit of Nebraska*, aircraft number 89-0128, is pictured inside its hangar at Whiteman Air Force Base. Hangar doors are open on either side, allowing the stealth bomber to taxi into the hangar and park for required maintenance. (Courtesy Whiteman Air Force Base, 509th Bomb Wing Public Affairs.)

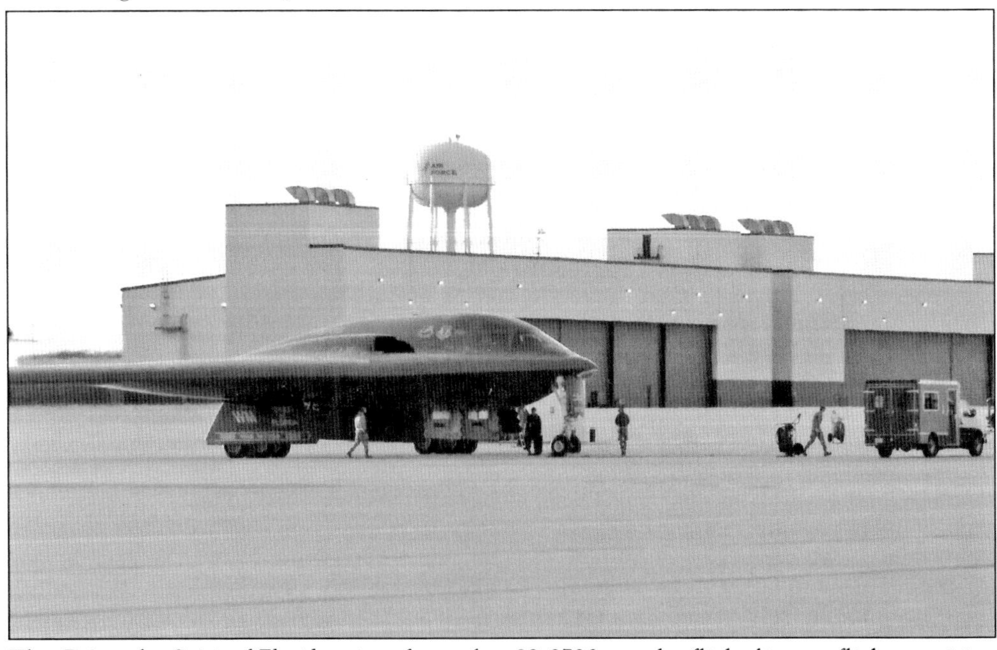

This B-2 is the *Spirit of Florida*, aircraft number 92-0700, on the flight line preflight, awaiting flight crew for takeoff on a training sortie. The view includes the exteriors of the B-2 hangars, with hangar doors closed. The base water tower is in the background. (Courtesy Whiteman Air Force Base, 509th Bomb Wing Public Affairs.)

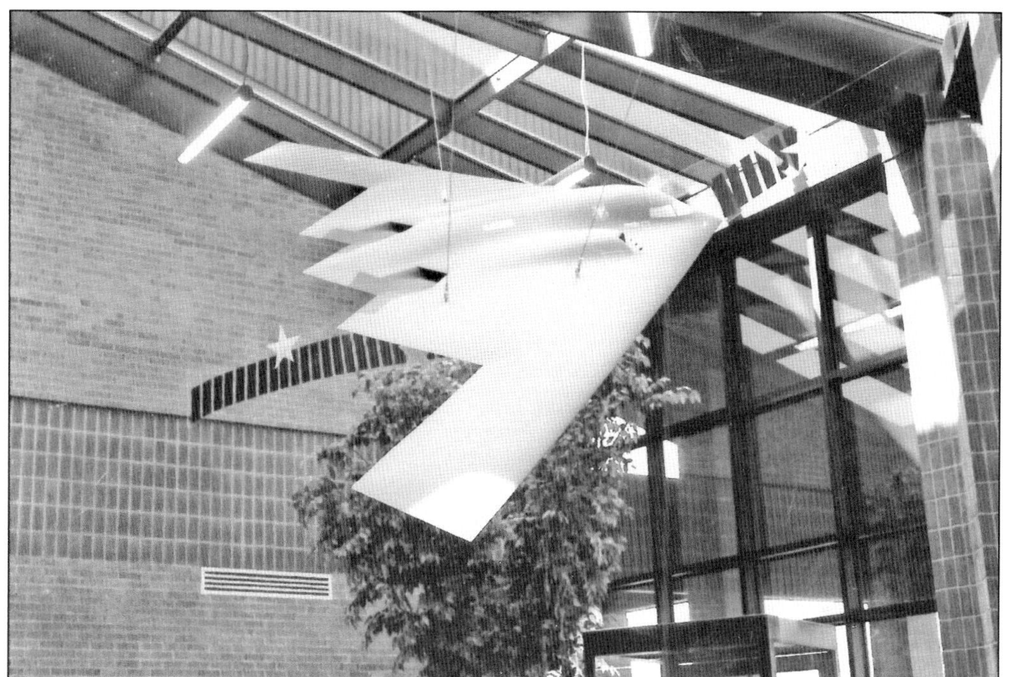

This large-scale model of Northrop B-2 Spirit bomber hangs from the ceiling at the entrance to the 509th Bomb Wing Headquarters on Whiteman Air Force Base. The entrance provides a small museum to the history of the 509th Composite Group and 509th Bomb Wing. (Author's collection.)

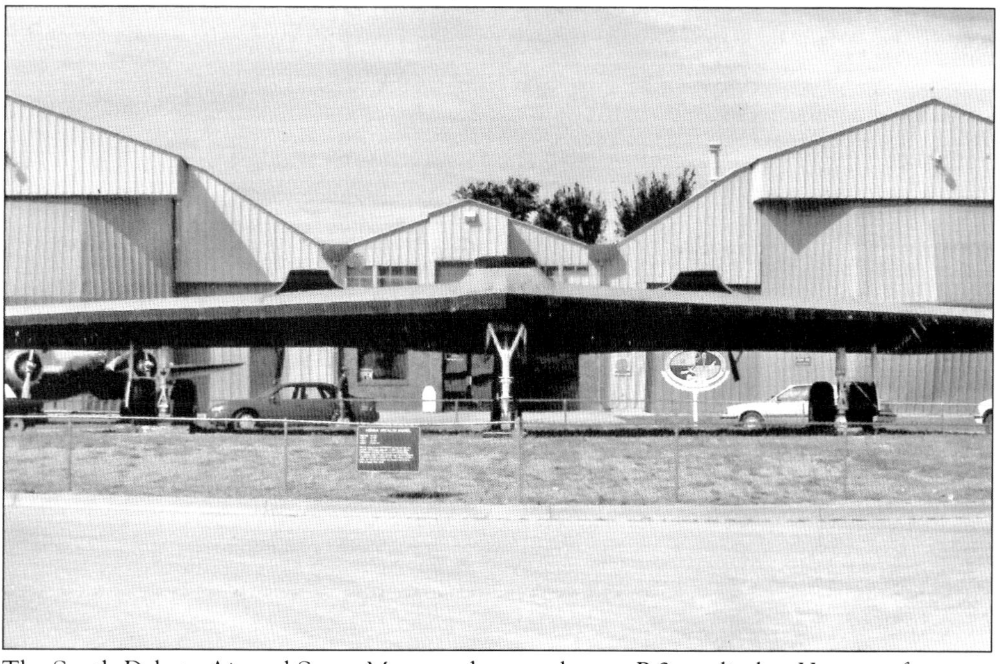

The South Dakota Air and Space Museum does not have a B-2 on display. However, for many years, the Honda Corporation provided a steel scale replica of the Northrop B-2 stealth bomber for display in front of the museum. In 1997, this replica was scrapped and replaced with a B-1B bomber. (Author's collection.)

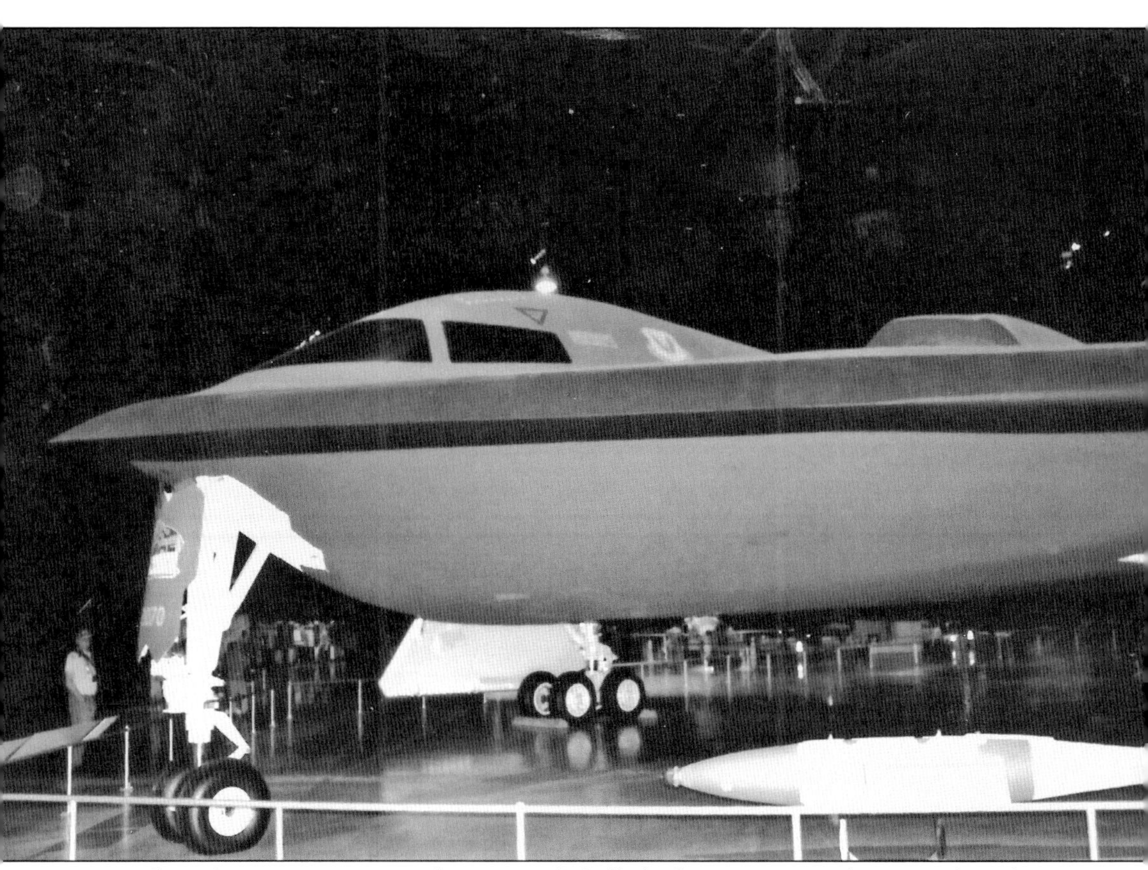

Northrop Grumman constructed two aircraft shells for fatigue testing. The *Spirit of Freedom* was built as a test shell and now is on display at the National Museum of the United States Air Force. (Author's collection.)

Seven

20th Reconnaissance Squadron, MQ-1B Predator 2010–Present

On June 21, 2010, the Department of the Air Force announced that Whiteman AFB was to receive a new mission and a new aircraft, the General Atomics Aeronautical Systems Incorporated MQ-1B Predator unmanned drone. Whiteman AFB likely stood apart from other candidates because of its status as one of five Global Strike Command bases and because it is home to the Northrup B-2 stealth bomber. Whiteman, with a base employment of 8,353, also has excess capacity for billeting, meaning it will not need to construct new housing.

The Predator can be deployed for worldwide operations. It can also be disassembled and loaded into a shipping container for transport to an overseas advanced operation location. The ground control system and Predator Primary Satellite Link (PPSL) are transportable in a Lockheed C-130 Hercules four-turbo-engine transport or the Boeing C-17 Globemaster III transport. The deployed system consists of four sensor/weapon-equipped aircraft, ground control station, PPSL, and spare equipment, along with operations and maintenance crew for long-duration missions. The Predator can operate from a 75-foot-wide, 5,000-foot-long hard-surface runway for loaded takeoffs and land within 2,000 feet, with clear line of sight to the ground data terminal antenna. The antenna provides line-of-sight communications for takeoff and landing. The PPSL provides necessary over-the-horizon communications for the aircraft and sensors. The primary concept of operations, remote split operations (RSO), employs a launch recovery element (LRE) ground control for takeoff and landing operations, while the crew based in the continental United States executes command and control of the remainder of the mission via beyond-line-of-sight links. RSO results in a number of personnel deployed to forward locations and consolidated control of the different flights in one location, and as such, simplified command and control functions as well as logistical supply challenges for the weapon system.

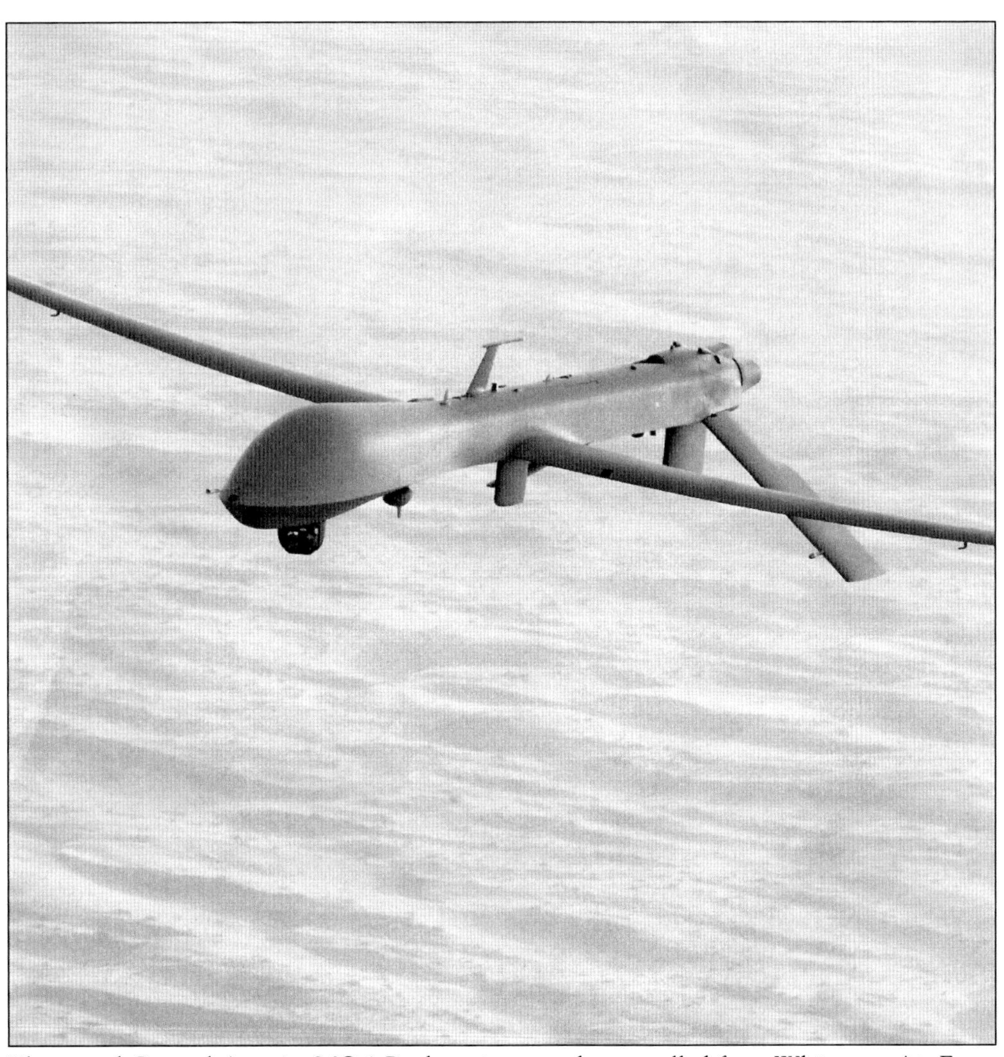

The armed General Atomics MQ-1 Predator is remotely controlled from Whiteman Air Force Base but is launched and recovered from undisclosed forward operating bases in Southwest Asia to strike enemy targets and personnel in Afghanistan, Iraq, and eastern Syria. (Courtesy General Atomics Aeronautical Systems.)

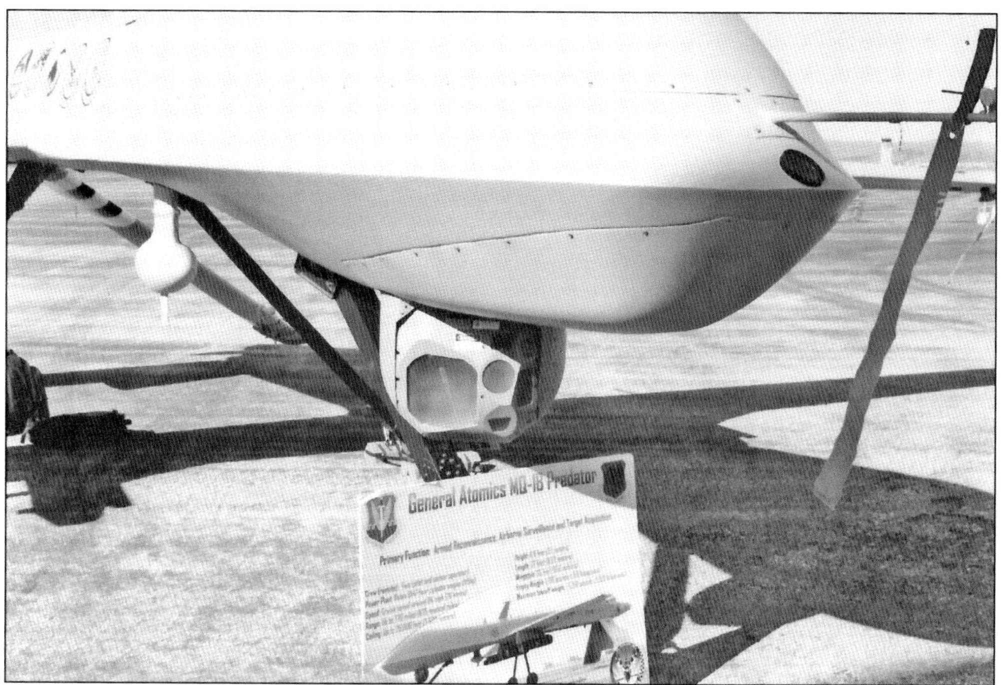

The General Atomics MQ-1B Predator is a medium-altitude, long-endurance, unmanned aircraft system. The Predator's primary missions are close air support; air interdiction; and intelligence, surveillance, and performance (ISR). This one is on display at the Ellsworth Air Force Base open house and air show. (Author's collection.)

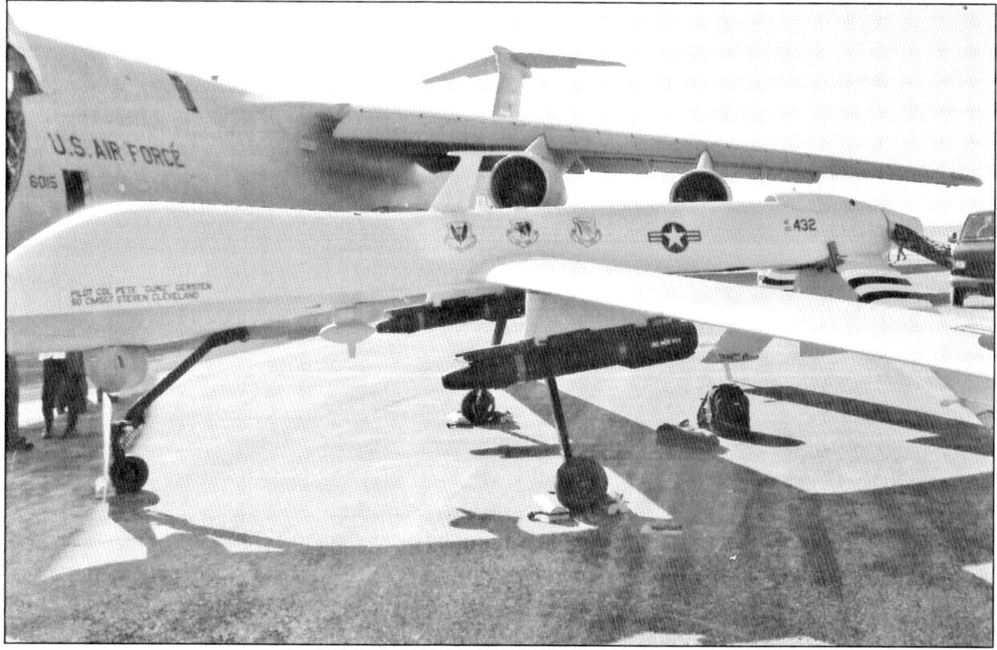

This MQ-1B Predator is on static display with two inert training AGM-114 Hellfire missiles. The Hellfire is a laser-guided, highly accurate, low-collateral-damage missile with anti-armor and anti-personnel capability. It is part of America's war on terrorism. (Author's collection.)

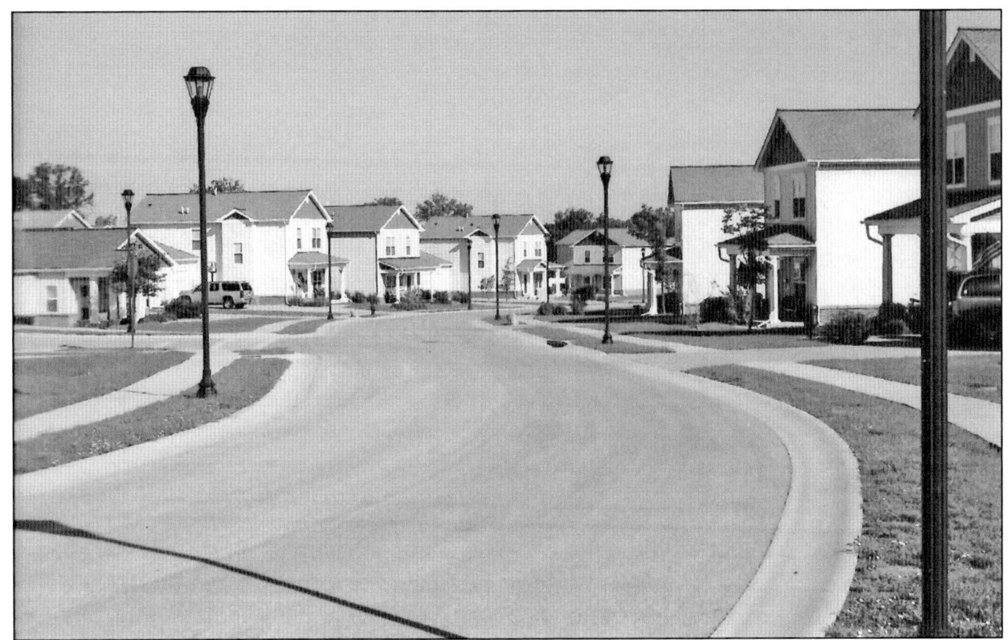

Whiteman Air Force Base housing is modern, supporting many different organizations that operate on the base, active duty as well as reserve units. These housing units were one of the factors for Whiteman Air Force Base becoming home for the 20th Reconnaissance Squadron, flying the MQ-1B Predator. (Author's collection.)

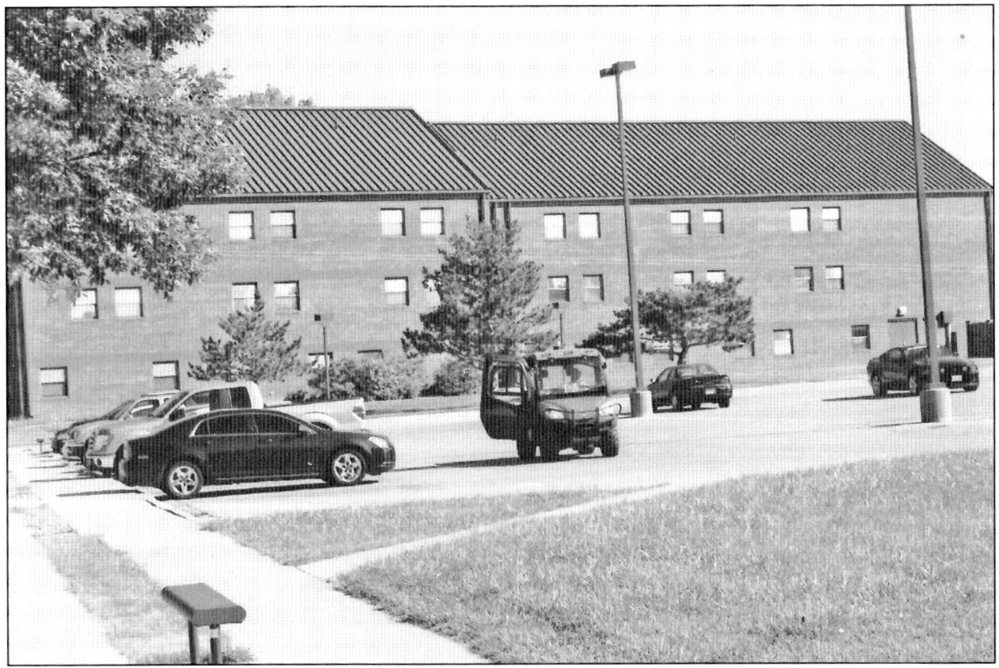

Whiteman Air Force Base provides five 125-personnel units with two-person rooms, along with modern conveniences to provide for off-duty residents while maintaining the morale of the airmen who perform technical work on the base. The barracks capacity tipped the decision to station the 20th Reconnaissance Squadron on the base. (Author's collection.)

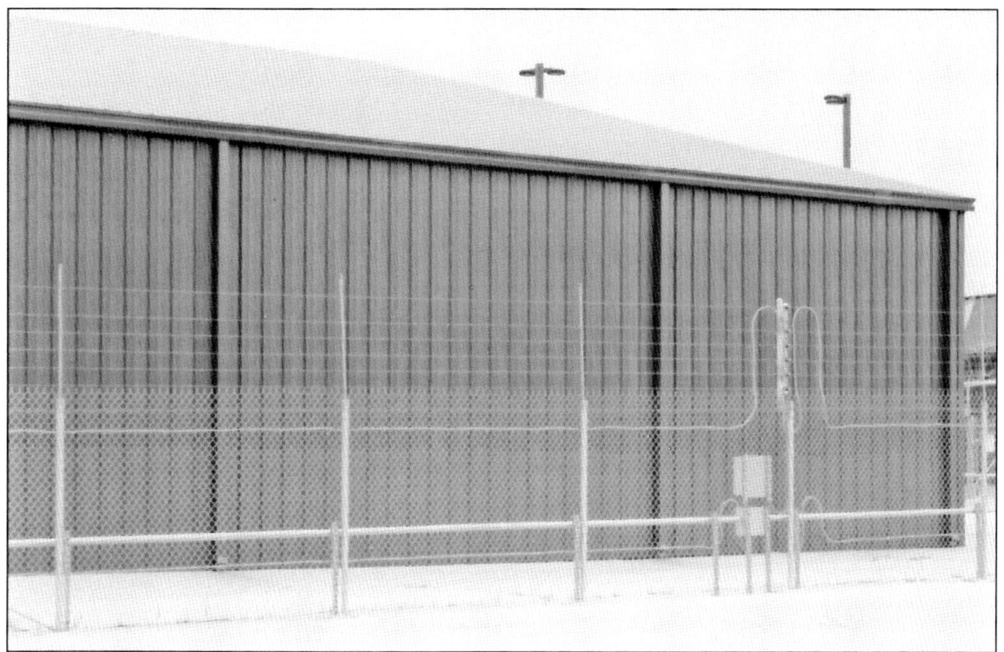

The 20th Reconnaissance Squadron operations center is an unassuming building with no windows behind a sensor-equipped security fence that is separated from the base proper and from flight line operations. It is a sensitive compartmented intelligence facility (SCIF) with no unauthorized entry or photographs allowed. (Author's collection.)

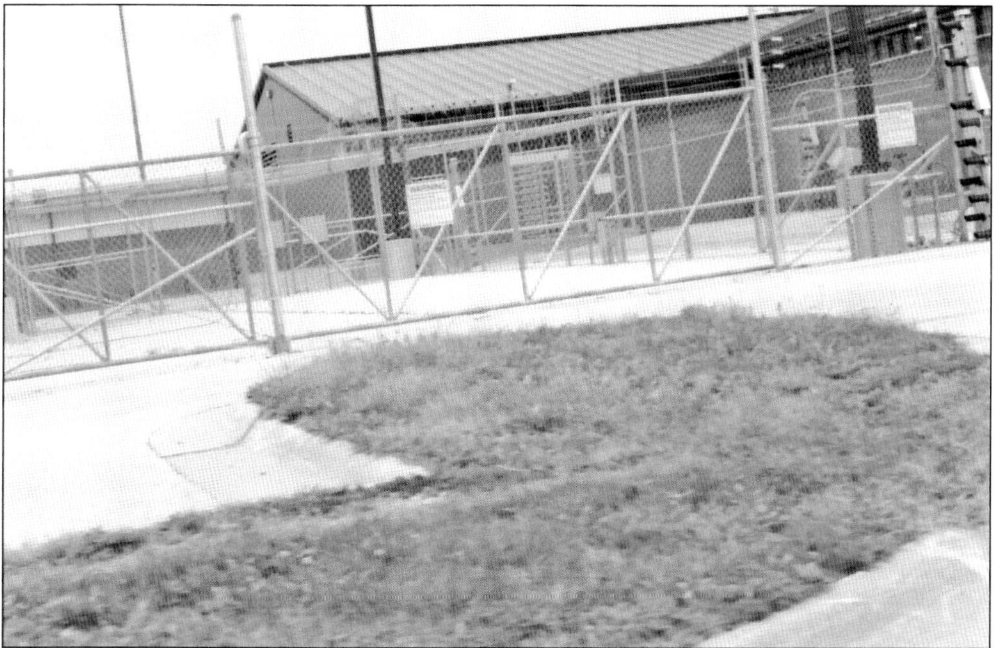

Shown is the personnel and vehicle security entrance to the 20th Reconnaissance Squadron. The gate electrically opens and closes. The security fence maintains the integrity of the SCIF. The outside area in the compound is monitored with cameras to prevent unauthorized entry. (Author's collection.)

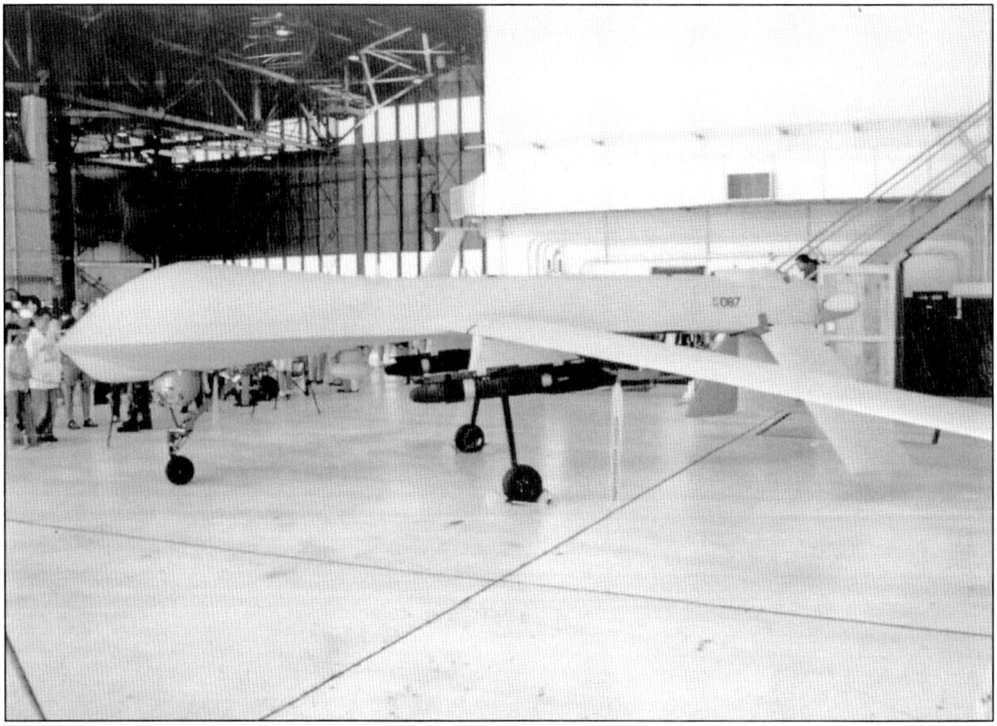

This Predator is on display at a Whiteman Air Force Base open house inside one the of the B-2 hangars, showing inert training laser-guided AGM-114 Hellfire air-to-ground missiles. (Courtesy Whiteman Air Force Base, 509th Bomb Wing Public Affairs.)

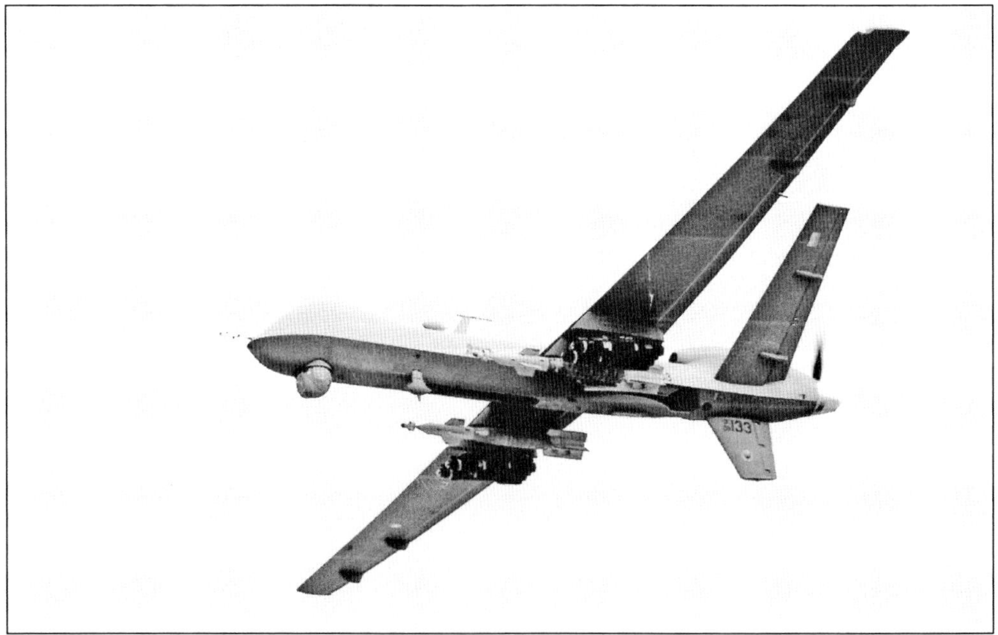

An airborne Reaper is armed with four AGM-114 Hellfire air-to-ground missiles and two GBU-15 laser-guided standoff munitions. (Courtesy Whiteman Air Force Base, 509th Bomb Wing Public Affairs.)

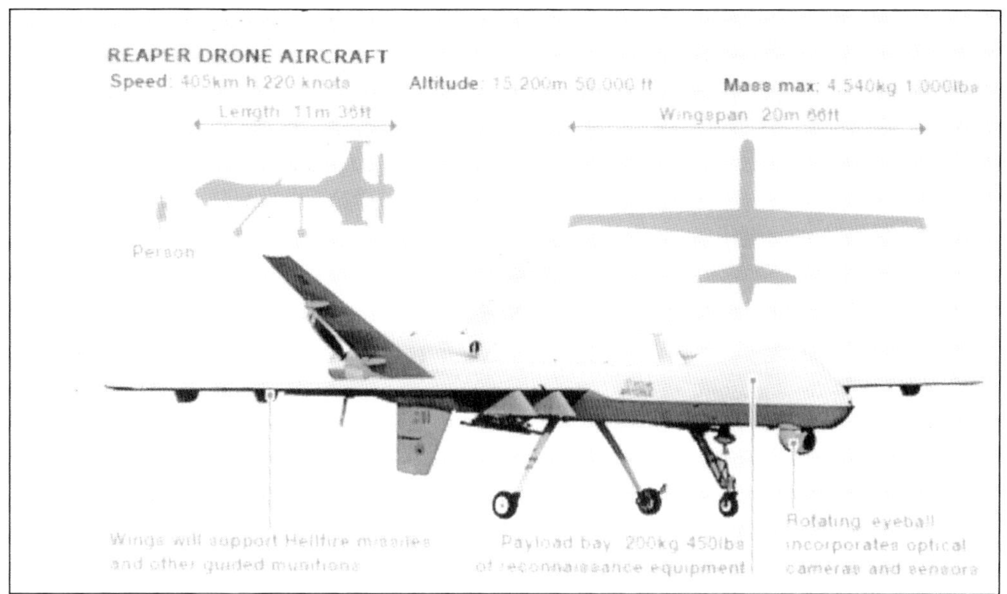

The unmanned, remotely controlled MQ-1B Predator is an advanced weapon system with many different sensors and munitions pylons. (Courtesy General Atomics Aeronautical Systems.)

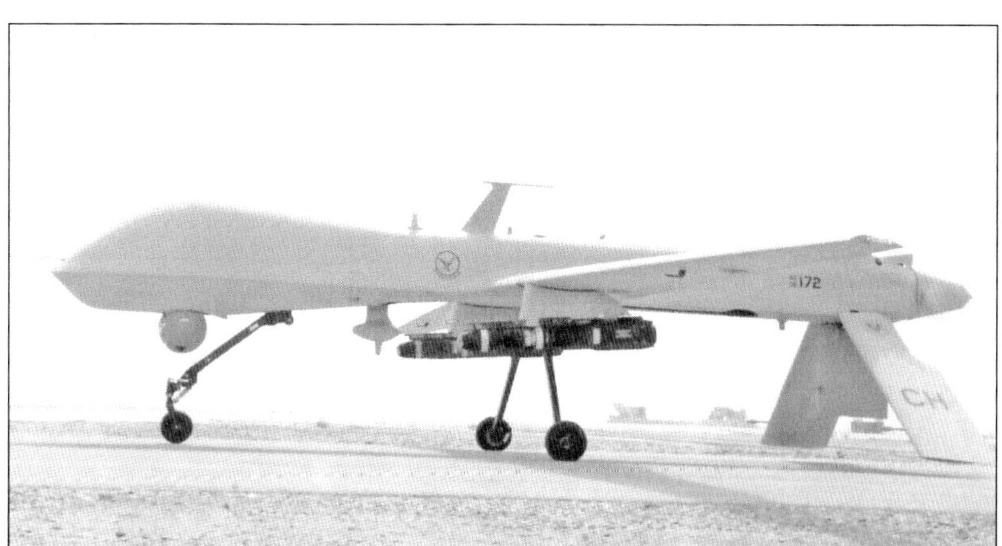

A MQ-1B Predator is shown at Ali Air Base, Iraq, a forward operating base in Southwest Asia, loaded with four AGM-114 Hellfire air-to-ground missiles at the end of the runway in preparation for takeoff and patrol. (Courtesy Whiteman Air Force Base, 509th Bomb Wing Public Affairs.)

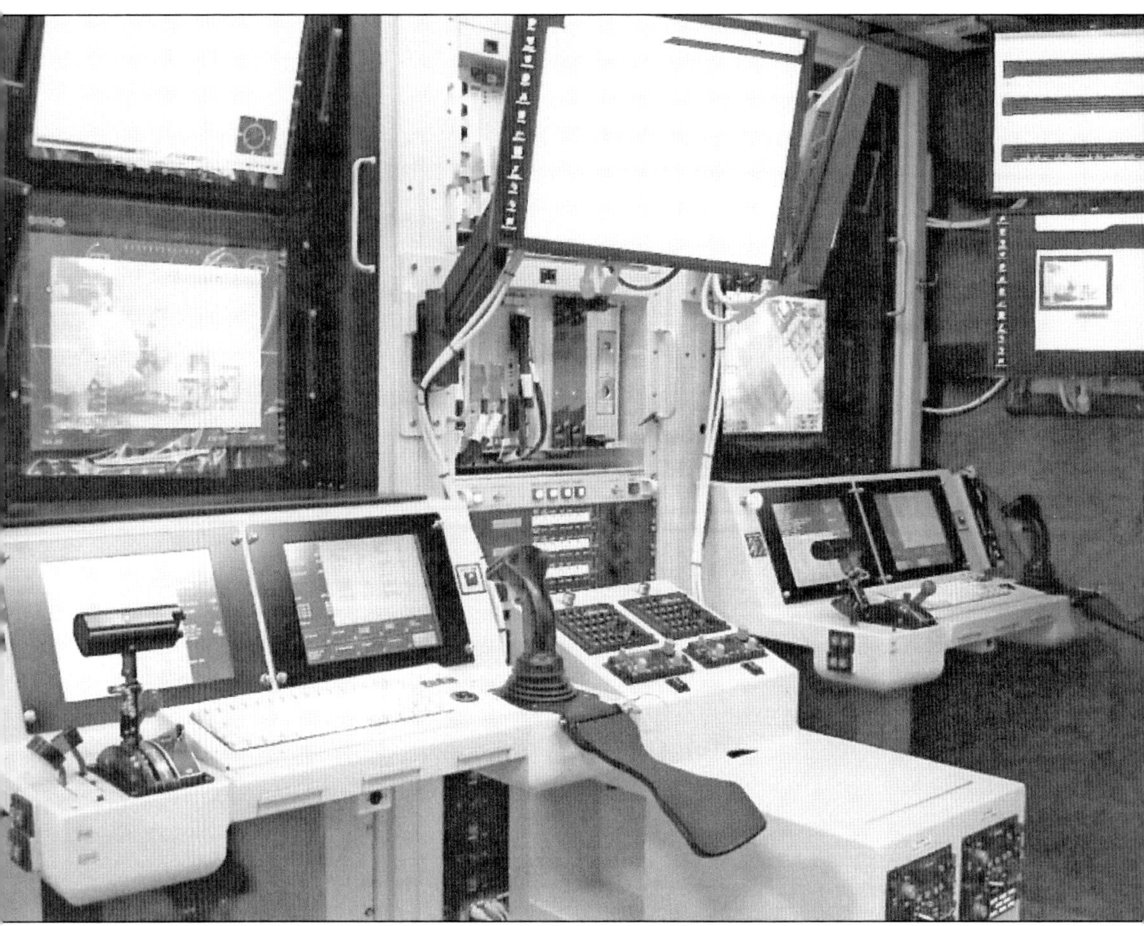

The General Atomics MQ-1B Predator crew console position is shown in this photograph. The aircraft and mission payloads are controlled via satellite data link. Sensor feeds are received at the mission control center via satellite and are processed and analyzed. (Courtesy General Atomics Aeronautical Systems.)

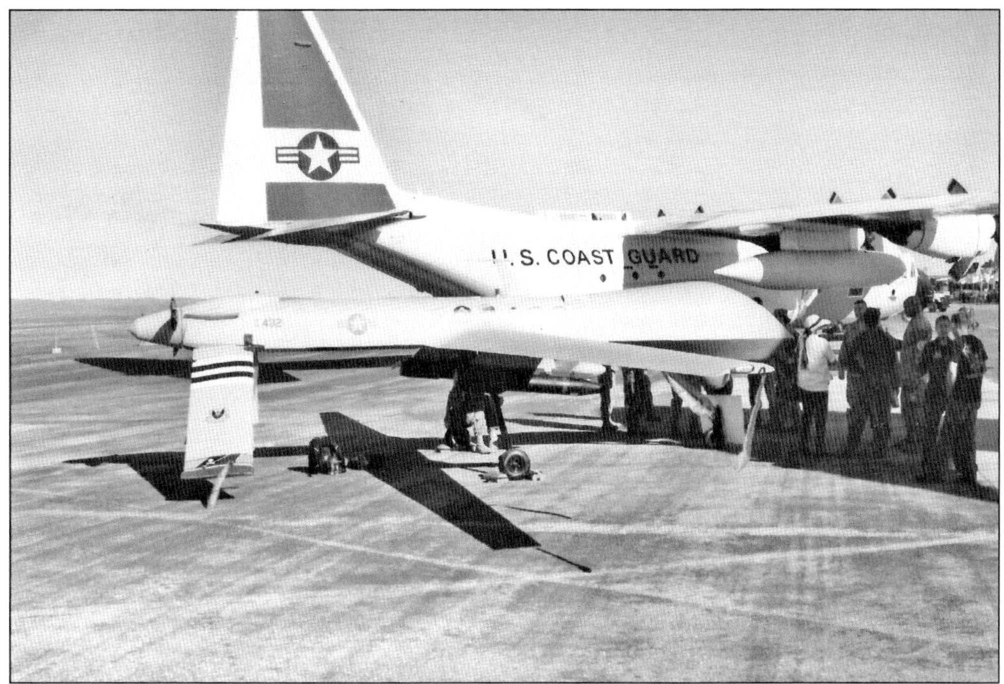

This Predator is on display at an Ellsworth Air Force Base open house and air show, allowing photographs to be taken up close of the side and rear of the aircraft showing the wings, downward V tail, and piston pusher engine. (Author's collection.)

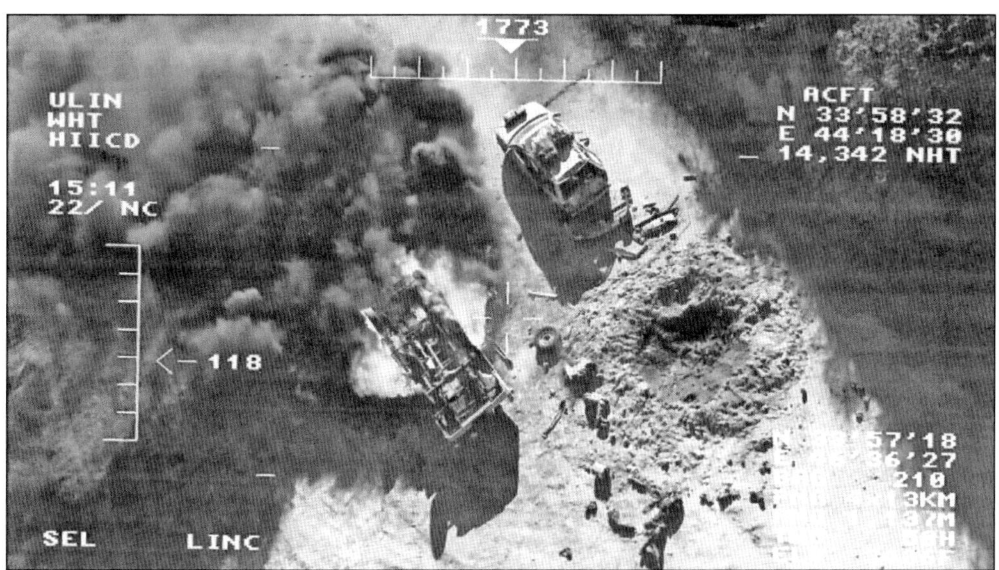

The Predator pilot's view of the ground provides real-time images of the target to be attacked—in this photograph, two vehicles north of Baghdad, outside Baqubah. The Predator can locate targets, attack, and provide damage assessment. (Courtesy Department of Defense, Department of the Air Force, Pentagon News Media.)

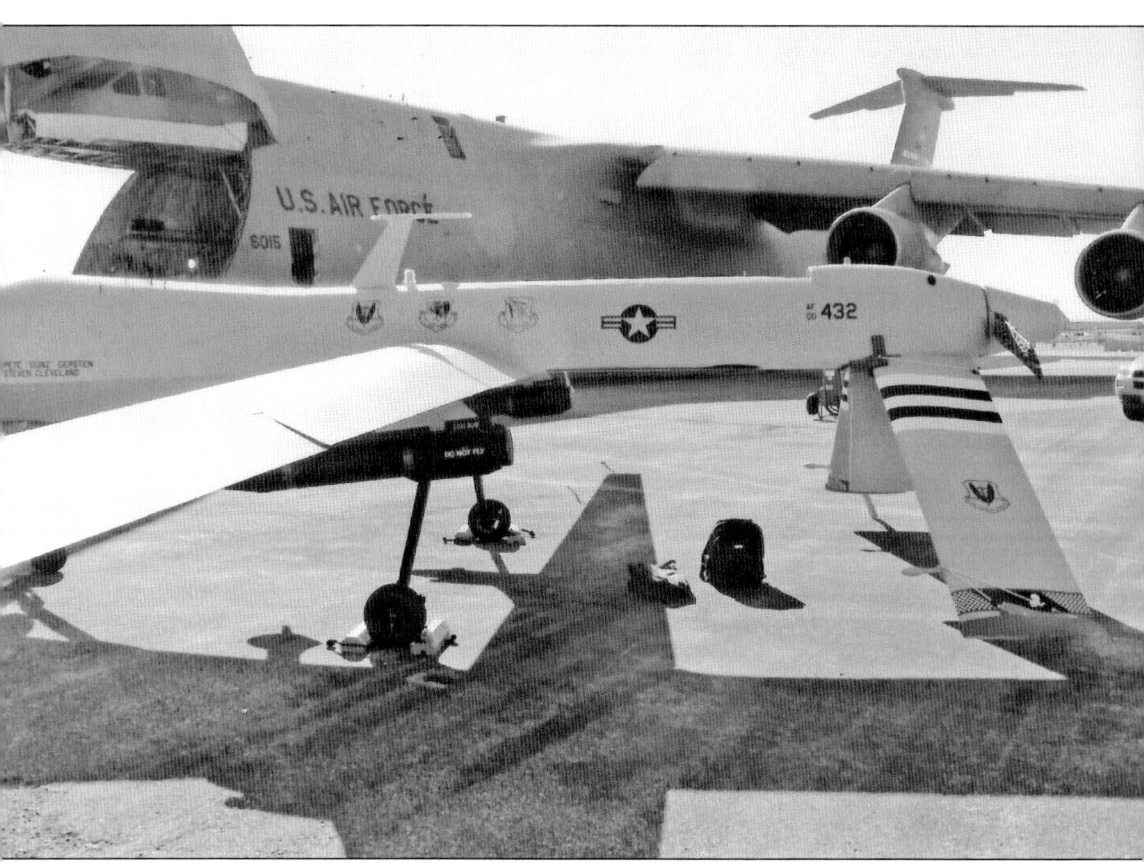

This Predator is on display at an Ellsworth Air Force Base open house and air show. The slim silhouette of the aircraft's fuselage and wings is visible. It is powered by a tail-mounted pusher engine that is undetectable at altitude, and its under-nose-mounted optics gives the remote operator a clear view below. (Author's collection.)

Eight

442nd Fighter Wing and 1-135th Attack Aviation Battalion 1949–Present

The lineage of the 442nd Fighter Wing (FW) began with the 442nd Troop Carrier Wing (TCW) (Medium) on May 10, 1949. It was activated in the Air Force Reserve on June 27, 1949. It was ordered to active service on March 10, 1951; inactivated on March 12, 1951; activated in the Air Force Reserve on June 15, 1952; redesignated the 442nd TCW (Heavy) on May 8, 1961; ordered to active service on October 1, 1961; and released from active service on August 27, 1962. It was redesignated the 442nd Air Transport Wing (ATW) (Heavy) on December 1, 1965; the 442nd Military Airlift Wing (MAW) on January 1, 1966; and the 442nd Tactical Airlift Wing (TAW) on June 29, 1971. The unit was inactivated on October 1, 1982; redesignated 442nd Tactical Fighter Wing (TFW) in November 1983; and activated in the Air Force Reserve on February 1, 1984, and equipped with the Fairchild Republic Company A-10 Thunderbolt II. Redesignated the 442nd FW on February 1, 1992, it was assigned to Whiteman AFB on April 1, 1994.

The 917th Fighter Group (FG), an Air Force Reserve unit out of Barksdale AFB, Louisiana, was deactivated on January 1, 2011, and realigned under the 442nd FW. The 442nd is comprised of approximately 1,000 personnel. Besides the 917th FG, the second geographically separated unit is the 476th FG at Moody AFB, Georgia. The wing is responsible for 48 A-10Cs: 24 at Whiteman, 12 at Barksdale, and 12 at Moody. The A-10 remains effective in protecting US ground forces in combat, mostly recently in Afghanistan and against ISIS to support US ground forces in western Iraq and eastern Syria.

The 1-135th Attack Aviation Battalion's mission is to conduct attack reconnaissance and security operations that complement maneuver forces. It controls 20 AH-64D Apache Longbow helicopters. The Missouri National Guard is to provide support when called upon by the president, which could be for overseas contingency operations or emergencies like the disaster caused by Hurricane Katrina, and to support the governor in times of state crisis.

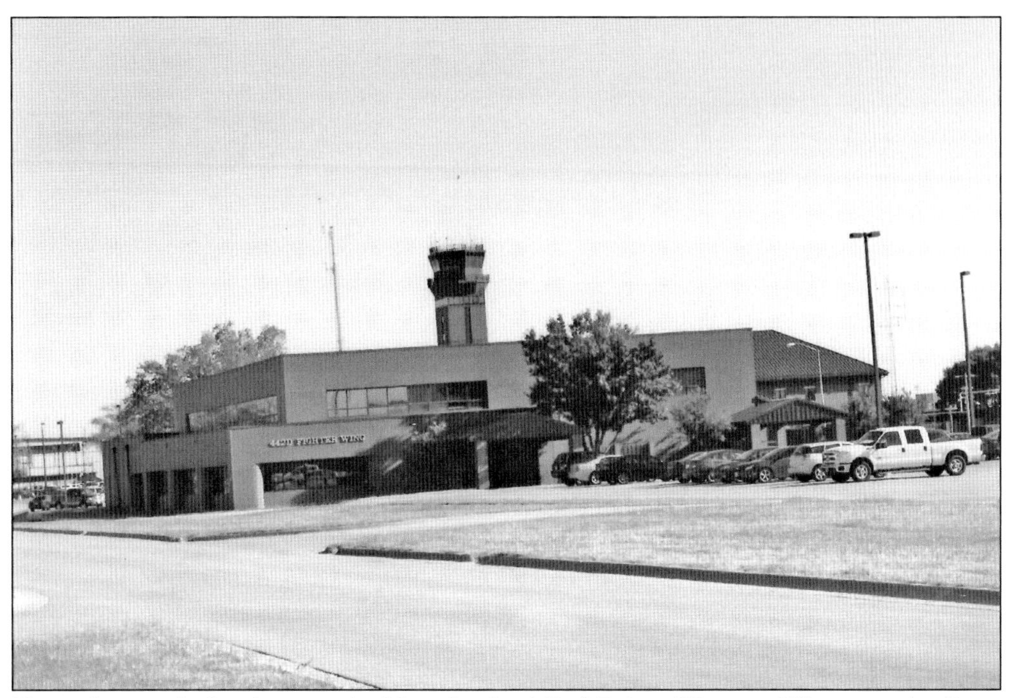

Shown here is the headquarters building for the 442nd Fighter Wing on Whiteman Air Force Base. (Author's collection.)

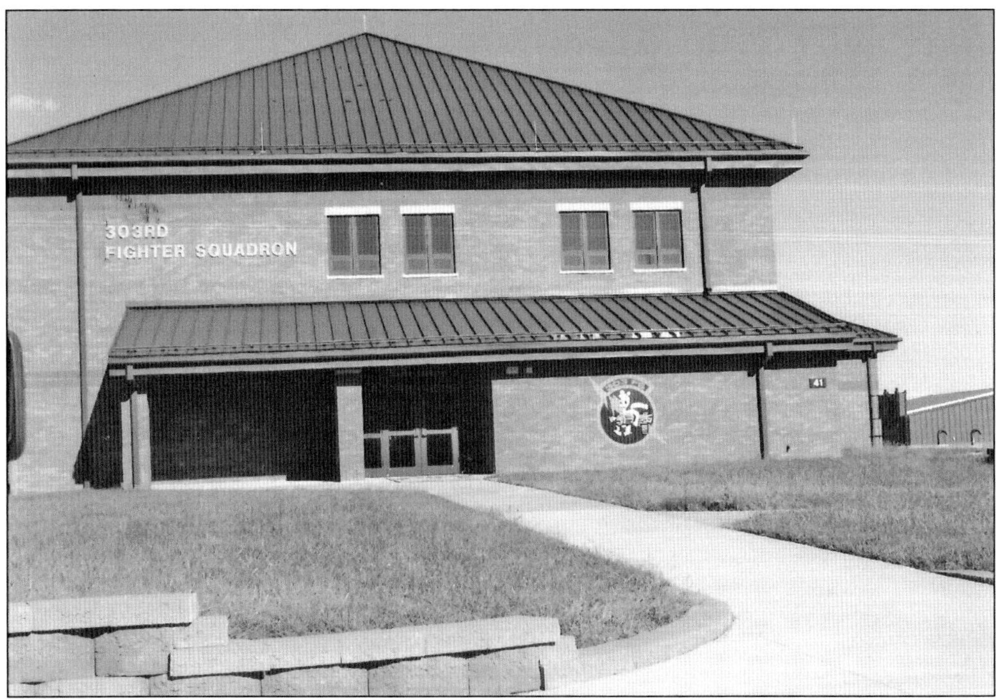

Pictured is the headquarters building for the 442nd Fighter Wing's 303rd Fighter Squadron. (Author's collection.)

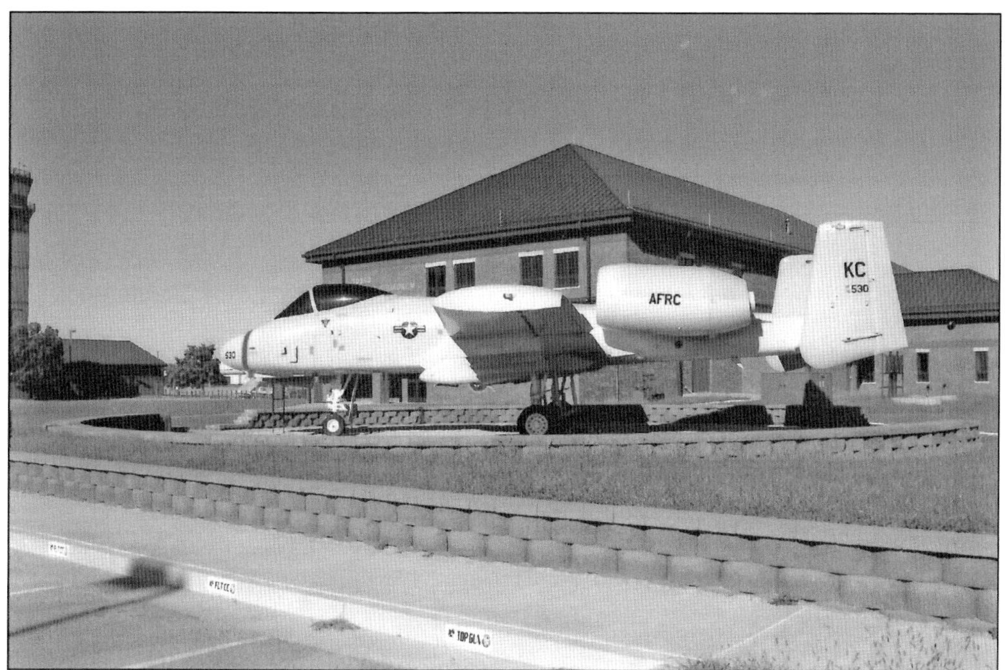

A Fairchild A-10C Thunderbolt II ground attack fighter is on display in front of the 442nd Fighter Wing Headquarters on Whiteman Air Force Base. The aircraft has been modified and technologically updated for operations in Southwest Asia. (Author's collection.)

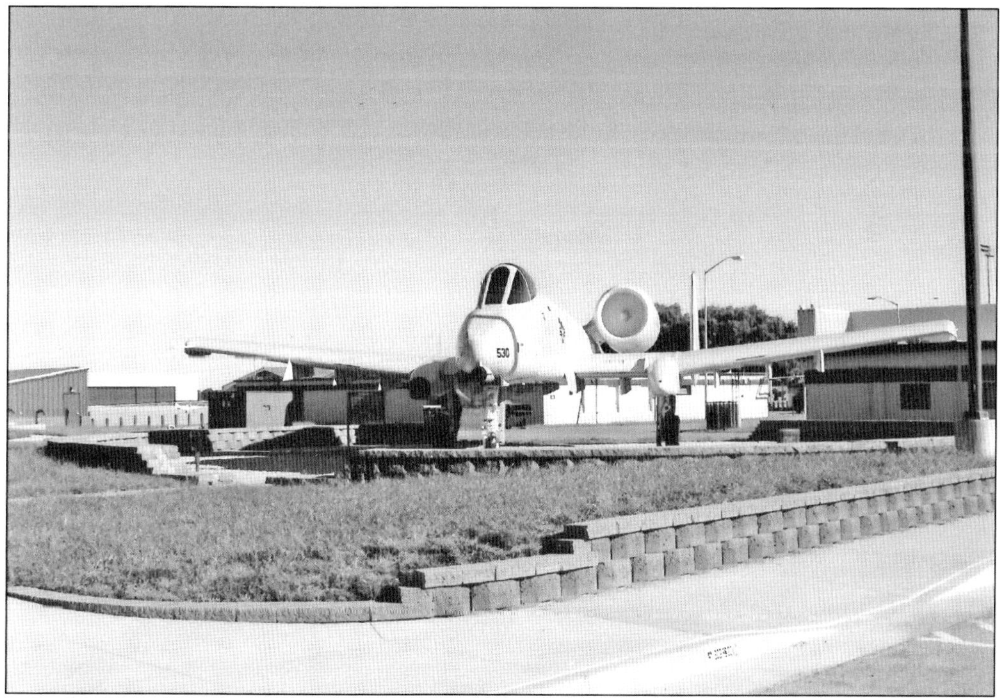

A head-on view of an A-10A shows the high-clearance tricycle landing gear, strongly built to allow rough airfield operations as in Southwest Asia. The high clearance also allows a wide variety of ordnance to be carried by the aircraft. (Author's collection.)

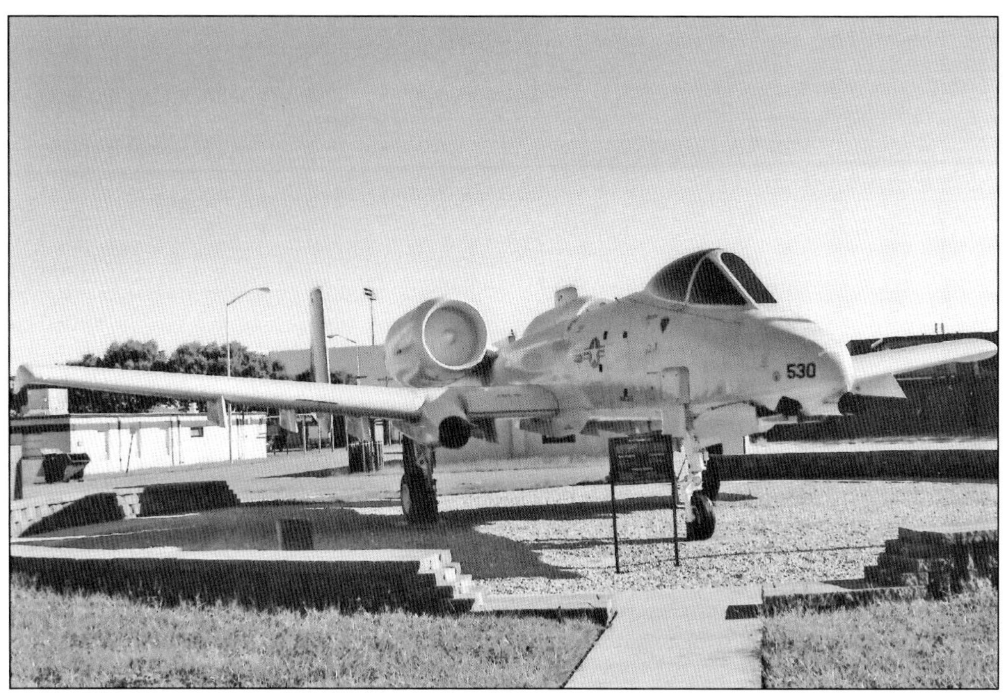

A close-up view of the right side of the aircraft shows the nose mounted 30-millimeter, seven-barrel GAU-8/A Gatling gun. The pilot has an excellent view over the nose of the aircraft for close ground support attack operations. (Author's collection.)

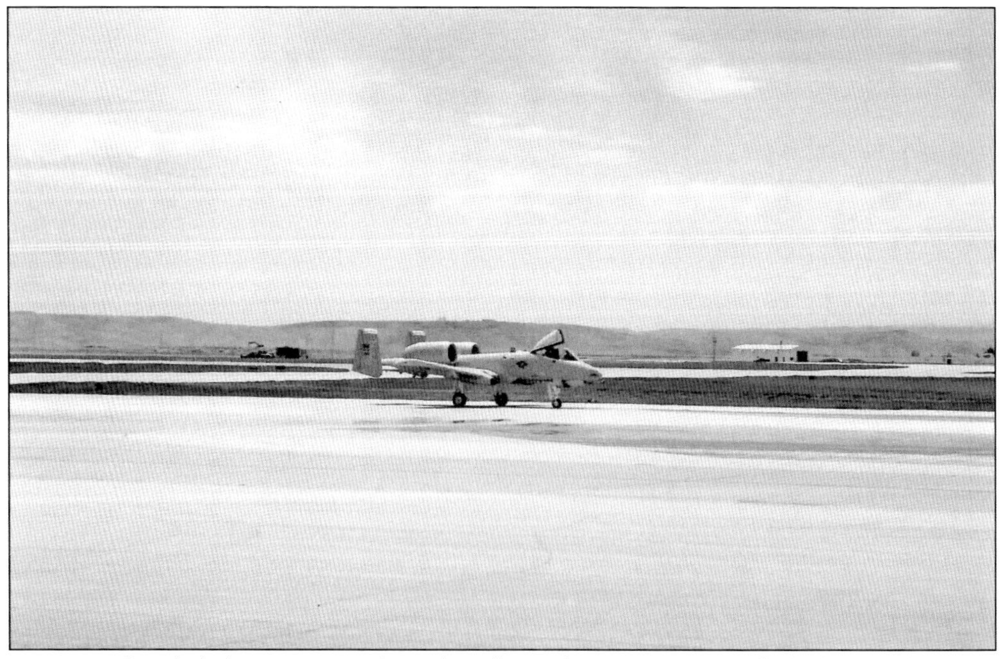
An A-10 Thunderbolt II taxis out from the Ellsworth Air Force Base flight line to the main runway during Dakota Thunder, the base's open house and air show on June 4, 2011. The aircraft performed low-altitude flight maneuvers over the main runway showing the fighter's performance envelope. (Author's collection.)

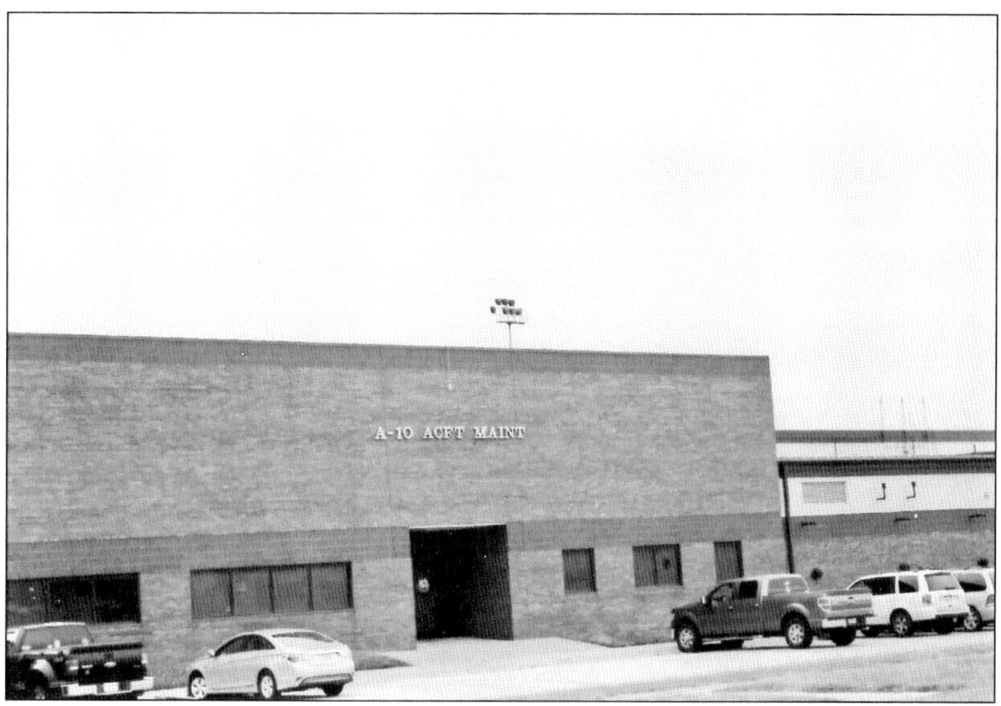

An important building for the 442nd Fighter Wing is the A-10 Aircraft Maintenance Facility on Whiteman Air Force Base. (Author's collection.)

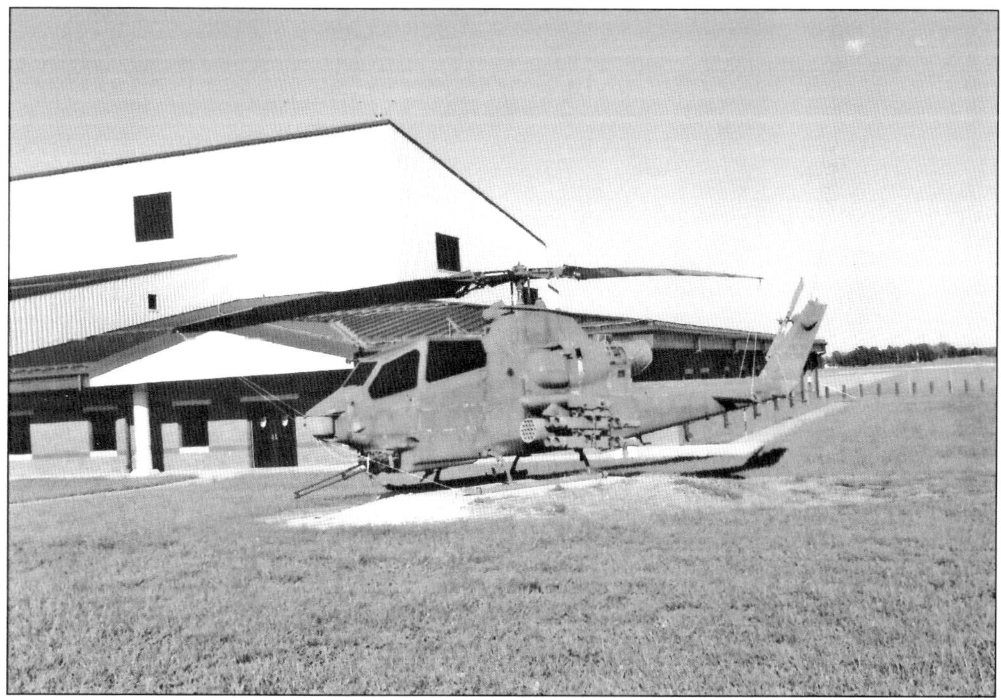
An AH-64 Apache helicopter is on display outside the Missouri National Guard 1-135th Attack Reconnaissance Battalion headquarters on Whiteman Air Force Base. (Author's collection.)

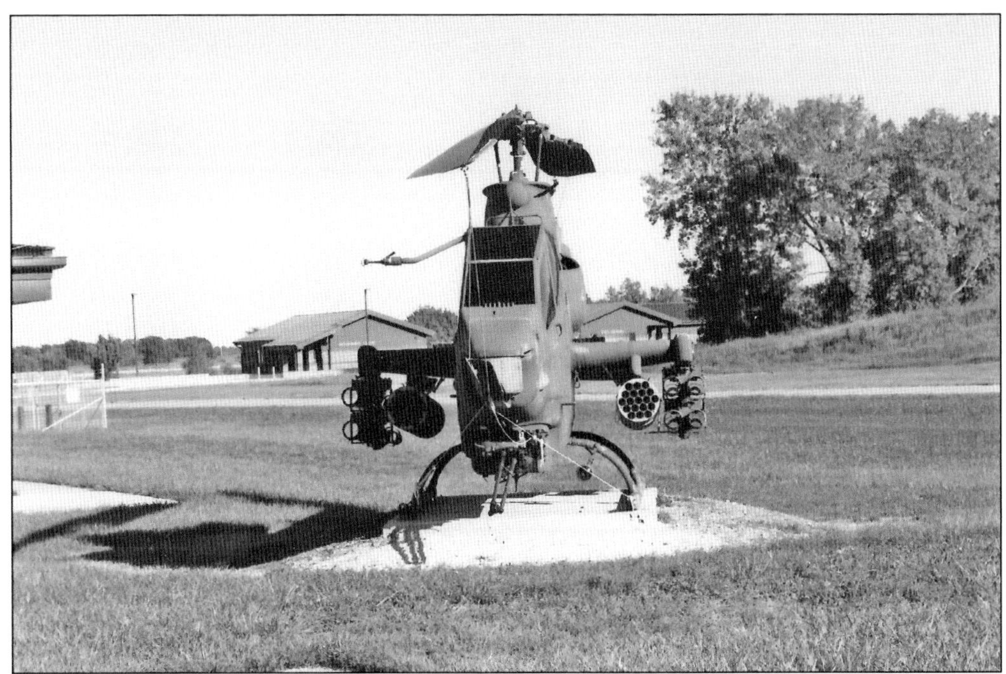

An AH-64 Apache helicopter is seen head-on. The fuselage-mounted stub wings hold four weapons positions (two on each side of the aircraft); each wing can carry one rocket launcher with 33 tubes to hold 70-millimeter high-explosive unguided rockets and four launch tubes. (Author's collection.)

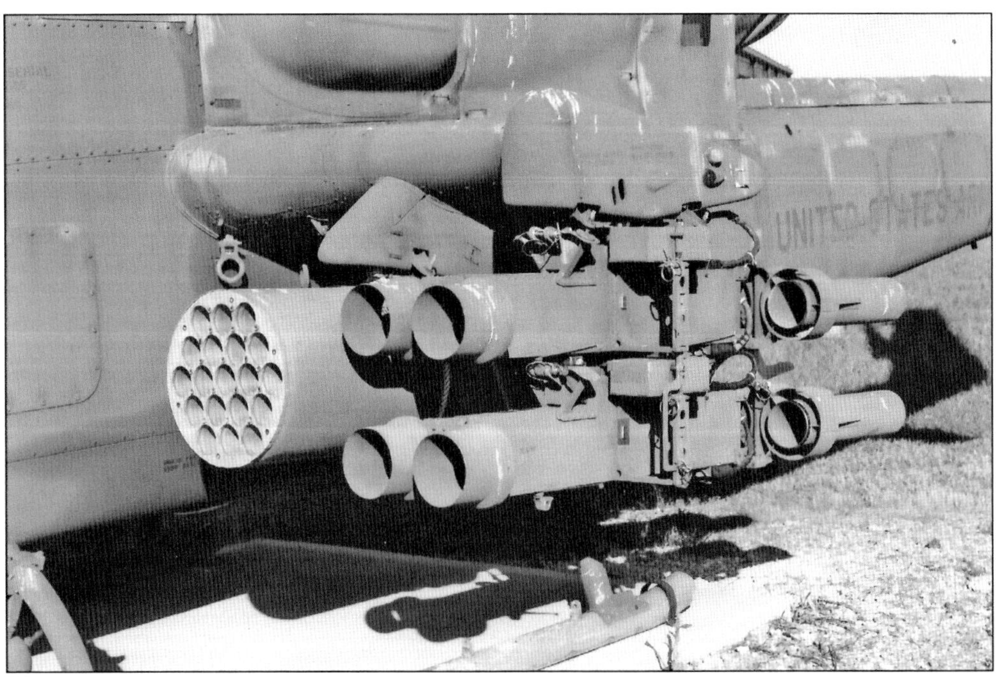

These munitions positions are visible on this helicopter. (Author's collection.)

Nine

Whiteman Air Force Base
The B-2 Bomber

Whiteman Air Force Base is home to the nation's only stealth bomber, the B-2 Spirit. The 509th Bomb Wing plays a major role in the nation's global power reach and long-range strike capability to deliver rapid, decisive, and survivable air power anytime and anywhere. To accomplish this mission, base facilities are modern and functional. These facilities support a large on-base military, dependent, and civilian workforce of approximately 11,000. These base facilities support not only the 509th Bomb Wing's Support, Operations, Maintenance and Medical Group, but also the Air Force Reserve's 442nd Fighter Wing, the Missouri's Air National Guard's 131st Bomb Wing (the only Air Force Reserve unit to fly the B-2 Spirit bomber), the Army National Guard's I-135th Aviation Battalion, and other tenant units. The base is a small city with the services and recreation of the surrounding communities in Missouri. Active-duty military personnel work and live on the base, using all the base facilities. The following photographs highlight a few of these facilities on the base.

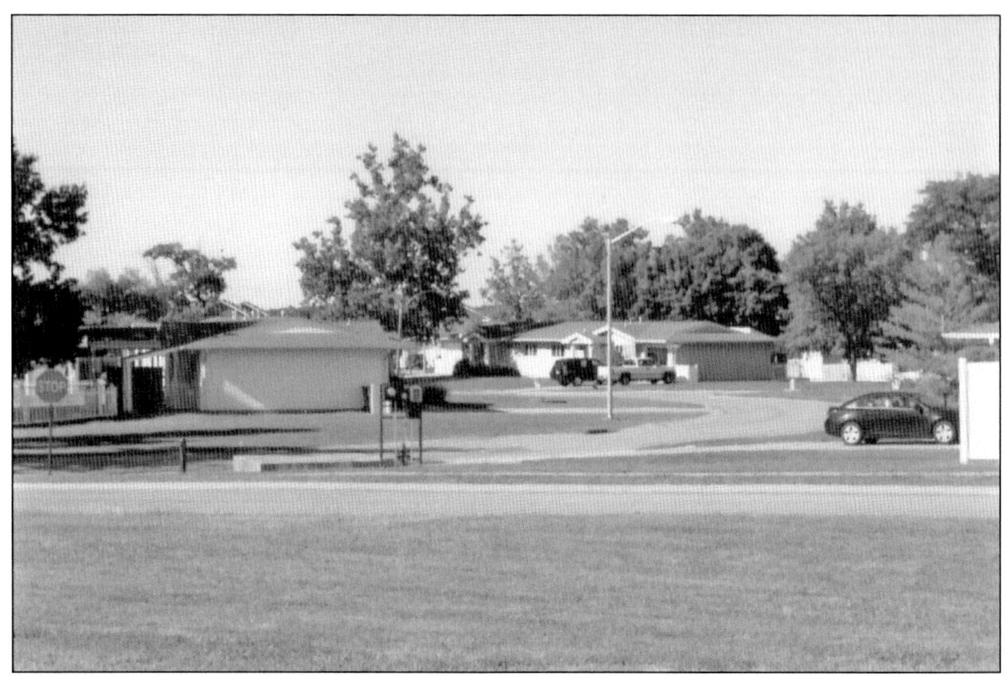

On-base housing for married military is run by a civilian company, Balfour Beatty Communities. Each unit is equipped with a stove, a refrigerator, electric connections for a clothes washer and dryer, patio cover, trash-holding fencing, an extended driveway, and central heating and air-conditioning and is ready to be furnished by the occupants. (Author's collection.)

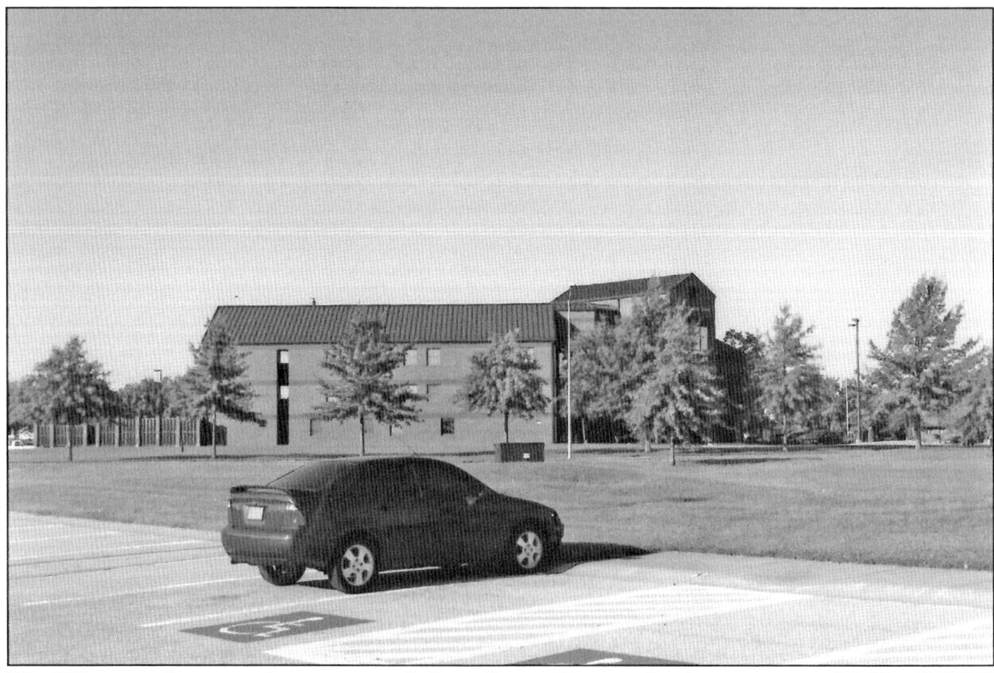

The Whiteman Inn provides temporary lodging for newly arrived military personnel, VIPs, START inspectors, headquarters inspectors, and military retirees. The Whiteman Inn's main facility and outlying buildings provide a total of 186 rooms. (Author's collection.)

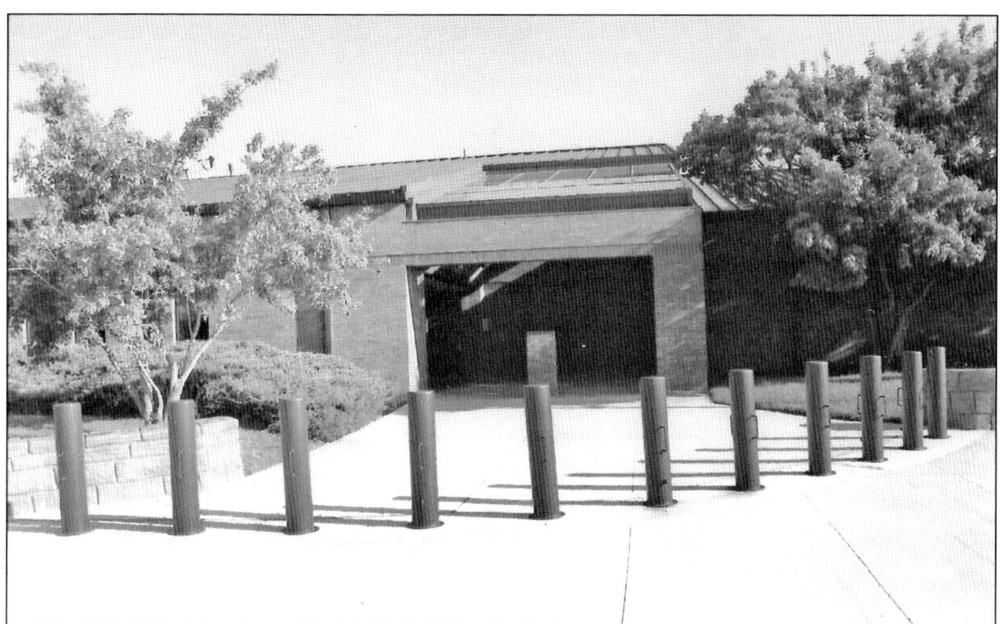

The 509th Bomb Wing Force Support Squadron Headquarters is shown in this photograph along with the Military Personnel and Non-Appropriated Fund Human Resources Offices. Squadron personnel are responsible for maintaining entry control and security of all base high-security areas. (Author's collection.)

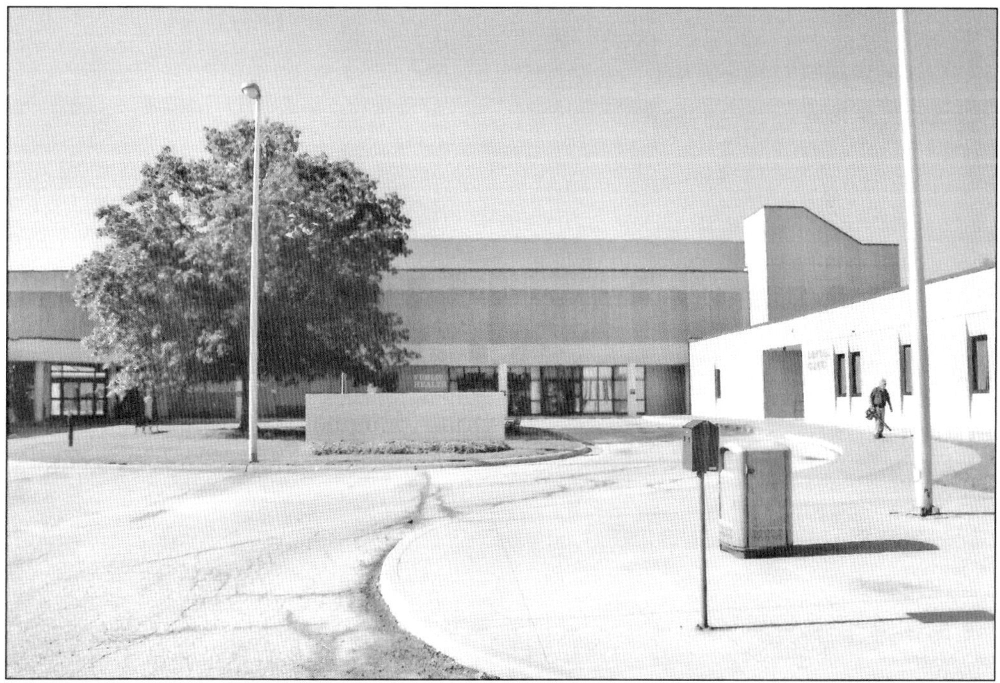

The 509th Medical Group provides on-base medical care for acute, routine, and specialty appointments for Tri-Care Prime enrollees. For Tri-Care for Life retirees 65 years and older, enrollment must be made through Social Security Part B for medical care from civilian health-care providers. (Author's collection.)

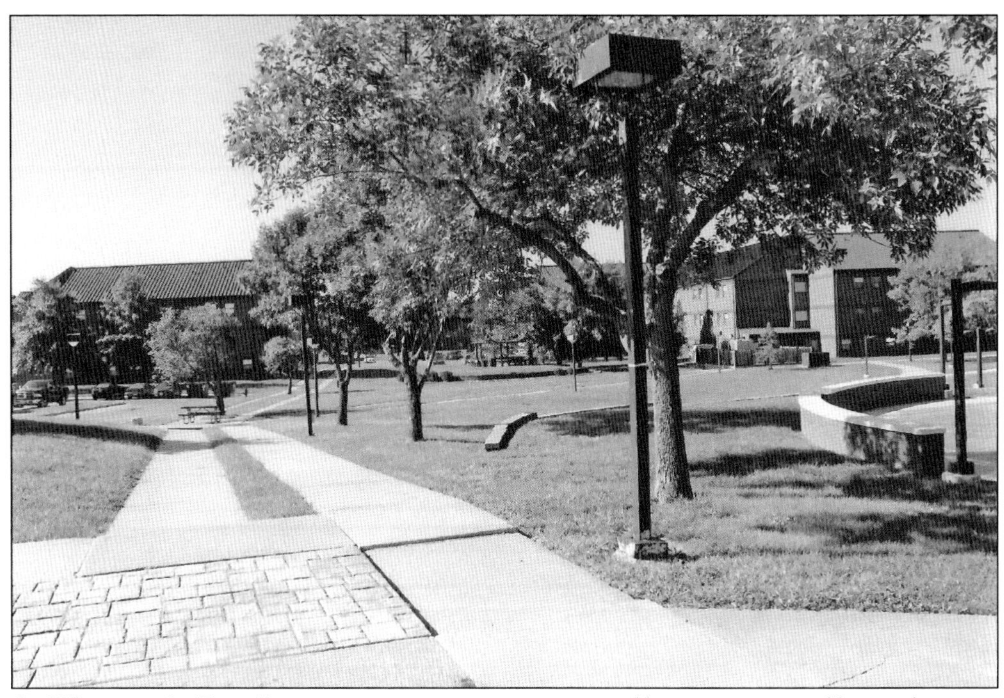

On Whiteman Air Force Base, permanent party unaccompanied housing consists of five modern two-by-two-room dormitories with an average capacity of 120 to 125 airmen. (Author's collection.)

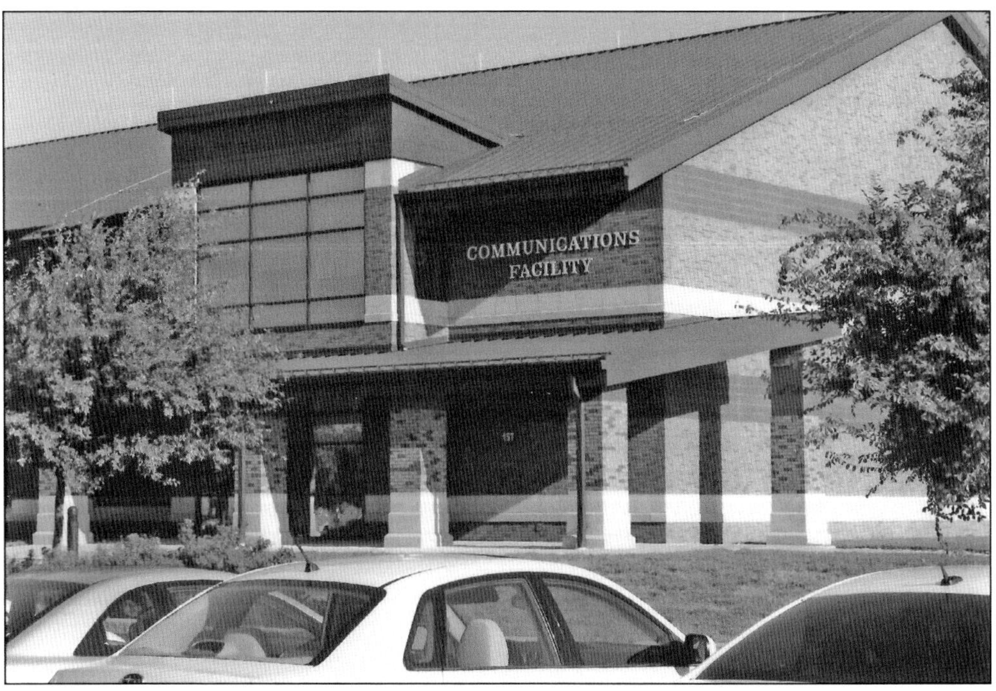

Secure communications are essential for the 509th Bomb Wing, supported by the 509th Communication Squadron to operate and maintain unclassified and classified communications. Today, with the threat of computer hacking, its services are essential. (Author's collection.)

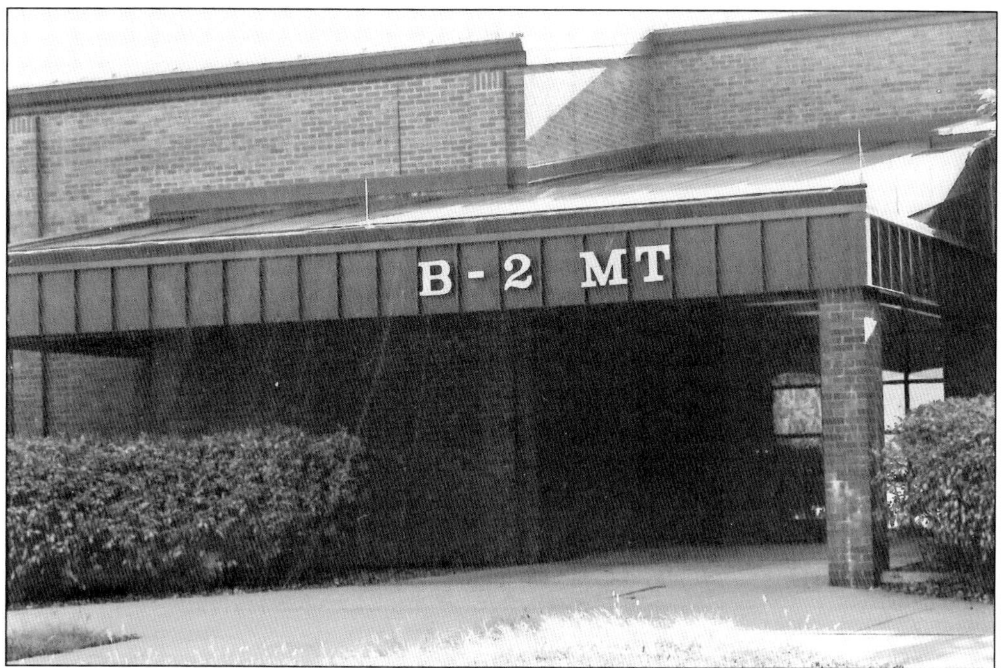

The B-2 Spirit requires extensive maintenance on the classified airframe to keep up the tempo of training and operational missions leveled by the Department of Defense to support America's presence in Southwest Asia. The planes are forward-deployed to Andersen Air Force Base, Guam. (Author's collection.)

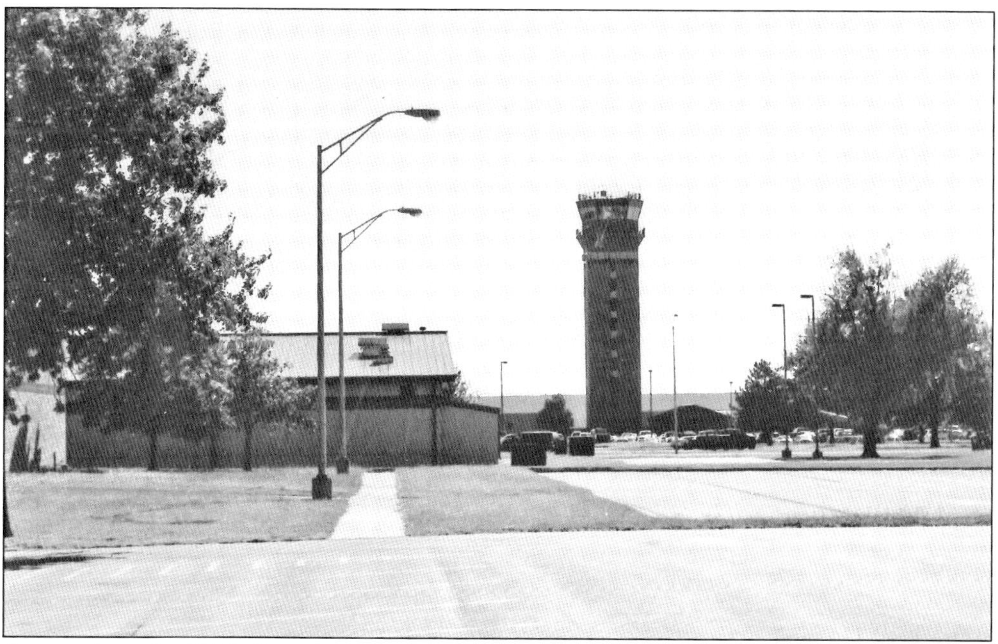
Airmen from the 509th Operations Support Squadron man the air traffic control tower 24 hours a day, seven days a week. They remain vigilant and communicate with aircraft to ensure that they take off and land safely. Airmen use a light gun to communicate safely and signal movements to individuals on the flight line. (Author's collection.)

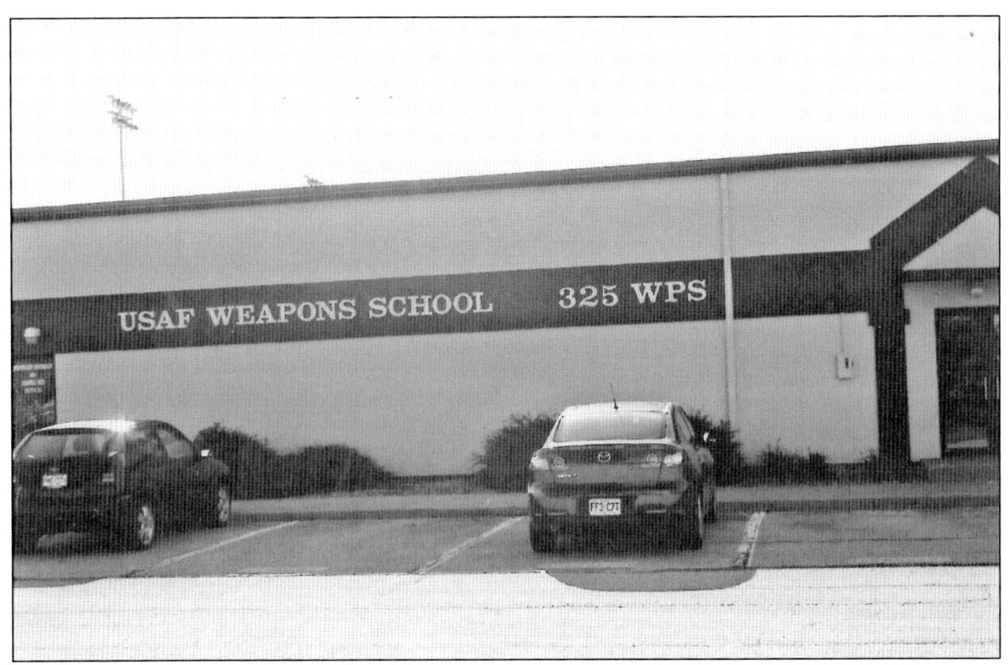

The 325th Weapons Squadron is a tenant unit on Whiteman Air Force Base whose mission is to teach graduate-level instructor courses, providing the world's most advanced training in weapons and tactics. It employs officers and a small number of Air Force–level board-selected B-2 instructor pilots. (Author's collection.)

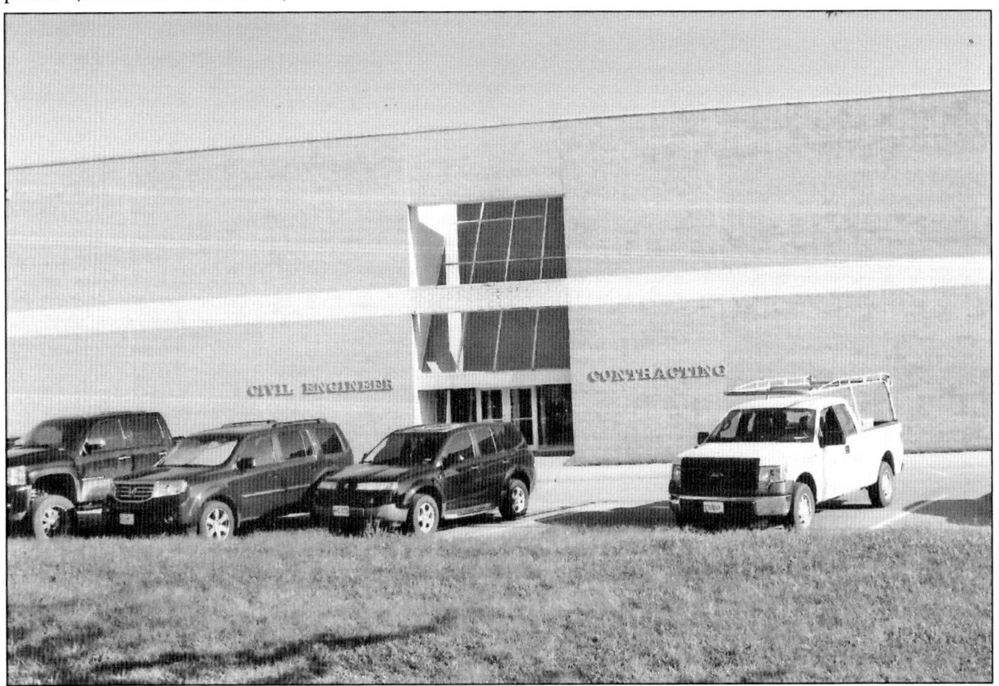

Whiteman Air Force Base is a large complex, comprising 4,916 acres enclosed by a perimeter security fence and numerous layers of security. The 509th Civil Engineering Squadron maintains and operates the base complex. (Author's collection.)

Bibliography

"131st Bomb Wing." //www.nationalguard.mil/news/articleview.

"442nd Fighter Wing." Whiteman Air Force Base, 442nd Fighter Wing, Office of Public Affairs.

"A Brief History of the 509th Bomb Wing." Whiteman Air Force Base, 509th Bomb Wing Historian Archives.

"Brief History of Sedalia Air Force Base, 1942–1954." Montgomery, AL: Maxwell Air Force Base, US Air Force Historical Division, Research Studies Institute, January 1956.

"Early US Army Glider Training Program." Bloomington, MN: National World War II Glider Pilots Association, Inc. www.ww2gp/training.php

"Gliders Away." *The Journal of the Army Ordnance Association*. Washington, DC: Army Ordnance Association, May–June 1944.

"History of 340th Bombardment Wing (M), Sedalia Air Force Base, Sedalia, Missouri, April 1954." Information on file at Headquarters Air Force Historical Research Agency, Maxwell Air Force Base, Alabama, August 2014.

"History of Whiteman Air Force Base." *Air Force Print News Today*, July 27, 2007. Washington, DC: Department of Defense, Department of the Air Force.

"Strategic Air Command Strategic Missile Wings." Strategic Air Command Association.

Technical Training Manual, Advanced Glider Training. TM 1-815, April 8, 1943. Washington, DC., War Department, Secretary of War (Gen. George C. Marshall, Chief of Staff). Courtesy US Army War College, US Army History Institute. Reference Section, Carlisle Barracks, PA.

US Army Corps of Engineers Ballistic Missile Construction Office (Los Angeles). "History of Construction Activities and Contract Administration Phases Encountered by Whiteman Area Office Corps of Engineers, CKBCO, during Construction of Minuteman Strategic Missile Wing IV, Whiteman Air Force Base, Missouri, June 27, 1989." The document was unclassified in accordance with 13526.

"Whiteman Air Force Base." *US Air Force Fact Sheet*. www.whiteman.af.mil/about-US/factsheets.

"Whiteman Air Force Base, 2014 Base Guide and Telephone Directory." 509th Bomb Wing, Public Affairs, 2014.

"Whiteman Air Force Base Lands Drone Assignment." US senator Kit Bond, Missouri, Washington, DC, press release, June 24, 2010.

Consistent with our mission to preserve history on a local level, this book was printed in South Carolina on American-made paper and manufactured entirely in the United States. Products carrying the accredited Forest Stewardship Council (FSC) label are printed on 100 percent FSC-certified paper.

MADE IN THE

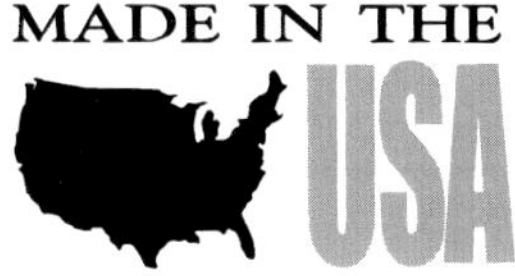